# Monitoring the Earth

## PHYSICAL GEOLOGY IN ACTION

## Claudio Vita-Finzi
*Natural History Museum, London*

TERRA

First published in 2002 by Terra Publishing

Terra Publishing
PO Box 315, Harpenden, Hertfordshire AL5 2ZD, England
Telephone: +44 (0)1582 762413
Fax: +44 (0)870 055 8105
Website: www.terrapublishing.net
E-mail: publishing@rjpc.demon.co.uk

ISBN:  1-903544-12-2


12 11 10 09 08 07 06 05 04 03 02
11 10 9 8 7 6 5 4 3 2 1

British Library Cataloguing-in-Publication Data
A CIP record for this book is available from the British Library

Library of Congress Cataloging-in-Publication Data are available

Typeset in Times New Roman and Helvetica
Printed and bound by Biddles Limited, Guildford and King's Lynn, England

*For Leo*

# Contents

# Preface

Floods, volcanic eruptions and earthquakes have long been monitored closely, especially where they impinge on towns or farmland. Consider the Nile, which has been gauged since the second millennium BC at least, or Pliny the Elder's observations of Vesuvius in action in AD 79. But major changes of the Earth's surface, such as the growth of mountains or the drift of continents, have until recent years eluded direct measurement.

Technical advances, especially in satellite technology and computing, have changed everything. We can now observe the rise of mountains and the opening of ocean basins from one year to the next, and sometimes even more closely. The ebb and flow of ice sheets and the shifting sea level, documented locally for centuries, are now being recorded continuously around the globe, and processes that appear too subtle to measure, such as the weathering of rockfaces and the infall of dust from space, are at long last within the reach of direct monitoring. Some of the names I toyed with for the book were terrametry, geometry, planetometry, developmental geology and geochrony.

In *Monitoring the Earth* I argue that these developments provide an opportunity to update both the scope and the character of physical geology. The title seems an oxymoron: can you have real-time history? But geology deals not only with the past, as volcanologists and highway engineers well know, and even when it does there remains a need for modern analogues: Charles Lyell's *Principles of geology* (1830–33) was "an attempt to explain the former changes of the Earth's surface, by reference to causes now in operation".

The point of measuring geological changes in action is, of course, to understand the underlying processes. And as our grasp of the mechanisms improves, so it becomes feasible to analyze the past and draw up forecasts. Physical geology is accordingly shifting from a historical perspective mainly concerned with description to an analytical one preoccupied with explanation. A helpful analogy is the distinction between anatomy and physiology, which have always overlapped substantially but which convey (at least to the outsider) an emphasis on structure in the former and on function in the latter.

The book outlines some of the crucial techniques and their bearing on studies of the Earth's shape and orbit, its response to a changing Sun and to bombardment by meteorites and comets, through the more traditionally geological topics of plate tectonics, rock deformation, erosion and deposition, to the geochemical activities of living organisms viewed at the microscopic level. As the table of contents shows, a subsidiary aim is to broaden the scope of physical geology to include material usually considered the preserve of astronomers and geophysicists. The text is intended for students of Earth and planetary science but it may also interest biologists and historians of science.

I thank Walter Alvarez and Luna Leopold for encouragement, Mike Audley-Charles and G. David Price for support, and Dominic Fortes, Joanna Haigh, Roger Jones, Mike Russell and Stan Trimble for advice.

Claudio Vita-Finzi
London
October 2002

# Acknowledgements

The following individuals, as well as the publishers and organizations acknowledged in the captions, kindly gave permission to use published illustrations as the basis for the figures in this book:

D. F. Argus, M. Bezzeghoud, G. Blewitt, D. E. Brownlee, A. B. Chamberlin, B. F. Chao, V. E. Courtillot, C. DeMets, C. S. M. Doake, H. Dragert, P. J. Dunn, L. A. Frank, J. D. Gage, C. Garcia, M. M. Grady, R. A. F. Grieve, D. V. Hoyt, C-A. Huh, M. Jackson, H-G. Kahle, J. Kalish, R. H. King, J. Lean, A. Lin, J. E. Lupton, H. Y. McSween Jr, D. Massonnet, S. Matsuzaka, T. C. Meierding, W. R. Osterkamp, C. F. Pearson, W. R. Peltier, G. Plafker, P. D. Quay, J. Sauber, G. Seeber, F. Sigmundsson, A. Soare, F. R. Stephenson, M. Stuiver, B. A. Tinsley, A. L. Washburn and the US Government. The illustrations are largely the work of S. Tapper of Geografx and R. Jones of Terra Publishing.

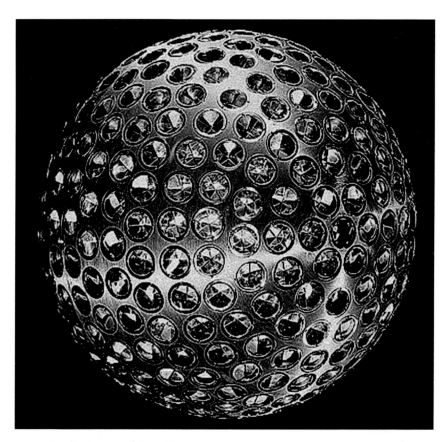

**Frontispiece: LAGEOS 1**     The LAGEOS (Laser Geodynamics) satellites, 60 cm in diameter, have a brass core that ensures a stable orbit. They are covered with 426 retroreflectors, used for laser ranging from ground stations to a precision of <1 cm. The results are used to measure changes in the Earth's rate of rotation and wobble, to map its shape and gravity, and to trace plate movements. LAGEOS 1 was launched by NASA in 1976; LAGEOS 2, which provides better coverage of seismically active areas, was launched in 1992 by NASA and the Italian Space Agency (ASI). Image courtesy of NASA.

# CHAPTER 1
# New rulers and clocks

*Progress in science depends on new techniques, new discoveries and new ideas, probably in that order.* Sidney Brenner 1980

On 26 November 1987 an editorial in *Nature* carried the headline "Tectonics in almost real time". It reported how the westward movement of California was being tracked with the help of mobile radiotelescopes. The author went on to suggest that the technique might soon compete with laser ground-ranging in determining which parts of the San Andreas Fault move smoothly and which parts are locked together until an earthquake releases the accumulated strain.

"Real time" is always a misleading term as there is bound to be a delay, if only microseconds long, before any data can be logged and then read, whether on an instrument or in one's brain; but it was as well for *Nature* to say "almost real time", because it took four years for California's drift to be securely established within the error margins of the method. Measurements of the Earth's ozone shield by the ERS-2 satellite are likewise called near real time by the European Space Agency: the data are sent by the satellite to a ground receiving station once every orbit (100 min), whence they are passed on to Kiruna in Sweden (about 5 min) to be processed (1 min) and distributed (98% of the observations reach the users within 3 h of collection).

There had been many previous attempts to measure regional deformation, as the reference to laser ranging made clear: mechanical strainmeters have been deployed across the San Andreas Fault at least since 1950, and displaced trees, walls and sidewalks have provided average rates of movement since 1850. The search for ages and rates has always been at the heart of much of Earth science. Yet *Nature*'s headline was justified. There is now in prospect the continuous monitoring of Earth movements at any scale and without the need for wires or unimpeded lines of sight. Moreover, the monitoring

---

*Note* Abbreviations and acronyms are explained where they first arise. The power notation (e.g. $10^{-2}$, $10^8$) is used when dealing with a wide range of volumes or masses to avoid compounds with tera, giga and so on, except where (as in μm for micrometre, or Myr for million years) the alternative is familiar or obvious. A large number of bibliographic references are included because a brief list of supplementary readings would have been an inadequate guide to a varied and rapidly growing field.

will be based primarily on measurement. Many traditional methods rely mainly on inference. A row of dead barnacles well above the reach of high tide implies a shift in the shoreline; a tide gauge or orbiting satellite shows the shift directly.

The application to physical geology of satellite altimeters and mobile radiotelescopes could hardly have been predicted, and it is still sometimes ignored in a subject traditionally based on field observation backed up by experience. Yet the new toolkit is helping to solve longstanding riddles as well as making some hitherto impenetrable problems appear soluble. New procedures are quickly adopted, and they link areas of Earth science that have previously appeared to have little in common. For instance, the use of measurements from orbiting satellites and other space techniques to investigate the Earth's shape and gravitational field has proved a boon to both structural geologists and geomorphologists; where the results overlap, say if active faulting affects river behaviour, there may be benefits for seismology. Other novel techniques may at first accentuate academic divisions because they are expensive or esoteric; yet, here too, barriers are falling or at any rate changing position. Typical of this category is the use of cosmogenic isotopes to date rock surfaces, a procedure once considered prohibitively expensive and scientifically suspect, but which is now being deployed with growing confidence to resolve the age of such diverse items as Meteor Crater in Arizona (also known as Barringer Crater or the Barringer Meteorite Crater), polar ice, and the Egyptian Sphinx.

The resulting advances bear primarily on location and timing – central concerns of Earth science from its beginnings. There has been equally momentous progress in chemical and physical analysis, but it is convenient at this stage in the book to concentrate on rulers and clocks.

# Location

For centuries cartographers have fretted over minute errors in their maps, without being able to specify their exact position on the globe. This was partly because the requisite astronomical methods were complex and required expensive instruments, and partly because, until the advent of canals and railroads, the primary concern was the shape of fields and coastlines. Even now, geologists may draw exquisite field sketches and geological sections whose precise latitude and longitude are not a material consideration.

The geodesists, professionally dedicated to measuring the Earth, quietly persevered. By the middle of the nineteenth century they attained accuracies for distance and angular measurement ($1:10^5$ and $1:10^6$ respectively) remarkably close to modern standards. Yet, although by now proficient in obtaining astronomical fixes, they were limited in what they could achieve by deficiencies in time measurement, and thus in establishing the relative position of their landmarks.

The introduction in the 1950s of electronic distance meters (EDM), using light or radar, rendered ground-based surveying much less laborious than traditional methods requiring distance measurement with tapes or chains (Fig. 1.1a); it was revolutionary

**Figure 1.1** Distance measurement. **(a)** Old style, using Invar wire (after Hinks 1947, by permission of Cambridge University Press). **(b)** One of the current alternatives, portable GPS (courtesy of SECO Manufacturing Company Inc.). **(c)** The Landsat 4 satellite (operational 1982–93), which carried a Thematic Mapper (30 m resolution) as well as the Multi-Spectral Scanner of its predecessors. The latest is the series in Landsat 7 (April 1999). **(d)** Radiotelescope at Medicina, Italy, used for VLBI.

in its potential for bridging significant bodies of water or impassable terrain. Precisions of $1{:}10^6$ – a tenfold improvement in a century – became commonplace for distance measurement.

The limit was set by atmospheric refraction, the distorting effect on light produced by differential heating. The geodimeter, for example, could yield precisions of $1{:}10^7$ over a distance of 10 km (Table 1.1) provided there was information along the entire survey line on average temperature to a precision of better than 0.1°C and on pressure to < 1 mb (millibar). Securing this information might involve flying a suitably instrumented light aircraft along the light path. A cunning way around this extravagant solution was to measure the distance using light of two colours (and thus at two wavelengths), as differences in the result could be used to evaluate the effect of refraction.

3

**Table 1.1** Applications and precision of GPS as function of network scale (adapted from Blewitt 1993).

| Scale | Geophysical application | Precision |
|---|---|---|
| Very local 10 m–1 km | 3-D geodetic ties for <br> – technique intercomparison <br> – reference frame unification | 0.1–1 mm <br> (in $10^2$ sec) |
| Local 1–100 km | Deformation in fault zones <br> – seismic and aseismic slip <br> – post-seismic relaxation <br> Surface topographic change <br> – mountain formation <br> – glaciology and ice sheets | 1–4 mm <br> (in $10^3$ sec) |
| Regional 100–1000 km | Plate boundary structure <br> Block rotation <br> Ice sheet volume change <br> Mountain-range formation <br> Far-field seismic displacement | 4–10 mm <br> (in $10^4$ sec) |
| Global 1000–10 000 km | Plate tectonics <br> Excitation of Earth wobble and spin rate <br> Sea-level change <br> Postglacial rebound <br> Sea-surface topography <br> High-resolution gravity field | ~10 mm <br> (in $10^5$ sec) |

The extent of variations in atmospheric pressure now had to be known to no better than 50 mb.

Yet, in order to get a reading, the surveyor still needed an uninterrupted line of sight (or its radio equivalent) between each pair of stations. Moreover, the longest baseline that could be measured by EDM was only about 12 km and, although longer lines could be extended from EDM baselines by triangulation (i.e. by using angular measurement), they could hardly bridge the oceans.

## GPS

The problem was sidestepped with the Global Positioning System or GPS, which was devised by the US Navy for fixing the position of two or more stations anywhere on Earth without the need for a line of sight between them. The two developments that made GPS possible were artificial satellites and the atomic clock. The former provided extraterrestrial reference points, the locations of which were continuously monitored; the latter is a means of determining the distance of the satellites from the observer by measuring the time of travel of radio signals sent out by them.

The GPS (Fig. 1.1b) was intended for navigation, and its potential impact on Earth science was not generally obvious. Receivers were expensive and the data required complex and time-consuming analysis. Moreover, the signals were purposely degraded for military reasons. But scientists soon recognized the revolutionary capability of space geodesy and circumvented the limitations that were inherent in the original design, as well as those imposed for security, to the point where precisions were sometimes attained that were three times better than originally intended. Signal degradation was abandoned by the US Government in May 2000.

The prototype GPS satellite was launched in 1967. By 1990 six were in position – the

Block 1 constellation – and by 1995 there were 24 in 12-hour orbits at an elevation of ~20 000 km on six orbital planes (Fig. 1.2b), thus ensuring that four or more GPS satellites were visible simultaneously at all times virtually throughout the globe (Yunck 1995). By 1999 the number had risen to 28. Europe is planning a system of its own.

The precision of GPS geodetic baselines improved by three orders of magnitude between 1992 and 1993 (Fig. 1.3a; Blewitt 1993). The major sources of error remain uncertainties in the satellite orbits and in signal propagation associated with variations in the water-vapour level in the troposphere and ambiguities in the carrier-phase cycle (Dixon 1991). But, although the atmosphere still sets limits of 3 mm per 3 km on line-of-sight distances (Fig. 1.3b), the same ratio ($1:10^6$) as with EDM, the limit of 3 mm applies over thousands of kilometres because the atmospheric contribution to errors remains unchanged beyond the horizontal equivalent of two atmospheric thicknesses (Bilham et al. 1998). In other words, distances of 1000 km or more can be measured by GPS at millimetre-level precision; if adequate data on atmospheric water vapour are

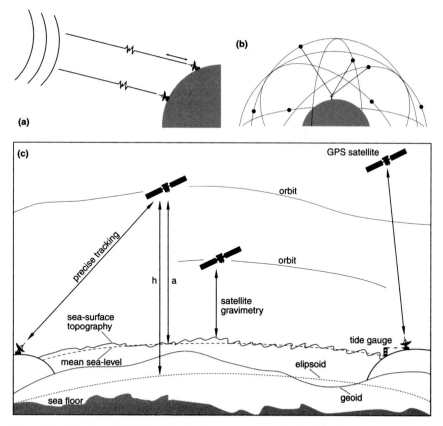

**Figure 1.2** Principles of **(a)** VLBI, with the double-headed arrow indicating time difference in arrival of the signal from the radio source at two terrestrial receivers; **(b)** GPS, with three satellites visible from the receiver; and **(c)** satellite altimetry and gravimetry, where a = true orbit and h = computed orbit. Other terms are discussed in the text.

5

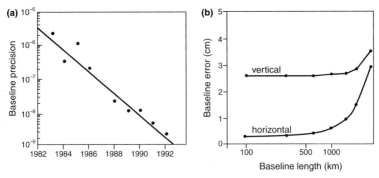

**Figure 1.3** **(a)** Improvements between 1982 and 1992 in the precision of baselines measured by GPS (after Blewitt 1993; ©1993 AGU). **(b)** GPS accuracies in east–west baselines in a South Pacific study to illustrate how the tropospheric effect has much greater effect on vertical than on horizontal accuracy, especially on relatively short baselines (after Thornton et al. 1986, by permission of Elsevier Science).

available, precisions of ~0.1 mm can be obtained after a few hours of observation for distances of less than 100 km (Yunck 1995). For much Earth science, lower precisions are of course acceptable, especially when economy and portability are critical (Fig. 1.1b).

By 1983 it was reasonable to distinguish between pre-satellite and satellite geodesy. "Revolutionary changes from established proven methods to radically new methods", the director of the US National Geodetic Survey commented, "only come about when the new method is so overwhelmingly superior in enough aspects as to render the old methods obsolete and uneconomic by comparison" (Bossler 1983). In his view, GPS (like VLBI, discussed below) heralded such a revolution in geodesy, not least because it did away with the optical stellar observations at up to 50 observatories around the world that were required to determine Earth rotation and polar motion and that could not be completed until long after the distance measurements to which they referred.

*Very long baseline interferometry*
Very long baseline interferometry (VLBI) came on the scene at about the same time as GPS. It too depends on radio signals beamed to Earth and it is essentially indifferent to weather and time of day or night. The radio sources in question are extragalactic, usually quasars; the differential time of arrival of the signals at two or more radio-astronomy antennas serves as a measure of the separation between them (Fig. 1.2a). As the calculation is complicated by the Doppler shift resulting from the Earth's rotation, several radio sources are used to secure independent measurements of the baseline. It is worth noting that the Doppler effect – the change in the wavelength of radiation received from a moving source from the wavelength at which it is emitted – was exploited in early attempts at satellite geodesy and it yielded accuracies as high as $1:10^9$.

Much effort has gone towards making VLBI sensitive to height variations and towards cutting down to a single day the time of observation for station coordinates at millimetre accuracy. Other improvements have come from judicious choice of quasars and standardizing azimuth coverage at each station (Herring 1995). But the practical difference between a set of GPS receivers and a trio of radiotelescopes seems unlikely to fade. Portable radiotelescopes have been used experimentally, but they are unlikely to approach the flexibility of the GPS receiver.

*Laser techniques*
When allied with space technology, the laser has also contributed to the revitalization of geodesy. Lunar laser ranging (LLR) and satellite laser ranging (SLR), like terrestrial laser ranging using the geodolite, measure distance by determining the round-trip travel time of a pulse of light bounced off a target. LLR depends on retro-reflectors left on the Moon by Apollo astronauts; its greatest contribution has been in the analysis of the Earth–Moon system. SLR measurements from several stations have proved valuable for determining satellite orbits: the position of near-Earth satellites at first depended on triangulation based on optical sighting and on Doppler ranging, but by the late 1960s SLR had become established as the most precise method. In 1972 the NASA laser-ranging system, using a spacecraft in near-circular orbit at an altitude of about 1000 km, had an error of ±70 cm; by 1976 this was 8 cm.

The major obstacle to further improvements was seen to be inadequate knowledge of the gravity field (Smith et al. 1979), but this too would soon benefit from the new technology. Similarly, an awareness that some land areas were too unstable to provide secure geodetic base stations prompted the thought that space geodesy might eventually permit the measurement of deformation. The first subject, the San Andreas Fault, was made as early as 1972, soon to be followed by variations in the rate of the Earth's rotation and in the alignment of its axis.

The flow of information is thus in both directions. LAGEOS, a satellite dedicated exclusively to laser ranging, was launched in 1976. Its height, perfect sphericity and high density render its orbit almost immune to distortion by gravity and air drag (Christodoulidis et al. 1985), but solar-radiation pressure has some effect on its trajectory, and, before the results of LAGEOS ranging can be applied to geodetic problems, allowance has to be made for the effects of polar motion, variations in Earth rotation and the location of tracking stations (Smith et al. 1990).

# Altitude

Table 1.2 summarizes the quality of the distance measurements obtained by the various techniques now in use (see also Fig. 1.4). The choice of technique may hinge more on flexibility than on bald statistics: GPS and EDM results are in good agreement over distances of 10–50 km (Tralli 1991), but the former will probably be favoured when (as in the study of strain across fault systems) the intention is to extend the study more than 50 km from the baseline.

Altitude is generally more poorly determined than horizontal distance, although the problem can sometimes be resolved by doubling the period of observation (Larson 1995). By 1999, GPS observations over 24 hours reportedly gave measurements of

**Table 1.2** Horizontal distance measurement (after Hinks 1947, Bannister et al. 1998, Bilham et al. 1998, NASA web pages and other sources).

| Method | Date | Precision* | Distance |
|---|---|---|---|
| Star fix | 1927[†] | lat | <1 naut. mile |
| Steel tape | ~1950 | 1:10$^5$ | Several km |
| EDM | | | |
| Microwave (e.g.Tellurometer) | 1957 | 1:10$^6$ | <50 km |
| Electro-optical (e.g Mekometer) | 1976 | 1:10$^5$ | <60 km |
| Infrared (e.g. Geodimeter) | 1980s | 1:10$^6$ | <2 km |
| Two-colour Geodimeter | | 1:10$^7$ | 1–12 km |
| Satellite | | | |
| Transit (Doppler) | 1967 | 1:10$^9$ | 5–100 km |
| Differential GPS | 1978 | 1:10$^7$–10$^{9+}$ | |
| SLR to Lageos I and II[#] | 1976 | <1 cm | |
| LLR[¶] | 1969 | 1–15 cm | |
| VLBI (for geodesy) | | 1 mm | |

\* The various measures of precision given reflect the different criteria favoured by practitioners.

† GMT broadcasts begin.

\# Mainly for rotation and deformation of the Earth; 25 years of observation on 15 satellites including Starlette and other satellites used for gravity studies.

¶ Neodymium laser gives 1 cm accuracies; the ruby laser system gave accuracies of 10–15 cm.

§ For SLR, LLR and VLBI (as for the other items) the error is for baseline precision and not for the distance measurement to the satellite, Moon or quasar.

+ 3 mm accuracies for distances ranging from a few kilometres to thousands of kilometres; near 1 mm accuracy with continuous observation over several weeks.

elevation to within 2 cm. When the critical process is too slow or non-uniform to be revealed satisfactorily by space geodesy, it may be necessary to revert to traditional levelling, with all its labour intensity and slowness. Similarly, direct measurement of gradient on short stretches may be better done by means of tiltmeters, which attain resolutions as good as 0.1 mrad (thousandths of a radian) and can be set to record short-term changes in the direction of tilt.

At sea and over ice sheets the answer may lie in satellite radar altimetry. The elevation of the ocean surface when derived from space is generally expressed above a reference ellipsoid of rotation rather than relative to a shoreline (Fig. 1.2c). The main source of error at present is uncertainty over the satellite orbit relative to the centre of the Earth, and it amounts to a root mean square (r.m.s.) value of ~20 cm for the ERS-1 satellite (Table 1.3); for the joint US–French Ocean Topography Experiment satellite, TOPEX/Poseidon, it is ~5 cm, not much greater than the other sources of uncertainty (Shum et al. 1995). TOPEX/Poseidon data have been used to correct ERS-1 orbits. DORIS (Doppler orbitography and radiopositioning integrated by satellite) was developed in the early 1990s for precise determination of satellite orbits specifically for determining sea-surface topography and related aspects of oceanic circulation, although it is proving valuable in geodynamics too; the system was placed aboard the French satellites SPOT 2 (launched in 1990) and SPOT 3 (1993) and on TOPEX/Poseidon (1992) (Fig. 1.5).

However precise, the products of radar altimetry are of limited value to oceanography without a long-term perspective. Tide gauges, which would supply such perspective, generally require decades of record for reliable secular trends to emerge from short-term fluctuations. The extra uncertainty introduced by possible movements of the land has been especially serious at some of the oldest gauges, notably at Amsterdam

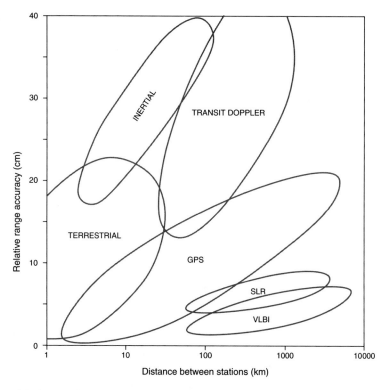

**Figure 1.4** Accuracy in the determination of relative position by various methods including terrestrial (as opposed to satellite) geodesy; note the wide range of distances for which GPS can be used (after Seeber 1993, by permission of Walter de Gruyter GmbH).

**Table 1.3** Accuracy of sea-level measurements from satellites (after Shum et al. 1995).

| Satellite | Launch date | Estimated accuracy of sea-level measurements (cm)* |
|---|---|---|
| Geos-3 | 1975 | 67 |
| Seasat | 1978 | 33 |
| Geosat | 1985 | 22 |
| ERS-1 | 1991 | 19 |
| TOPEX/Poseidon | 1992 | <5 |

* Root mean square combined error of orbit and altimeter.

(Netherlands), where the readings extend over 300 years. Sea-level marks in Sweden dating from 1731 onwards are similarly compromised (Sjöberg 1986).

If purely tectonic, the uncertainty can be isolated by comparing the record for a range of different locations; but, where the deformation results from loading and unloading of the sea floor by the very sea-level changes being investigated, the correction is more elusive. At all events the satellite data have to be combined with the tide-gauge records

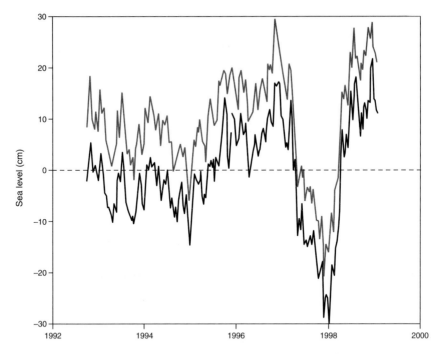

**Figure 1.5** Agreement between satellite altimeter (TOPEX/Poseidon) (grey line) and tide-gauge record (black line) at Pohnpei, in the central Pacific (7° N, 158° E). The heights are offset on the figure by 10 cm for ease of comparison. (After Nerem & Mitchum 2001, by permission of Elsevier Science.)

if there is to be any hope of identifying the contribution to sea level made by changes in ocean temperature and salinity, ocean-basin volume and the distribution of water in the atmosphere, the solid Earth, the oceans and ice bodies.

Under project IRIS (International Radio Interferometric Surveying), GPS and VLBI are being used to link tide gauges to a global geodynamic network, one of its aims being to separate sea-level effects from crustal deformation (Carter et al. 1986). Longer-term changes spanning the past millennium (Varekamp & Thomas 1998) have to depend on dated estuarine deposits and saltmarsh sequences.

## *Radar mapping*

Mapping (as distinct from measurement) by radar is rapidly gaining support for terrestrial studies, in part because of its great success on Venus. Synthetic aperture radar (SAR) simulates an increase in the diameter of the satellite antenna, typically from about 10 m to about 4000 m, by adding radar echoes along the satellite track. The expectation is that radar maps of Earth with a resolution of 3 m will soon be feasible. Besides being unimpeded by clouds or the absence of solar illumination, radar imaging yields information on surface properties as well as topography. But its real impact has been through InSAR, or synthetic radar interferometry, which exploits the phase difference between two synthetic aperture radar images of a target area obtained on separate satellite orbits.

InSAR was first used in 1974 for topographical mapping. In 1985 Massonnet showed that, provided that the ground response to the radar signal was unchanged (which would not be the case if, for example, there had been a heavy fall of snow between the two passes of the satellite) and the satellite orbits were well enough known for coherence between the images, the interference pattern produced by combining the two images was a measure of any intervening topographical change (Massonnet et al. 1993, Zebker et al. 1994, Feigl et al. 1995).

Successive tests have found that one-day intervals are well suited to topographical mapping and analysis of glacier motion (Fig. 1.6), whereas deformation measurements on volcanoes and the like often require intervals of six months between images (Rosen et al. 1996). Displacements of 1 cm have been detected in artificial targets, and milli-metre-level resolution is confidently expected. Even though atmospheric effects can complicate the analysis (Meade & Sandwell 1996), displacements of 3–10 cm along a swath 50–100 km wide have been identified in field tests.

Because SAR interferometry is not confined to a survey line or to an area selected for re-mapping or repeat aerial photography, it may reveal topographical changes in un-expected or inaccessible locations, something that has proved especially valuable in

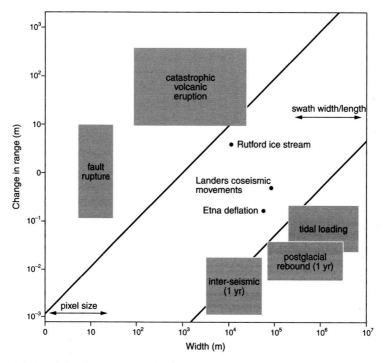

**Figure 1.6** Resolution of measurements of surface change by interferometry based on synthetic aperture radar (InSAR) (after Meade & Sandwell 1996; ©1996 American Association for the Advancement of Science). Ice flow, volcanic deflation and coseismic deformation are well within its capability (diagonal zone). For Rutford ice stream see Ch. 6, for Etna deflation see Ch. 7, for Landers coseismic movements see Ch. 8.

studies of ground deformation during earthquakes and that outweighs the greater precision of GPS or ground-based geodesy. But the timing of the repetition is dictated by the satellite managers. Here GPS scores because, provided that five satellites are visible, it can track ground motion as often and as quickly as required at centimetre-level accuracy (Bannister et al. 1998).

The demands of dynamic surveying have pressed into service many of the conventional tools of geophysics. For instance, gravimeters are now sensitive enough to detect changes of less than 1/1000 mgal (a mgal being 1/1000th of the mean surface value of *g*), equivalent to shifts in topography of less than 5 mm. Magnetometers are routinely used to detect premonitory displacements on restless volcanoes. In a mere four decades, the determination of distance and height has moved from being a vexing and often insoluble chore to a rich source of valuable information.

# Time

How far back in time to take the narrative of the ensuing chapters is governed by the nature of the data. Thus, it makes sense to discuss the Earth's magnetic field over the past few millennia, as internal and external sources of magnetism cannot otherwise be differentiated, whereas the infall of dust and meteoritic material, which would undoubtedly benefit from a perspective spanning at least 65 million years, has been adequately quantified only for the past 10 years.

## Timekeeping

Laser altimetry, like EDM, depends on the accurate timing of the signal round trip. Horizontal positioning also increasingly requires precise time measurement. The NAVSAT navigational system (like that of some altimetric satellites) is based on the Doppler effect on a broadcast signal; the receivers measure the time needed for a number of beat cycles between the received signals and those generated by ground stations. With GPS, the distance (range) between satellite and receiver is measured by multiplying the transit time of the radio signal emitted by the satellites by the speed of light.

The best mechanical clocks have daily errors of a few thousandths of a second (Fig. 1.7). Quartz frequency standards, introduced in the 1930s, were at least ten times more accurate (Ward 1970). Clocks based on molecular or atomic vibration, first devised in 1948, had attained an accuracy of $1:10^{12}$ (i.e. 1 second in 30000 yr) by 1970. GPS satellites employ cæsium or rubidium clocks, the receivers generally cheaper quartz clocks; for VLBI (Anderson & Cazenave 1986), hydrogen-maser clocks are used at the two radiotelescopes.

The need in space geodesy is not only for good time resolution but also clock stability, both at the local station and on the satellite, so that calibration from high-performance devices is maintained within acceptable limits during the satellite pass or other critical interval. Oscillator stability of $5:10^{11}$ is equivalent to an uncertainty of 5 ms (Anderson & Cazenave 1986); for a satellite moving at $7 \, km \, s^{-1}$ it would lead to an error in the satellite position of 3.5 cm.

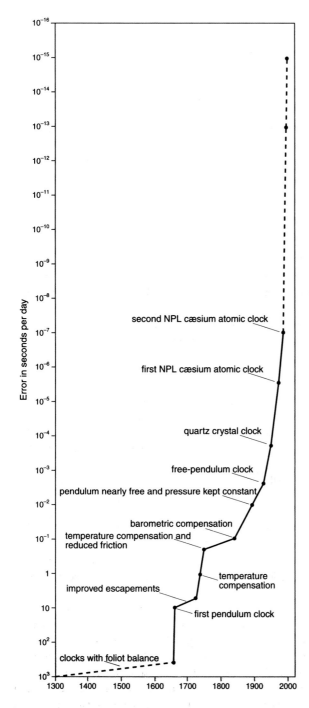

**Figure 1.7** Progress in timekeeping. The uppermost dot represents the precision (1.7 parts in $10^{15}$) of cæsium atomic clock NIST-F1 in 1999, an improvement of five orders of magnitude since 1950 (modified after Ward 1970, by permission of the Science Museum, London). Precisions of one part in $10^{18}$ are in prospect.

## Geochronometry

The dating of rocks and land surfaces has also experienced rapid progress in recent decades. Most of the existing techniques had a resolution measured in thousands or at best hundreds of years, and could be applied only to a narrow range of materials. Laminated lake beds (Fig. 1.8a) and tree rings can sometimes be counted confidently to the nearest year, but the results may be applied securely only to nearby parts of the same bed or ring, otherwise we have to make assumptions about the perfect equivalence of adjoining sequences or use other dating methods, such as the radiocarbon ($^{14}$C) technique, to bridge the gap between parts of a sequence or between two sequences.

A major source of uncertainty in $^{14}$C dating was the possibility that the atmospheric level of $^{14}$C, by which a "modern" sample is defined, had fluctuated. Calibration of $^{14}$C ages by dating tree rings of known age made possible the conversion of $^{14}$C ages to calendar ages (Becker 1992). The next key development was the introduction of accelerator mass spectroscopic (AMS) $^{14}$C dating in 1977. Although early hopes that it would extend the range of $^{14}$C dating to 100 000 yr have not been fulfilled, it has led to a dramatic reduction in the size of sample that can yield acceptable results – from 20 g to less than 1 mg – and therefore greatly expanded the range of locations that can be dated by $^{14}$C and the resolution with which it can be performed. Individual $^{14}$C ages for the Turin shroud had errors of $\pm 30$ yr and the weighted mean (for a total of 12 determinations shared between 3 laboratories) was $689 \pm 16$ yr (Damon et al. 1989).

In the light of these advances, the convention of using BP (before present) as the normal way of expressing $^{14}$C and some other numerical ages may no longer be acceptable, as "present" is traditionally 1950. The ambiguities and additional error values created by conversion to calendar dates on the basis of tree-ring calibration makes BC/AD equivalents in his respect even less satisfactory. The answer may lie in the inclusion of the date of measurement (i.e. the "present" for that age estimate) in the $^{14}$C determination.

The mass spectrometer has had a similar impact on U-series dating: high-precision $^{230}$Th ages on corals derived by TIMS have standard errors of $\pm 3$–5 yr (at two standard deviations or s.d.) for specimens less than 500 yr old, so that, for example, coastal uplift can be ascribed to an earthquake because two intertidal coral heads (Fig. 1.8b), which were killed by emergence, have the same age to within that margin of error (Edwards et al. 1988).

New isotopic methods have come into play. The potassium/argon (K/Ar) method suffered from uncertainty about the possible loss of argon gas from the sample; the $^{40}$Ar/$^{39}$Ar method can show whether there has been any loss (or gain) in argon after a mineral has crystallized. It is also helping to trace sea-level changes closely, because the small samples it requires can be drawn from well defined waterlines.

Some of the newer methods exploit isotopes with very short half-lives ($t_{1/2}$), the period during which the content in the radioactive parent isotope is halved. The polonium 210/lead 210 ($^{210}$Po/$^{210}$Pb) technique provides ages of lavas erupted on the sea floor during the past 2.5 yr (Rubin et al. 1994). $^{210}$Pb has a half-life of 22.26 yr. It is a decay product of radon 222 ($^{222}$Rn), which forms part of the decay series of uranium 238 ($^{238}$U) and it escapes into the atmosphere, where it remains for about ten days (residence time) before being washed out by rain or snow. $^{210}$Pb is therefore useful for dating snow and

**Figure 1.8** **(a)** Annual layers in Lisan Marls, Dead Sea, which may allow faulting (and thus earthquakes) to be dated to the nearest year. **(b, overleaf)** Micro-atoll, southwest coast of Simeulue (Indonesia), which is undergoing uplift. These coral structures, in combination with thermal ionization mass spectrometric (TIMS) [230]Th dating, can provide high-resolution age information on coseismic uplift in coastal areas.

sediments less than a century old; as its residence time in the ocean is 1–2 years, $^{210}$Pb is also used to analyze inshore marine deposits.

As some $^{210}$Pb is produced by the decay of radium 236 ($^{236}$Ra) rather than $^{222}$Rn in the sediment, it is important to analyze the top layers of the deposit to establish the local initial activity of $^{210}$Pb of atmospheric origin (Faure 1986). In freshwater peat (Oldfield et al. 1978) $^{210}$Pb does not work so well because the measurements are complicated by its downward diffusion; in the case of cæsium 137 ($^{137}$Cs) the problem is uptake by plants living in the peat.

## Cosmogenic isotopes

Ultra-sensitive mass spectrometers allow the study of radioactive nuclides, other than $^{14}$C, that are produced when galactic and solar cosmic rays interact with atoms in the atmosphere and on the surface of the Earth. The list includes two with suitably short half-lives: argon 39 ($^{39}$Ar, $t_{1/2} = 269$ yr) and silicon 31 ($^{31}$Si, $t_{1/2} = 276 \pm 32$ yr). There are others that bear on real-time geology indirectly. Beryllium 7 ($^{7}$Be) decays to lithium 7 ($^{7}$Li) with a $t_{1/2}$ of 53 days and thus is useful for studying atmospheric processes and sedimentation. Despite its relatively long half-life ($t_{1/2} = 1.5 \times 10^{6}$ yr), $^{10}$Be is critical to understanding the reasons for oscillations in the $^{14}$C level of the atmosphere (Faure 1986), as its residence time in surface ocean waters is a mere 16 yr.

Cosmogenic isotopes also hold the key to dating certain kinds of rock surface (including meteorites) and glacier ice. Since the 1980s, helium 3 ($^{3}$He), $^{10}$Be, $^{14}$C, neon 21 ($^{21}$Ne), aluminium 26 ($^{26}$Al) and chlorine 36 ($^{36}$Cl) have been used in landform studies (Bierman 1994). A thousand years of exposure history may produce enough cosmogenic isotopes to be measured (Cerling & Craig 1994), and advances in mass spectrometry for stable rare gases, as well as accelerator mass spectrometry for radio-nuclides, will doubtless further improve the resolution of this procedure.

Model calculations suggest that exposure ages can approach measurement precisions for surfaces eroding at less than 1 cm per 1000 yr, and that erosion rates can be estimated within $\pm 0.2\,cm\,yr^{-1}$ by using two suitable isotopes. In practice the uncertainties are much greater (Gillespie & Bierman 1995). But the resolution of the measurements is not the major problem facing interpretation of the data. Some of the isotopes may be produced in the atmosphere (meteoric) or by the decay of thorium and uranium (radio-genic), inherited from an earlier surface or depleted by erosion. Moreover, cosmogenic isotope production varies with depth and with the strength of the Earth's magnetic field. And analysis in terms of surface age or erosion rates requires consideration of geological history, which may of course include erosion itself (Bierman 1994).

Analyses of Apollo 15 lunar cores provide an independent estimate of the flux of solar cosmic rays. On Earth, short-lived nuclides such as sodium 22 ($^{22}$Na) and iron 55 ($^{55}$Fe) are thought to respond to individual solar-particle events and indeed to show evidence of the high solar activity that characterized the period 1954–64 (Jull et al. 1998). Cosmogenic isotopes are also used for discovering when a meteorite reached the Earth, as its cosmic irradiation then ceases and radioactive decay begins. $^{26}$Al ages for meteorites in east Antarctica include some younger than 100 000 years (Faure 1986), raising hopes of an independent measure of meteorite flux.

## *Biological markers*

Geochronology has benefited from advances in the life sciences besides radiobiology. Amino-acid racemization or epimerization (according to which of the amino acids is involved) is the process by which the spontaneously left-handed configuration (L-enantiomer) that characterizes protein-bound amino acids is transformed into D-enantiomer. Its speed is correlated with temperature, and the D:L ratio is thus not a simple measure of age. Initially exploited mainly for dating shell and bone beyond the range of $^{14}$C (i.e. >60 000 years), the method required calibration by uranium-series ages. Amino-acid dating is now applied independently of other dating techniques and to very recent centuries. Fossil shells provide results more reliable than bone, because their non-porous structure retains protein well (Goodfriend 1987), and dates for specimens a few millennia old have errors as low as $\pm 700$ years.

Another strategy for gauging recent events is to identify time markers representing radioactive fallout from nuclear weapons testing (or accidents). This is analogous to identifying a meteorite impact boundary by the iridium it is thought to have injected into the atmosphere. $^{36}$Cl, for example, has a long half-life of $3.08 \times 10^5$ years, but a pulse was apparently produced by nuclear fission devices in the atmosphere and was detected in Greenland ice dating from 1951 to 1974. Other possible bomb-produced markers are strontium 90 ($^{90}$Sr), silicon 32 ($^{32}$Si), which has been detected in rainwater, and $^{137}$Cs. Ashfalls provide a similar service, but unless they can be shown by their context to be extremely recent, as at Pompeii, they have to be dated by K/Ar or $^{14}$C, and are thus subject to the limitations of these methods.

Archaeology and history continue to make their own contribution to short-term Earth monitoring. Through archaeomagnetism (the study of the magnetism of archaeological remains) they help to calibrate shifts in the magnetic field, which elsewhere can be used to date artefacts and lavas that retain the magnetic field prevailing when they were baked. The dating of geological features and changes with the help of historical and documentary sources is a well established device (Fig. 1.9). Archbishop Ussher immortalized its dangerous charms by calculating the age of the Earth from the number of generations listed in Genesis. The underlying calculation – $n$ units each of $y$ years – is at the root of other less controversial methods such as tree-ring counting, but like them it is sensitive to the choice of year zero, as well as to the assumption that the governing process was periodic.

Yet Earth scientists who rely on history for chronology now benefit not only from enhanced scepticism but also from remarkable advances in archaeological and textual analysis. Direct dating of geological events is predictably most successful when the event is a disaster. Pompeii and Herculaneum are grandiloquent fossils with which to fix the timing and duration of Vesuvian eruptions. There are Chinese time observations for much of the period 145 BC to AD 1636, of which 87 refer to solar eclipses and 72 to lunar eclipses (Li 1987), valuable pegs on which to hang other chronologies.

Analysis of the 1200 or so non-mathematical Babylonian astronomical texts dating from 700 BC to AD 75 sometimes permits precise dating of individual earthquakes. For example, "The 19th, in the middle part of the day, the earth quaked" refers to 14 January 251 BC (Aaboe 1980), but the truth of these reports remains contentious, especially in view of the part played by earthquakes in Babylonian omens (Parpola 1983). This is a

**Figure 1.9** **(a)** Marine terrace at Boso, southwest of Tokyo (Japan), uplifted during the Kanto earthquake ($M_S = 8.1$) of 1 September 1923. **(b, opposite)** Keystones at Kalat Nimrud (Israel) border reportedly dislodged by an earthquake in 1202.

pity, as earthquakes were apparently rarer in some parts of the empire than in others and displayed some kind of periodicity (Ambraseys & Melville 1982). More recent eye-witness accounts in less rarefied circumstances fare no better. Not long after the earth-quakes that hit Corinth in 1980 (Vita-Finzi & King 1985) there was disagreement between local inhabitants, even man and wife, over how far the adjoining shoreline had been displaced.

The multi-pronged approach to terrestrial changes promoted by this book may some-times founder on such ambiguities; but shipwrecks help to reveal sandbanks and the currents by which they were fashioned.

# CHAPTER 2
# Rain from space

*Questa è polvere che viene dalle stelle . . . più anni passano, più ce n'è, di modo che funziona come un orologio.* ("This is dust from the stars . . . as the years pass there is more of it, so that it works like a clock.")
Carlo Levi, *La chiave a stella* ("The ring spanner") 1978

When Galileo saw through his telescope that Jupiter had moons and that Venus had phases, the Earth lost two claims to uniqueness. Galileo also saw that the Moon was cratered, yet it has taken over three centuries for astronomers to accept that the Earth is not immune from the plague of meteorites that has scarred its solid neighbours. Indeed, it was not until 1893 that G. K. Gilbert pointed to clear evidence for an impact origin of the lunar craters; and even then the volcanic alternative continued to be preferred by geologists "presumably not wishing to allow catastrophism, expelled by Lyell from their science, in by the back door of lunar studies" (Runcorn 1974). Gilbert himself dismissed a volcanic origin for Meteor Crater in Arizona, which to modern eyes looks archetypally the product of an impact.

Satellites and astronauts then revealed that cratering had pockmarked the surfaces of Mercury, Mars and, less obviously, Venus, as well as many of the planetary moons. The Earth's acknowledged craters, meanwhile, slowly increased from a handful in 1930 to over 170 by the turn of the century (Fig. 2.1), not counting features less than 10 m across that are ascribed to recent meteorite showers (Grieve & Pesonen 1992), such as the 200 pits produced by a single event in Russia in 1947.

Some early accounts had stiffened the prevailing scepticism by identifying as impact structures any large and roughly circular feature, including Hudson's Bay and the Gulf of Mexico. Even field studies founded on geochemical and petrological data, as well as morphology, earned little or no mention in standard textbooks. Then, in 1980, Luis and Walter Alvarez presented both chemical and circumstantial evidence that an extra-terrestrial source was responsible for the mass faunal extinction that occurred at the Cretaceous/Tertiary (K/T) boundary. Perhaps the most persuasive item of evidence they cited was an enrichment in iridium (Ir) of the sediments at the boundary to about a thousand times above the background level (Alvarez et al. 1980). Many asteroids and comets are much richer in iridium than the Earth's crust. Moreover, the Ir peak could be sought throughout the globe. It was duly found at several sites, and in 1993 the point

21

**(a)**

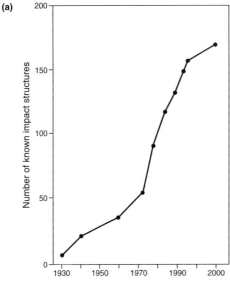

Number of known impact structures

**(b)**

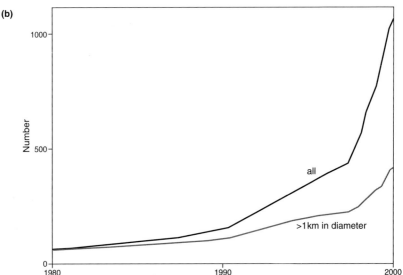

Number

**Figure 2.1** **(a)** Increase between 1980 and 2000 in the accepted number of impact craters on Earth (after Grieve 1991, by permission of *Meteorites and Planetary Science*). **(b)** Increase in number of known near-Earth asteroids since 1980 (after Alan B. Chamberlin, Minor Planet Center, JPL/NASA website 8 August 2000, with permission).

of impact itself was identified with the Chicxulub crater, straddling the northern coast of Yucatán (Mexico), which was first recognized by oil geologists in borehole data and subsequently mapped using geophysical methods (Sharpton et al. 1996). Yet the nearest to a real-time record of a terrestrial impact remained the Tunguska (Siberia) event of 1908, which presents many problems of interpretation. That is why trying to reconstruct an impact from the crater and associated debris requires both computer modelling and reference to explosion experiments by mining engineers and bomb designers.

In July 1994, there was a splendid demonstration of the energies that are produced

**Table 2.1** Chances of dying in the USA (from Chapman & Morrison 1994).

| | |
|---|---|
| Motor vehicle accident | 1 in 100 |
| Murder | 1 in 300 |
| Firearms accident | 1 in 2500 |
| Asteroid/comet impact | 1 in 3000 to 1 in 250000 |
| Passenger aircraft crash | 1 in 20000 |
| Flood | 1 in 30000 |
| Venomous bite or sting | 1 in 100000 |
| Fireworks accident | 1 in 1000000 |
| Food poisoning by botulism | 1 in 10000000 |

by impact, when comet Shoemaker–Levy 9 collided with Jupiter to release energies measurable in $10^6$ megatons of TNT (1 megaton = $4.2 \times 10^{15}$ Joules). Those who were still reluctant to include impact as a routine event in Earth history could argue that the exceptional size of Jupiter and its non-rocky exterior were hardly representative of terrestrial conditions. But the pendulum had swung decisively, and catastrophic impacts soon ranked fifteenth on a list of causes of mortality in the world as a whole after "venomous bite or sting" and before "airline hijacking aftermath" (c.f. Table 2.1).

In 1999 the Torino impact hazard scale was proposed by R. P. Binzel and adopted by the International Astronomical Union in the same year. It runs from zero for an object with virtually no chance of causing damage to Earth to ten for certain climatic catastrophe at global scale, and thus combines the probability of an impact with its severity. But, unlike seismic hazard assessment, which can take historical evidence into account in one way or another, estimates of impact hazard suffer from the serious difficulties that face any attempt to evaluate the environmental effects of dust or debris (Baillie 1999).

# Meteorites

Estimates of the total interplanetary influx of material on Earth are based on a mixture of direct and indirect sources. They include extrapolation from radar and photographic observation of incoming bodies, and astronomical records of potential impactors in orbit around the Earth; the microcraters left on artificial satellites or recorded on spaceborne instruments, and the size and distribution of impact structures on Earth, other solid planets and moons; sampling from observational balloons; and the collection of meteorites and dust on the ground, in polar ice and in deep-sea cores.

## Records
Dependable estimates for the size range 10–100 m or $10^5$–$10^{10}$ kg were not possible until 1990, when the Spacewatch telescope revealed several such bodies. Asteroidal bodies are classified in terms of their perihelion (their closest approach to the Sun, the farthest being the aphelion) and the semi-major axis, the shorter of the two axes defining the elliptical shape of their orbits, both expressed in astronomical units (AU), the average distance of the Earth from the Sun. Those bodies currently with orbits that are

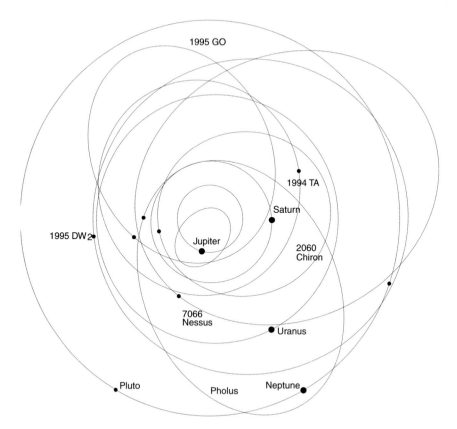

**Figure 2.2** Orbits of objects, some of them from the Kuiper belt, outside the orbit of Jupiter. Comets such as 2060 Chiron can be deflected by gravitational forces into the inner Solar System. (After McSween 1999, by permission of Cambridge University Press).

not Earth crossing may be perturbed into Earth-crossing orbits (Fig. 2.2) to qualify as near-Earth objects (NEOs), which are defined as having a perihelion < 1.3 AU. Apollos, named after asteroid 1862 Apollo, have a semi-major axis > 1 AU and perihelion < 1.017 AU. Amor objects, named after 1221 Amor, have orbits between those of Earth and Mars, with a semi-major axis of > 1 AU and perihelion 1.017–1.3 AU. Atens, named after asteroid 2062 Aten, have semi-major axis of < 1.0 AU and aphelion > 0.983 AU. In other words, Amors are Mars crossing but not Earth crossing; Apollos include most Earth-crossing asteroids, and Atens have orbits mostly inside that of the Earth.

Between 1985 and 1995 the number of known Apollo and Aten asteroids more than quadrupled (Steel 1995); by August 2000 the totals were listed as 496 Apollos, 79 Atens and 484 Amors (HSCFA 2000); many authors assume that there is a similar number of comets. The largest Earth-crossing asteroid is 1627 Ivar, with a diameter of 8 km and a mass of some $10^{15}$ kg; 1036 Ganymed is 100 times larger but at present merely in Earth-approaching orbit (Morrison et al. 1994).

Direct observations include fireball records, which amount to estimates of large

**Table 2.2** Influx of material in $kg\,yr^{-1}$ for entire Earth (after Ceplecha 1992).

| Material | Stony | Carbonaceous | Cometary |
|---|---|---|---|
| Dust | $8.3 \times 10^5$ | $2.4 \times 10^6$ | $4.7 \times 10^5$ |
| Mass ablated in atmosphere | $5.1 \times 10^7$ | $6.1 \times 10^7$ | $1.0 \times 10^8$ |
| Terminal mass after ablation | $1.1 \times 10^8$ | $1.0 \times 10^8$ | $6.5 \times 10^7$ |
| Meteorites (non-explosive impacts) | $4.1 \times 10^6$ | $3.1 \times 10^5$ | $8.0 \times 10^{-6}$ |
| Explosive impacts | $1.1 \times 10^8$ | $1.0 \times 10^8$ | $6.5 \times 10^7$ |
| Total | $1.7 \times 10^8$ | $1.7 \times 10^8$ | $1.7 \times 10^8$ |
| Bulk density | 0.5 | 0.75 | 1.45 |

bodies prior to entry into the atmosphere (Grady 1997). The Canadian Meteorite Observation and Recovery Project of 1971–85, for example, observed some 900 fireballs, interpreted as equivalent to a flux of about 50 tonnes a year for meteoroids with preatmospheric masses greater than 100 g.

The satellites Explorer I and Sputnik III carried microphone systems for the detection of micrometeorites. Many later satellites have continued to search the vicinity of the Earth and Venus, using a variety of systems other than microphones, such as pressure-sensitive detectors, conductive wires whose breakage produces a signal, photomultipliers that measure the luminous intensity emitted during the impact of a particle with sufficient velocity, and microcondensers, which discharge when an impact leads to vaporization of a conducting gas (Delobeau 1971). The two crucial problems (Brownlee 1985) are low collection rates and high velocities, typical values for particles of $10\,\mu m$ being $1\,m^{-2}\,day^{-1}$ (compared to $1\,m^{-2}\,yr^{-1}$ for $100\,\mu m$ particles) and impact velocities of about $15\,km\,s^{-1}$.

Even at the lowest impact velocity possible ($c.\ 3\,km\,s^{-1}$), the particle is destroyed, so that all structural and chemical information is lost unless (as in one of the Gemini 10 experiments) the solid surface experiencing the impact develops a crater that retains some of the sample. The capture cell technique employs a membrane pierced by the particle, which vaporizes beneath the diaphragm; the condensed vapours can then be analyzed isotopically in place or later in the laboratory.

In the stratosphere, the first incontrovertibly extraterrestrial particles were sampled by a balloon-borne collector in 1970 and, after 1974, by U2 aircraft. The preferred size range is $2–50\,\mu m$, because larger particles are rare and smaller ones are swamped by sulphate aerosols (Brownlee 1985). Velocities are $10^6$ lower than in space and the concentration of $10\,\mu m$ particles is correspondingly enhanced. Most of the particles of diameter $5–100\,\mu m$ recovered from the stratosphere are similar to carbonaceous chondrite meteorites, but they do not appear to encompass the full range of compositions indicated by reflection spectroscopy of the main-belt asteroids, and it has accordingly been suggested (Flynn 1994) that they are dominated by recent collisional events supplemented by some cometary material.

## Craters

Thanks mainly to computer modelling, there has been rapid progress in evaluating impactor size from crater geometry. The known impact structures are inevitably concentrated in areas that are well explored and subject to little erosion or tectonic activity (Fig. 2.3). The only well attested oceanic structures are the Montagnais Crater off Nova Scotia, 45 km in diameter and 50 Myr old, and the 2.15 Myr-old Eltanin Crater in the southeastern Pacific Ocean (Gersonde et al. 1997).

The observed number of large impact craters on terrestrial and lunar surfaces of known age suggests that there is an average of $900 \pm 400$ terrestrial impacts by 0.5 km-diameter objects per 100 Myr that might produce craters 10 km in diameter (Wetherill & Shoemaker 1982). The cratering rate indicated by actual structures about 120 Myr old is $(5.5 \pm 2.7) \times 10^{-15} \, \text{km}^2 \, \text{yr}^{-1}$; the current production rate for craters with diameters of about 20 km, taking comets as well as Earth-crossing asteroids into account, is the very similar figure of $(4.9 \pm 2.9) \times 10^{-15} \, \text{km}^2 \, \text{yr}^{-1}$ (Chyba et al. 1994, Grieve & Shoemaker 1994).

Comparison with other planetary bodies, even after allowance is made for relative position, differences in mass and atmospheric shielding, and extent of erosion and deposition, is prey to the quality and interpretation of imagery. For instance, there is general acceptance of a period prior to $3.9 \times 10^9$ yr ago when many large bodies bombarded the Earth and its Moon, but the evidence from the far side of the Moon obtained by the Clementine mission for an increase in the cratering rate by a factor of about 0.5 over the past 120 Myr has found little favour.

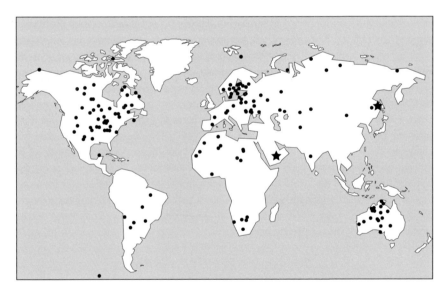

**Figure 2.3** Distribution of known impact craters, with inevitable shortage of undersea structures; Wabar (~150 yr old) in Saudi Arabia and Sikhote Alin (12 February 1947) are marked by stars (after Grieve & Shoemaker 1994 and Grady et al. 1998).

Confident recognition of an impact origin generally hinges on certain shock meta-morphic effects and geochemical anomalies produced by the projectile (Grieve 1991), rather than on morphology alone. Nevertheless, initial assessment hinges on two classic categories:

- simple craters, bowl shaped with an uplifted and overturned rim
- complex craters, where there is a central peak or ring.

For example, Meteor Crater is a simple structure that was formed about 50 000 yr ago by an iron meteorite with an impact velocity of $25\,\mathrm{km\,s^{-1}}$, equivalent to the release of $10^{16}\,\mathrm{J}$ of kinetic energy or 60 megatons of TNT (Grieve & Pesonen 1992). Superimposed craters of varying degrees of freshness, commonplace on lunar images, are rare on Earth, although analogy with the Moon led to the suggestion that the Campo del Cielo chain of craters in Argentina had been produced by low-angle bouncing projectiles (Schultz & Lianza 1992); current interest in the possibility that impacts triggered the emplacement of flood basalts on Earth doubtless draws some of its inspiration from images of the lunar maria, even if the age of the basalts conflicts with an impact origin.

In general the true crater floor is concealed by a breccia lens consisting of collapsed material from the walls of the initial (transient) cavity produced by the impact (Melosh 1989). The ratio between apparent depth ($d_A$) and true depth ($d_T$) for seven simple craters with diameter $D$ is

$$d_A = 0.13D^{1.06}$$

$$d_T = 0.28D^{1.02}$$

the lunar equivalent having greater apparent depths

$$d_A = 0.20D^{1.01}$$

presumably because greater $g$ on Earth promotes cavity-wall collapse (Grieve & Peso-nen 1992).

Complex craters have central-peak craters, central-peak basins with peak and ring, peak-ring basins with only a ring, and multi-ring basins. The last category includes the Sudbury structure (Ontario), which is some 200 km in diameter. The central structures consist of uplifted shocked rocks, which represent the floor of the transient cavity. Measurements on five complex craters suggest that the final form reflects the intrinsic strength of the target rocks. Thus,

$$d_A = 0.12D^{0.30}$$

for sedimentary rocks, and

$$d_A = 0.15D^{0.43}$$

for crystalline rocks But erosion may destroy all topographical trace of a complex crater, apart from the central positive structure.

Calculations show that comets and stony and carbonaceous meteorites with energies <10 megatons would not impinge materially on the surface. Iron–nickel meteorites, which make up 6 per cent of observed main-belt asteroids and Earth-crossing asteroids, would crater the ground enough to produce a 500 m crater on land every 1400 yr or thereabouts (Chyba 1993). Figure 2.4 shows the estimated number of Earth-crossing asteroids of a range of diameters; Figure 2.5 shows the cumulative energy-frequency curve for impacts on Earth based on the average interval between impacts equal to or greater than the energy yield shown on the $X$ axis.

At sea, a 1000-megaton impact could produce a 5 m sea wave or tsunami with a range of 1000 km (Morrison et al. 1994). Three quarters of the Earth's surface consists of ocean basins with depths averaging 4–5 km. A 10 km stony body hitting an ocean 5 km deep at 20 km s$^{-1}$ would generate a water wave 4 km high; 37 seconds later the wave would be 1 km high and 18 km from the impact site (Adushkin & Nemchinov 1994). Much effort is now being expended on the search for tsunami deposits that can be shown not to be the product of earthquakes or large landslides.

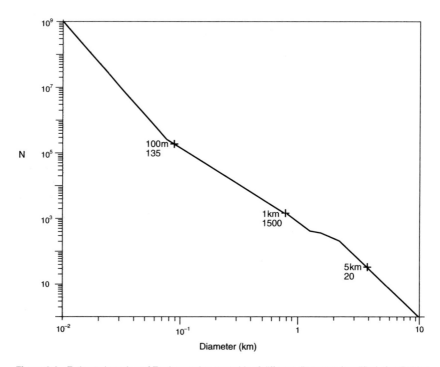

**Figure 2.4** Estimated number of Earth-crossing asteroids of different diameters (modified after Rabinowitz et al. 1994, by permission of the University of Arizona Press, © 1994 The Arizona Board of Regents).

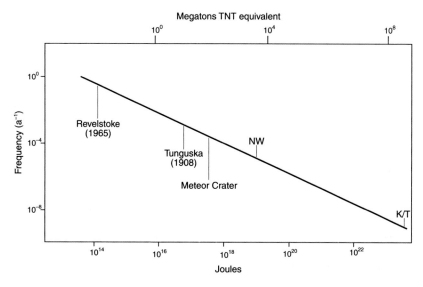

**Figure 2.5** Estimated frequency of impacts per year plotted against the impact in megatons of equivalent TNT explosive. (After Shoemaker 1983 and others). The figure also shows estimates for the energy of the Tertiary/Cretaceous (K/T) boundary event and other impacts and for the energy thought to be required to initiate nuclear winter (NW). Both Revelstoke and Tunguska were probably atmospheric impacts.

# Debris

Metallic spheroids were found to be present during exploration of the ocean floor in 1876. It soon became clear that they were extraterrestrial material and that coring would yield estimates of the annual influx. Values of several million kilograms per day were obtained for the Pacific Ocean, with an accretion rate of 2 mm per 1000 yr on average for the past 7.5 Myr (Delobeau 1971). One estimate for the total influx of all interplanetary bodies across the mass range measuring up to $10^{15}$ kg is $1.7 \times 10^8$ kg yr$^{-1}$; however, measurements of $^{187}Os/^{186}Os$ (osmium) ratios in deep-sea sediments and manganese nodules (Love & Brownlee 1993) indicate a much lower mass-accretion rate of about $49$–$56 \times 10^6$ kg yr$^{-1}$.

The atmosphere provides effective protection against stony bodies that weigh less than $10^5$ kg, carbonaceous bodies weighing less than $10^7$ kg, and cometary bodies weighing less than about $10^{11}$ kg. For stony and carbonaceous bodies (Ceplecha 1992), two thirds of the total influx comes from explosive impacts and a third from ablated material.

For a given energy, deepest penetration is at the slowest velocity (the escape velocity or 11.2 km s$^{-1}$ for Earth) because a bolide will explode, and thus contribute debris without producing a significant impact on the ground surface, at a pressure proportional to $Fv^2$, where $F$ is the atmospheric pressure and $v$ the bolide velocity (Chyba 1993). Thus, it can happen that a small meteorite is decelerated high in the atmosphere and survives complete ablation or pulverization; a stony asteroid of the dimensions proposed for the Tunguska event (see below) could penetrate deep into the atmosphere and experience sufficient aerodynamic loading to break up into many fragments no larger than 10 cm but widely dispersed (Svetsov 1996).

Asteroids and short-period (<20 yr) comets generally strike at velocities of about 15 km s$^{-1}$ (Chyba et al. 1994), and small asteroids (<50 m) probably at about 13 km s$^{-1}$, whereas long-period comets may do so at much greater speeds, a figure of 50 km s$^{-1}$ sometimes being cited. Although the nature of the meteoroid is evidently important in determining its fate, the effect, especially of the larger ones, is a matter of kinetic energy and therefore a combination of mass and velocity. Aerodynamic stresses break up meteoroids with diameters of up to some tens of meters; modelling suggests that rocky meteorites >50 m in diameter and comets >100 m can penetrate deep into the atmosphere.

Convincing eyewitness accounts of meteorite falls are few. The Barwell meteorite fell through a window in Leicestershire (England) on Christmas Eve 1965; the Pavlovka in Sartov (Russia) in 1882; the Junivas in Ardèche (France) in 1821; the Stannern in Jihomoravsky (Czechoslovakia) in 1808. The first is a chondrite, and contains chondrules or once-molten droplets that are thought to originate in the solar nebula before the planets formed. The other three have a structure that suggests they came from an asteroid, perhaps Vesta, which was large enough to have melted (S. Russell, pers. comm.). The US early-warning satellites recorded for 1972–2000 an annual average of 30 events of 1 kiloton of TNT or greater, most of which were not detected on the ground.

Calculations based on the collection of actual meteorites on the ground are subject to the vagaries of sampling and the mass lost by weathering and, if the number of falls is at issue, the extent to which several specimens may represent a single event. Areas deemed suitable for sampling are rocky deserts and Antarctica. In a recent study, a collection of 98 chondrite meteorites from accumulation sites in New Mexico, the Sahara and the Nullarbor region of Australia were dated by $^{14}$C and examined spectroscopically in order to determine how far they had been oxidized on Earth. The results, together with data on the number and distribution of paired meteorites in each region, made it possible to estimate the number of meteorite falls of >10 g as 36–116/ $10^6$ km$^{-2}$ yr$^{-1}$. The total mass flux to the Earth's surface of meteorites of 10–1000 g was placed at 2900–7300 kg yr$^{-1}$. These estimates are consistent between the three regions and agree closely with the estimate of the present flux from camera network data, suggesting that the flux of meteorites to the Earth has remained essentially constant over the past 50 000 yr (Bland et al. 1996).

The Earth's atmosphere, which is known to vaporize small projectiles, may in fact discriminate against the survival of large ones. The Tunguska event in Siberia on 30 June 1908 was once ascribed to a comet, both because its main effect was to flatten trees within an area of 10 000 km$^2$ and because no craters or meteorite fragments were reported. But it is now considered the product of an asteroid measuring tens of meters in diameter and entering the atmosphere at typical supersonic velocity (Chyba et al. 1993, Svetsov 1996): the flux of radiation inside and outside the fireball may have been sufficient to ablate most of the fragments, and those that escaped the fireball as a consequence of accidental collisions probably gained sufficient lateral velocity, say $1 \, km \, s^{-1}$ at a height of 15–20 km, to land 3–10 km away from the bull's-eye.

Conversely, the meteorite population may yield useful information on the surface on which it lies. The length of stay of the meteorite on Earth can be estimated from cosmogenic radionuclide abundances, their sojourn on an icecap from thermoluminescence analysis. The temperature problem that often complicates thermoluminescence dating can be countered either by making assumptions about both the original thermoluminescence level and the surface temperature or by taking several samples at different depths within a single meteorite. Some blue icefields in Victoria Land, Antarctica, have yielded many meteorites, none of which appears to have been exposed on the ice for more than 300 000 yr (Benoit 1995), suggesting that a pulse in ice thickening had disposed of any older meteorites.

## Dust

The youngest dated crater-forming events are at Wabar in Saudi Arabia (about 150 yr old) and at Sikhote Alin (12 February 1947). Forest strikes other than Tunguska are thought to have occurred in Brazil (1930) and Guyana (1935). But meteorites are exceedingly rare in comparison with cosmic dust, which is so abundant that "every footstep a person takes contacts a fragment of cosmic dust" and which "can be recovered from historical deposits in deep-sea sediments and collected in real time in space and the stratosphere" (Brownlee 1985).

The dust is probably more representative of the entire meteoroid complex at 1 AU than conventional meteorites, but its major source lies in comets, as asteroids generate dust only during collisions. Even then, cometary dust is mostly lost to space by collisions between dust grains and the pressure drag produced by solar radiation, and it has been argued that the latter is so effective at sweeping micro-particles out beyond the Earth's orbit that any measuring $<0.2 \, \mu m$ must represent the breakdown of larger bodies (Delobeau 1971). Samples from the bottom of the South Pole water well (Taylor et al. 1998), which represent all the material falling on the pre-industrial snow there, suggest that 90 per cent of the micro-meteoroid flux evaporates during entry into the atmosphere.

The zodiacal light – a phenomenon attributed by Cassini three centuries ago to diffraction by interplanetary dust and now simply explained by reflection – is consistent with a density of between $5 \times 10^{-21} \, g \, cm^{-3}$ and $10^{-23} \, g \, cm^{-3}$ (Delobeau 1971). According to observations by the spacecraft Luna X, the Moon is surrounded by a density of dust a hundred times greater than in the space between it and the Earth, which may indicate an origin in the ejection of material by the impacts that produced the Moon's craters. Indeed, the possibility has been raised that some Earth-crossing objects originate in lunar impacts (Chyba 1993).

If the peak of the micro-meteoroid mass distribution does indeed lie at about 200 μm, as is generally thought (Brownlee 1985), it is below the limit of detection of spacecraft

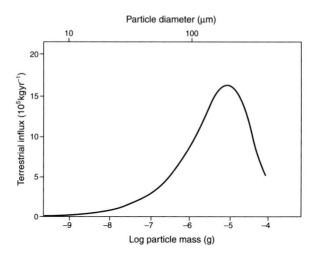

**Figure 2.6** Mass of micrometeorites accreted annually by the Earth judging from the cratering record on the Long Duration Exposure satellite device (after Love & Brownlee 1993, ©1993 American Association for the Advancement of Science). Note peak at diameter of 220 μm.

studies prior to 1993. The kinetic energy liberated by this size range is too low for optical detection (Love & Brownlee 1994), and sampling by radar meteor studies has an uncertainty of at least half an order of magnitude. Hence the importance of the Long-Duration Exposure Facility (LDEF) satellite, which provides large, solid aluminium targets always orientated within 1° of the zenith. Of a set of 761 craters on 5.6 m$^2$ of surface exposed for 5.77 yr at altitudes of 331–480 km, an estimated < 10 per cent were produced by orbital debris (Love & Brownlee 1993).

In order to calculate projectile energies, the average depth:diameter ratio (0.527) had to be applied to those craters whose depth was unknown. Laboratory experiments have shown that crater volume under the conditions in question is nearly proportional to the projectile kinetic energy, and the component of the projectile speed normal to the target is 12 km s$^{-1}$, a value derived from photographic evidence as well as crater rate measurements on the LDEF.

Integration of the mass-flux curve (Fig. 2.6) gives a total accretion rate of $40 \pm 20 \times 10^6$ kg yr$^{-1}$, the error being estimated from uncertainties about meteoroid velocity and the velocity component of the formula for penetration depth. The total is consistent with estimates based on measurements of the manganese 53 ($^{53}$Mn) component of marine sediments (Love & Brownlee 1993). This is a substantial portion of the total of $49–56 \times 10^6$ kg yr$^{-1}$ for meteoroids of all sizes mentioned earlier and it could indicate that the Spacewatch results exaggerate the long-term contribution by bodies with masses $> 10^6$ g.

Iridium, the telltale element at the K/T boundary, can similarly serve to trace the rate of sediment accumulation in oceans if its infall is assumed to be relatively constant except when large impacts take place. The relation between Ir and sediment accumulation is

$$I_{SED} = \frac{M_{COS} \cdot I_{COS} + M_{TER} \cdot I_{TER}}{M_{COS} + M_{TER}}$$

where $I_{SED}$, $I_{COS}$ and $I_{TER}$ are respectively Ir concentrations in the sediment, cosmic matter and terrigenous material, and $M_{COS}$ and $M_{TER}$ are respectively the cosmic and terrestrial mass accumulation rates (Bruns et al. 1995). The principle should make it possible to discriminate between hiatuses in sedimentation and breaks resulting from erosion, as a low supply of terrigenous sediment leads to high Ir concentrations, whereas erosion does not affect Ir levels.

## Comets

Shoemaker has suggested that half the impact craters on Earth that are > 20 km in diameter and nearly all those > 100 km diameter were produced by cometary impacts "late in geological time" (McCall 1997).

Earth-crossing comets (ECCs), like Apollo objects, have perihelia shorter than the aphelion distance of the Earth (or 1.017 AU), although in some definitions near-Earth comets must have a period of < 200 yr to qualify. Analysis of the cometary flux leads to the estimate that a long-period comet with a diameter of over 100 km crosses the Earth's orbit every 400 yr (Bailey et al. 1994). More specifically, of the known 26 active Earth-crossing periodic comets, 13 have a period of 20 years (Jupiter family) and 13 have a period of between 20 and 200 years (Halley family). The longest record belongs to Halley's comet (P/Halley), which has been seen 30 times since its first observation in 240 BC; the closest approach was by P/Lexell in 1770 (0.00015 AU or $2.2 \times 10^6$ km) (Shoemaker et al. 1994).

The closest Earth approach this century to be made by a known short-period comet will be by Finlay to 0.0473 AU on 27 October 2060. (The Aten asteroid 2340 Hathor will approach to 0.0066 AU in 2069 and 0.0057 AU in 2086.) Besides the uncertainties introduced by observation noise, and the effect of each successive close planetary encounter on succeeding ones, an active comet produces non-gravitational effects as a result of outgassing and discrepancies between its centre of mass and its centre of brightness. Long-period comets may be visiting the inner Solar System for the first time or have an unknown non-gravitational component (Yeomans & Chodas 1994), and in any case they may prove difficult to observe if approaching from the Sun.

The collision probability with Earth is estimated to be 1.3 per $10^9$ yr for the Jupiter family of comets and, mainly because of their longer orbital periods, as low as 1.6 per $10^{10}$ yr for the Halley family. On the other hand, their most probable impact velocities are 19.9 km s$^{-1}$ and 52.3 km s$^{-1}$ respectively (Shoemaker et al. 1994).

The cometary catalogue continues to grow, witness the recent discovery in 1994 of two more extinct comets: comets that do not exhibit a detectable coma and which may therefore be mistakenly reported as asteroids. One of them, 1994 EQ3, was a ~30 km-diameter Jupiter crosser that was subsequently identified on films taken as long ago as

1937. There is even some support for the suggestion (Zahnle & Grinspoon 1990) that the K/T extinction was the product of a cometary impact rather than a meteoritic one.

Debris from the large comet to be captured most recently into the inner Solar System may be the source of the Taurid Complex, a meteoroid stream that includes 10 per cent of the Earth-crossing asteroids and most of the dust derived from meteoroids (Bailey et al. 1994). The complex itself is a potential source of impacts by bodies resembling that responsible for Tunguska (i.e. a diameter of $\leq 100$ m), as well as an atmospheric dust load sufficient to provoke significant climatic cooling (Asher & Clube 1993) comparable to the climatic deterioration of the Holocene Little Ice Ages (Bailey et al. 1994). An apparent match between peaks in the accumulation of $^3$He from interplanetary dust particles (IDPs) and evidence for fluctuations in global ice volume with a period of about 100 000 yr has led to the suggestion that cyclic changes in the Earth's orbital inclination caused periodic blockage of solar radiation (Muller & MacDonald 1997) and hence triggered the glacial cycles.

Large impact events have been invoked to resolve other conundrums, including the angle and direction of planetary rotation. There is also the suggestion that major bombardment episodes, of which six have been proposed for the Moon for the past 3.8 Gyr, coincided in time (given resolution errors of $\pm 100$ Myr) with what are sometimes termed the six major episodes of mountain building on Earth (Stothers 1992). The old belief that the Earth was affected by worldwide orogenic events is contradicted by the available ages, and runs contrary to the current view that much tectonic activity results from plate interaction, which is rarely synchronous at several locations. On the other hand a major impact could trigger an episode of plate reorganization (Price 2001).

Interplanetary dust fine enough to be adequately decelerated could also have served to convey organics. Comets are unlikely to have been decelerated sufficiently for any organic molecules carried by them to survive impact (Chyba et al. 1990), but through shock vaporization they could have created reducing mixtures of gases from which organics were synthesized (Chyba & Sagan 1992). Comets may also have served both to deliver water (Fig. 2.7) and gases that led to acute greenhouse conditions (Chyba et al. 1994). The rain from space thus bears on the origins as well as the vicissitudes – past and future – of life on Earth.

**Figure 2.7** Multiple exposure ultraviolet image by NASA's Polar orbiter at an altitude of 47 400 km on 15 September 1996, showing 500 km trail of atomic oxygen ascribed to a mini-comet (courtesy of NASA and Louis A. Frank, University of Iowa).

# CHAPTER 3
# Earth and Sun

*E tanti furono i suoi capricci, che filosofando delle cose naturali attese a intendere le proprietà delle erbe, continuando (ed) osservando il moto del cielo, il corso della luna, e gli andamenti del sole.* ("So many were his passions, that in his studies of nature he paused to scrutinize the grass underfoot before turning to observe the movement of the heavens, the path of the Moon and the behaviour of the Sun.")
Giorgio Vasari on Leonardo da Vinci, in *Le Vite* (2nd edn) 1568

Most of the processes discussed in this book are influenced to some extent by the Sun, whether they are driven by its luminosity or modulated by the solar wind. The narrative itself is coloured by that interaction: the validity of [14]C ages, for example, hinges in part on the intensity of the cosmic-ray flux, to which the Sun makes a substantial contribution and from which the Earth is shielded by its variable magnetic field. The solar energy impinging upon the Earth depends on changes in the Earth's orbit, angle of tilt and precession (see Ch. 4). The solar constant varies, and therefore enters discussion of those climatic byblows – the atmospheric circulation and the distribution of ice bodies and oceans – that impinge on the Earth's rotation. How it varies, and why, are therefore questions that cannot be dismissed as purely astronomical.

Until the era of direct satellite measurement, the truth of solar variability rested primarily on the evidence of sunspots and was therefore not generally recognized. Aurorae have been described since antiquity, but their interpretation is problematic. The corona is poorly recorded (Stephenson 1988a). The sunspot record goes back at least to 165 BC in China. In the West, scattered sunspot observations have long been made but largely ignored, because the Sun was considered to be too perfect to bear such blemishes. When they were too obvious to be disregarded, they were sometimes explained away as planetary transits across the solar disk, with Mercury or Venus generally implicated. Among those who were thus misled are Ptolemy in AD 150, Averroes in the late twelfth century and Johannes Kepler in 1607 (van Helden 1995). Estimates of variations in the Sun's diameter had been derived previously from the timing of solar eclipses and of genuine transits of Mercury across the solar disk, but even now there is uncertainty over the relationship between diameter and solar output (Stephenson 1988a). The available measurements (Parkinson et al. 1980) yield evidence of a negligible trend since 1715

(−0.008±0.007%) and of a more convincing periodicity of about 76 yr (half amplitude 0.02%), the significance of which is obscure.

Since 1983, photoelectric measurements have been made of the vertical and horizontal diameters of the Sun, and spacecraft have monitored directly the character and level of its energy output down to the level of outbursts of flare activity measured in minutes, but no clear trend has yet emerged.

## Sunspots

Galileo's observations of sunspots began in 1611 but were not detailed until 1612, when his adoption of the projection method made recording both safe and more precise. Galileo's view soon prevailed – that the spots were not planets but features analogous to clouds on Earth (van Helden 1995) – but their cyclical nature was not recognized until 1843, when H. Schwabe identified a period of about 10 yr.

The subject was formalized by Wolf in Zurich, who introduced the annual index that is still in use and inaugurated a regular survey of the Sun, although almost daily sunspot surveys were already available since 1818 (Stephenson 1988a). The index $R$ is intended to convey an annual mean sunspot number:

$$R = k \, (10\,g + f)$$

where $f$ and $g$ are counted numbers of spots and groups respectively and $k$ is a calibration factor (Eddy 1988). Using the records back to the start of the telescopic era, Wolf refined the cyclical length to 11.1 yr.

There is a hint of some longer-term cyclicity with a period of about 80 yr, which is sometimes named after W. Gleissberg. Much more striking is an apparent gap in sunspot records between approximately 1645 and 1715 (Fig. 3.1), which was interpreted by Eddy (1983) as a period of weak solar activity and named by him after W. A. Maunder, who in 1894 had recognized a period of depressed sunspot activity. Historical accounts for the period had yielded 600–1000 individual sunspot records, compared with several hundred in a single day during years with moderate to high solar activity (Eddy 1988). But there are those who explain the Maunder minimum by changing attitudes to celestial observation, differential survival of the records, or a paucity of

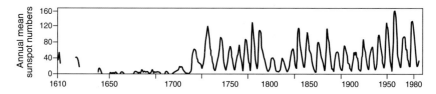

**Figure 3.1**  Annual sunspot numbers 1610–1988; note apparent deficit before about 1720 (after J. Eddy in Stephenson 1990, by permission of the Royal Society).

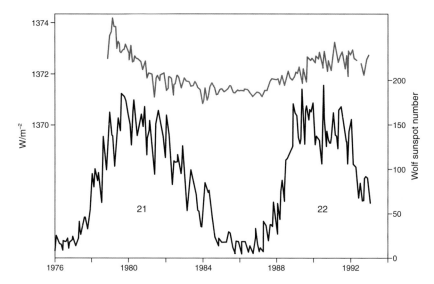

**Figure 3.2** Monthly mean solar irradiance (from Nimbus 7 upper curve and left hand scale) and sunspot numbers for cycles 21 and 22 (lower curve and right-hand scale) (courtesy of NASA and D. V. Hoyt).

observations – and observers – highlighted by improvements in the recording and communication of scientific data in the late seventeenth century (Stephenson 1988a).

## Measurement by spacecraft

The fact remains that the relationship between sunspots and solar output (let alone climate) remains obscure. The first step to resolve the issue is evidently to measure the Sun's luminosity directly. In order to minimize atmospheric interference, Langley attempted to determine the solar constant from the summit of Mt Whitney (4418 m). These and other mountain-top observations in North and South America and Africa remained subject to errors of about 1 per cent because of uncertainties about atmospheric transmission. The problem was finally solved when radiometers on the Nimbus 7 satellite and on the Solar Maximum Mission (SMM) satellite assessed the solar constant with an internal precision of 0.01 per cent, the former from 1978 and the latter from late 1979 to 1989 (Eddy et al. 1982, Hansen & Lacis 1990; Fig. 3.2).

The results showed variations in solar output at the 0.1–0.3 per cent level, about ten times more sensitive than ground-based measurements, with a maximum of 0.5 per cent (but generally 0.1 per cent or less) and 1–2 weeks in duration. More recent data put the variability at <0.1 per cent over the 11 yr cycle and up to 0.3 per cent over a period of centuries (Lean et al. 1992). The SMM record also suggested that the major dips coincided with the passage of large sunspot groups across the Sun, the effect of which could be modelled (Eddy et al. 1982) on the basis of geometrical foreshortening combined with the lower contrast of sunspots near the edge (or limb) of the Sun's apparent disk, where it is less bright than near the centre.

Two important conclusions flowed from these findings. First, short-term variations

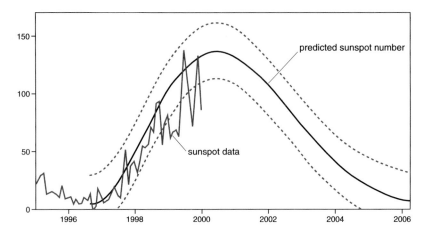

**Figure 3.3** Prediction of sunspot maximum by combining geomagnetic (sinusoidal curve) with sunspot data (after D. Hathaway et al. at www.spacescience.com).

in the solar "constant" could be forecast a few days in advance from sunspot observations combined with the known rotational properties of the Sun (Fig. 3.3). Secondly, solar activity could now be reconstructed from sunspot records.

Nevertheless, there was mounting evidence that sunspot blocking accounts for less than half the variance observed during the Sun's 27-day rotation. The photosphere, the 500 km-deep layer at the boundary of the visible solar disk, and the chromosphere, a much hotter zone that extends 5000 km above it, contain bright regions known as faculae, where photoemission is enhanced rather than reduced and which are as significant as sunspots in governing changing net solar luminosity. In addition, the SMM and Nimbus readings, like the modelled sunspot data, hinted at a longer-term trend amounting to about 0.02–0.04 per cent per year.

If the sunspots and faculae mostly compensate for each other in terms of energy over periods of weeks to months, as seems to be the case (Lean 1991), their contribution to both cyclical and cumulative change must be small, and appeal has to be made to some other variable such as emission from extended magnetic regions not associated with sunspots (Foukal & Lean 1988, Lean 1991). In fact by 1995 it was clear that, at solar-activity maxima, facular emission exceeds the sunspot deficit by a factor of 1.5. Yet, although the mechanism of irradiance changes is less straightforward than originally thought, the sunspot index remains a dependable means for tracking the Schwabe cycle – a reassuring conclusion given the continuing need to rely on sunspot records for information on solar activity prior to 1980.

## $^{14}C$ and $^{10}Be$ as proxies of solar activity

For periods before about 1715, studies of solar activity are probably better based on proxy records (Stephenson 1990). The search for a solar history that might complement the sunspot chronicles and encompass earlier centuries led to radiocarbon. $^{14}C$ is produced in the upper atmosphere by high-energy galactic cosmic rays through the interaction of neutrons with atmospheric nitrogen. Solar cosmic rays have lower energies (1–100 MeV compared with 1–100 GeV for galactic cosmic rays) and contribute little to the total atmospheric $^{14}C$ production (Cerling & Craig 1994).

Although $^{12}C$ is much more abundant (the ratio between $^{14}C$ and $^{12}C$ being $1:10^{12}$), $^{14}C$ at the levels found in nature is readily traced by several laboratory techniques. The rate of $^{14}C$ production is controlled not only by the flux of galactic cosmic rays but also by the Earth's geomagnetic field, which acts as a shield, and the solar wind, which deflects cosmic rays (with the greatest effect at low energies) away from the Earth. It has been calculated that the production of cosmogenic isotopes can vary by about 20–25 per cent between solar minima and maxima (Beer et al. 1990).

The oceanic circulation influences the rate of take-up and release of $CO_2$. The $^{14}C$ residence time in the deep ocean is about 1000 yr, and decay ($t_{1/2}= 5730$ yr) reduces deep-water $^{14}C$ activity. Diffusion by atmospheric circulation will further blur any short-term periodicities in $^{14}C$ production.

The atmospheric $^{14}C$ is incorporated in living organisms by photosynthesis, the formation of carbonate shells from ocean waters into which $CO_2$ has become dissolved, and so forth. The organic record thus offers the promise of extending solar history back several millennia. Tree rings are used for this research because they provide an independent calendric timescale, as well as raw material for isotopic measurements.

To judge from $^{14}C$ averages for coral dated by $^{234}U/^{230}Th$, the atmospheric $^{14}C$ curve has declined since 22 000 yr BP from 450‰ to the negative value of the early centuries AD. Analysis of $^{14}C$ in tree rings now extends back 7500 years. It shows a gradual fall by ~8 per cent in the $^{14}C/^{12}C$ ratio (usually expressed as $\delta^{14}C‰$) between 6500 and 1500 years ago, followed by an increase still in progress on which short-term fluctuations are superimposed. The data for the second millennium AD (Stuiver & Quay 1980) show

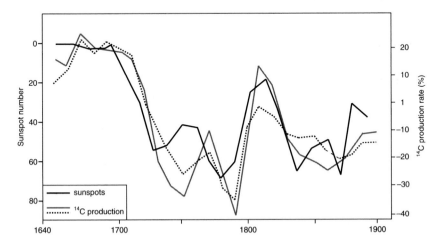

**Figure 3.4** Comparison between inverse sunspot number record and $^{14}C$ production rate (relative to 1000–1860 average), calculated assuming radiocarbon has a residence time in the atmosphere of 20 yr (grey line) and 60 yr (dotted line) (after Stuiver & Quay 1980; ©1980 American Association for the Advancement of Science).

that the period of the Maunder minimum was indeed characterized by an increase of $^{14}C/^{12}C$ by about 2 per cent (Fig. 3.4). In addition, it highlights other minima: the Oort (1020–1065), the Wolf (1275–1350), the Spörer (1395–1530), the Dalton (1800–1835) and an unnamed one in 1880–1915 (Stuiver & Quay 1980). Two independent tree-ring series for 1564–1780 (Attolini et al. 1993) show enhanced $^{14}C$ levels during the Maunder minimum and also time variations in $^{14}C$ production during the minimum that have been ascribed to solar modulation, even though net solar activity was low at the time.

Tree rings dating from 1600–1940 have been found to display both the familiar 10–12 year cycle and the Gleissberg cycle, which some take as evidence that they responded to cosmic-ray intensity connected to solar wind-flux variations. But others contend that the Gleissberg cycle, at any rate, is the product of changes in the Earth's magnetic dipole moment (Mazaud et al. 1991). In other words, the tree rings tell us more about the Earth's magnetic shield than about changes in solar output. It would seem to follow that the solar component can be teased out of the net $^{14}C$ measurements only by allowing for the geomagnetic effect (see Ch. 4).

On the theoretical front, global average $^{14}C$ production rates (in atoms $s^{-1}\, cm^2$) calculated from observed cosmic-ray neutron fluxes (O'Brien 1979) appear to be linearly related to the sunspot record. To test the association further, changes in $^{14}C$ production have been derived from the tree-ring data using a reservoir model that takes account of the atmosphere, the oceanic mixed layer, the deep sea and the biosphere. Two other periods besides the Maunder minimum were associated with an increase in production of 10 per cent above the 1000–1860 baseline: the Wolf and the Spörer. Both corresponded closely with intervals of low sunspot activity, the former in 1280–1350 and the latter in 1400–1600.

The argument is to some extent circular. Fortunately, the interaction of cosmic rays with the atmosphere produces another radioisotope that can be recovered from geological evidence: $^{10}Be$. Unlike $^{14}C$, which has been assessed in various ways since 1950, $^{10}Be$ could not be pressed into service in the study of the Sun until the advent of AMS. $^{10}Be$ becomes attached to aerosols and is removed from the atmosphere mainly by precipitation. Its atmospheric residence time is 1–2 yr and it therefore reflects local rather than global conditions. Data from a 300 m ice core in southern Greenland showed clear anti-correlation between $^{10}Be$ and solar activity, with a phase lag of a year (Beer et al. 1990). There were discrepancies in the records, especially at times of minimum sunspot number, but the main culprits appear to have been atmospheric mixing, precipitation rate and other climatic factors operating at the collecting site. $^{10}Be$ thus promises to complement $^{14}C$ usefully in extending the solar narrative (Beer et al. 1990), both by virtue of its short atmospheric residence time and because it is not influenced by nuclear bomb tests or the burning of fossil fuels.

For the measurement of long-term solar activity outside the atmosphere, the analysis of cosmogenic isotope titanium 44 ($^{44}Ti$) in meteorites is a promising technique, as it appears to detect century-scale fluctuations in the galactic cosmic-ray flux, which is, of course, modulated by solar activity (Bonino et al. 1994). The first meteorite analyzed to this end was the Rio Negro meteorite, which fell in Argentina in 1934.

Visual auroral observations, which span some 500 years, appear to corroborate the Spörer, Maunder and Dalton minima, as well as one in about 1765; they also show that the Dalton may be the deepest (Silverman 1991), as it saw a marked fall in the number of aurorae in middle and low latitudes (Stephenson 1988a). A period of high $^{14}$C production (Eddy 1988) coincides with a hiatus in auroral sighting during 1040–1050, the closing stages of the Oort.

# Variability of the Sun's ultraviolet irradiance

Ultraviolet radiation (300–1000 nm) makes up only 1 per cent of the Sun's radiative output, but it is a major influence on the composition and behaviour of the middle and upper atmosphere, and it is at the ultraviolet end of the spectrum that the amplitude of solar fluctuation is at its greatest. Figure 3.5 depicts solar variability during cycle 21 (1976–86), during which total irradiance varied by about 0.1 per cent, whereas that part of the ultraviolet spectrum with wavelengths below about 150 nm varied by almost 100 per cent over the 11 yr cycle (Lean 1991). A solar backscatter ultraviolet instrument on the NOAA 9 satellite showed that, from solar minimum in September 1986 to solar maximum in 1989, solar irradiance changed by 8.6 per cent at 205 nm, 3.5 per cent at 250 nm and < 1 per cent beyond 300 nm (Cebula et al. 1992).

Solar radiation provokes the destruction and also the production of ozone in the stratosphere; ozone content in the stratosphere echoes the Sun's 27-day rotation period as well as the 11 yr cycle. Absorption of ultraviolet by ozone is the main mechanism of energy input into the stratosphere. In the upper atmosphere, variations in solar energy at wavelengths of < 170 nm within the 11 yr cycle can change the temperature at the top of the thermosphere (100–160 km above the ground) from 750 to > 1250 K, primarily owing to emissions at wavelengths < 110 nm (Lean 1991).

All the solar flux in the extreme ultraviolet band is absorbed within the thermosphere; 20 per cent of this energy contributes to bulk heating (Gorney 1990). At < 242 nm the increased flux promotes additional photo-dissociation of molecular oxygen (Haigh 1994), and the resulting molecular oxygen combines with $O_2$ to produce higher concentrations of ozone ($O_3$), which in turn absorbs more radiation at 200–350 nm and also across the visible part of the spectrum.

The effect on the irradiance that reaches the lower atmosphere varies with latitude. In the winter hemisphere at middle and higher latitudes, less solar radiation reaches the troposphere during periods of higher solar activity (Haigh 1994). In other words, the resulting ozone variations may shield the lower atmosphere from variations in the overall radiative flux.

Direct measurement of the response of the middle atmosphere to ultraviolet fluctuations is possible with LIDAR (LIght + raDAR; that is to say, using laser rather than microwaves) which, in contrast with most satellite systems, can be confined to a single location and prolonged as much as necessary. One such study, of the 30–90 km zone above southern France, measured over a hundred profiles a year between 1981 and 1991

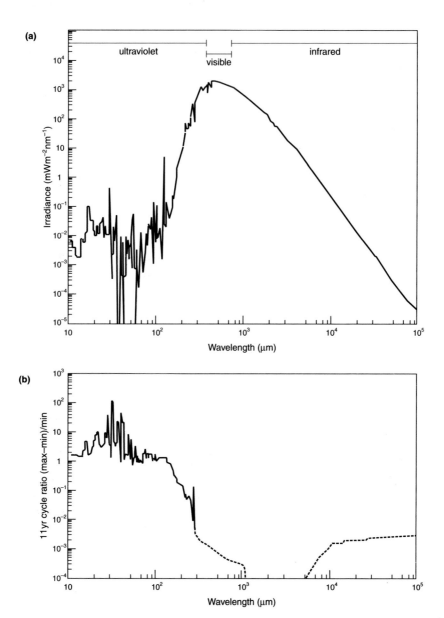

**Figure 3.5** **(a)** The Sun's spectral irradiance at solar minimum conditions. **(b)** Irradiance variation from maximum to minimum of 11 yr cycle (solid line: derived from direct satellite observations during solar cycle 21; dashed line: estimated). (After Lean 1991; ©1991 American Geophysical Union.)

at better than one degree Kelvin (at 50 km). Solar ultraviolet flux variability data were not accurate enough throughout, and reliance was placed on data obtained by the Solar Mesosphere Explorer in 1982–6 and then by ultraviolet-proxy data from the Nimbus 7–NOAA 9 readings (Keckhut & Chanin 1992). The 27-day solar rotation effect was clear in a positive correlation between temperature and solar flux at 65–70 km. In half the cases, however, there was a negative correlation at 40–60 km (Hood & Zhou 1998). Purely radiative and photochemical factors are evidently complicated by dynamical processes within the atmosphere, and analysis of the 27-day cycle cannot be used as proxy for the 11 yr cycle.

An alternative link between solar activity and atmospheric dynamics is the flux of MeV–GeV particles, primarily galactic cosmic rays, which could promote electro-freezing of supercooled droplets, with a consequent release of latent heat (Tinsley & Heelis 1993), and thus account for the correlation between the cosmic-ray flux with winter cyclone intensity and storm-latitude shifts (Tinsley & Deen 1991; see Ch. 9). In the shorter term, changes in cyclonic activity and tropospheric winds follow strong coronal mass ejections by a few days, with increases of up to 7 per cent in zonal flow (Anderson 1992).

## Solar activity and the surface record

Once the Sun was revealed to be inconstant, the climatic implications appeared self-evident. William Herschel was one of the first to raise the matter, and he suggested in 1801 that the wheat prices given by Adam Smith in *The wealth of nations* could be attributed to "more or less copious emissions of the solar beams" (Meadows 1975). The links between climate and geological processes become obscure once we leave such obvious categories as sandy deserts and arctic tundra, although even there the association is by no means straightforward, especially when we are dealing with former climates and their geological imprint. For many years the evidence of Ordovician glaciation was disregarded in the Saharan rock record; and, conversely, deposits long taken to be glacial tillite are now dismissed as alluvial-fan material.

Oil companies see the issue as of the highest practical importance, as extrapolation away from expensive boreholes is successful only if based on intelligent palaeo-geographical reconstruction. Today, climatic change gains urgency from the possible impact of an accentuated greenhouse effect on agriculture, settlements and nuclear-waste repositories.

A simple link between solar irradiance and global temperature has long been sought, but it remains elusive (Kelly & Wigley 1990, Gillett et al. 2000). The calculation is complicated by the fact that global climate may fluctuate without any change in external forcing: a 100 yr run of a model with constant solar irradiance and greenhouse gases gave variations of as much as 0.4°C in mean surface temperature, doubtless because the solutions for the nonlinear equations for atmospheric structure and motion display chaotic behaviour (Hansen & Lacis 1990). There are also many feedback effects, notably cloud cover. Proxy records suggest that solar variability since 1600 may explain as much as ~30–55 per cent of climatic variance at decadal–centennial timescales (Crowley & Kim 1996), and a correlation of 0.95 has been reported between the length of the 11 yr sunspot cycle and surface temperature in the Northern Hemisphere between 1865 and 1985 (Lassen & Friis-Christensen 1995). On the other hand, there is some evidence that higher sunspot numbers are associated with global cooling rather than warming.

Some 30 per cent of the irradiance of $1370\,w\,m^{-2}$ incident on the Earth is reflected back out; as the Earth's surface area is four times its cross section, the mean solar heating of the Earth is $240\,w\,m^{-2}$ and a 0.1 per cent change in solar irradiance amounts to a climate forcing of $0.24\,w\,m^{-2}$ (Hansen & Lacis 1990). There was a decline in irradiance of 0.1 per cent between 1979 and the mid-1980s, followed by partial recovery since 1989. The human greenhouse effect is estimated to have been $2$–$2.5\,w\,m^{-2}$ between 1850 and 1989. It would seem to follow that, if the response time is measured in decades, short-term solar change will have little impact, especially as, unlike the greenhouse factor, it is concentrated towards lower latitudes and, once we consider the ultraviolet component, high in the atmosphere. Solar irradiance would have to decline by 2 per cent to counteract greenhouse forcing if this amounted to, say, $4$–$5\,w\,m^{-2}$ following a doubling of atmospheric $CO_2$.

A promising independent measure of global temperature change over recent centuries, which may help to reduce the area of doubt, is provided by boreholes. Analysis of geothermal data hinges on sound understanding of the local temperature gradient, which depends on thermal conductivity of the rock and deep heatflow. Short-period temperature fluctuations will evidently penetrate less deeply than long-period ones: daily oscillations penetrate about 1 m and seasonal ones about 15 m. Five centuries is deemed sufficient to yield a robust signal. Measurements from 616 boreholes from all the continents except Antarctica confirm that the twentieth century has experienced warming, but the amount it indicates is about 1°C more than suggested by multi-proxy sources (Huang et al. 2000).

Realistic analyses consider not only the energy balance and circulation patterns but also such topics as the greenhouse effect attributable to chlorofluorocarbons (CFCs), methane ($CH_4$) and nitrous oxide ($N_2O$), the impact of industrially produced aerosols and of sulphate from volcanic eruptions, and the modification of albedo by changes in land use.

The debate has always been hampered by the statistical problems that face any attempt to interpret climatic series (Pittock 1983, Burroughs 1994). We may set aside the comparison of solar behaviour with temperature, rainfall and other time series, and start by identifying a mechanism that will conceivably transfer solar changes to geological processes. The kinds of process that are generally considered (Gorney 1990, Tett et al. 1999), besides variations in the Earth's heat budget governed by the solar constant, are those produced by changes in the chemistry of the middle atmosphere that affect radiative and dynamic processes, and those in the magnetosphere and ionosphere that perhaps influence weather patterns.

During 1948–66, a period of sunspot maximum, there was increased frontal activity

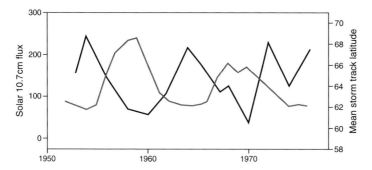

**Figure 3.6** Mean latitude of storm tracks in the North Atlantic, north of latitude 50° (black line) and solar flux (grey line), for quasi-biennial oscillation west-phase winters (after Tinsley 1988; ©1988 American Geophysical Union).

in the North Atlantic, and the cyclonic tracks of the North Atlantic were displaced southwards by as much as 3° (Herman & Goldberg 1985). Variations in the mean latitude of winter storm tracks in the eastern North Atlantic have now been found to coincide with the sunspot cycle for six cycles (Tinsley 1990). It had already been shown in 1874 that the number, size and duration of cyclones in the Indian Ocean during 1847–73 – and the number of ships putting into Mauritius for repair after damage by heavy seas – were all enhanced at solar maximum (Meadows 1975).

Stratospheric warming caused by ultraviolet absorption by ozone appears to be associated with shifts in the circumpolar vortex and the jet stream, and therefore in the mid-latitude storm tracks (Landscheidt 1987). Some support for the proposal comes from global circulation modelling (Haigh 1996). Moreover, the match between solar flux and latitude is better during the west phase of the quasi-biennial oscillation (Fig. 3.6; Tinsley 1988). During half of the quasi-biennial oscillation, the tropical stratospheric winds blow predominantly westwards and during the other half mainly eastwards; the west phase is characterized by a close parallelism between polar stratospheric temperatures and the 10.7 cm (radio) portion of the solar flux (Labitzke & van Loon 1990). UV would seem to be the elusive link between solar variability and climate.

# CHAPTER 4
# Global changes

*'Tis not impossible but that some of these great alterations may have alter'd
also the magnetical Directions of the Earth; so that what is now under the
Pole or Aequator, or any other Degree of Latitude may have formerly been
under another . . .*
Robert Hooke, *On earthquakes and fossils* (1668)

Besides making available to geology many new techniques and devices, space science
has brought to the forefront a subject formerly too often relegated to cursory prefaces:
the study of the Earth as a whole. We are speaking not of neglect but of obscurity born
of mathematical complexity, as well as the tradition of allocating whole planets to
astronomy and bits of planets to geology. The imagery sent back by the Voyager and
Mariner spacecraft created the new field of planetary geology. Its reliance predominantly on digital data removed one of the barriers between geology and geodesy, and,
what is more, made possible analysis of the images with respect to time.

Real-time measurement of terrestrial change has a far longer pedigree. In 1881–2, for
example, Darwin's sons Horace and George carried out experiments designed to isolate
the gravitational effect of the Moon; instead they found that "the ground on which we
live is probably everywhere in what is practically an incessant state of vibration", and
they set up special apparatus to record the motions "with the hope of eventually discovering the laws by which they were governed" (Milne 1886). Even if any such laws
remain elusive, the improved evidence continuously highlights the interplay between
the many moving parts and driving forces and, in so doing, shows how progress in one
area may accidentally illuminate another.

## The figure of the Earth

It stands to reason that our understanding of the shape of the entire Earth should be one
of the greatest beneficiaries of advances in satellite technology and the analysis of
satellite orbits. The figure is the product of forces within the planet, as well as the
stresses imposed on it by its rotation and by its interaction with other planets and the

Sun, and it is therefore an obvious candidate for repetitive scrutiny from space.

The archaic phrase "figure of the Earth" benefits in English from the ambiguity of "figure" to denote both shape and number, as it has long been used to mean the search for a numerical expression for the deviation of the planet from exact sphericity. Newton concluded that the Earth was flattened at the poles by 1/230th of the equatorial diameter, an effect he ascribed in his *Principia* to the action of gravity and rotation on a body that was originally fluid. The flattening allowed Newton to explain the precession of the equinoxes, known to the Greeks since 130 BC, whereby the point of equinox is shifted eastwards each year. The reality of flattening was in due course confirmed by expeditions to Lapland in 1735 and Ecuador in 1736, which showed that the length on the ground of a degree of latitude varied with latitude, but the severity of the flattening and the processes responsible for it are topics that are by no means exhausted even today. Thus, although the value of 1/298.25 is used for many purposes, the International Union for Geodesy continues to update the figure.

Satellite technology has influenced the field in two ways. Satellites provide targets for laser ranging and Doppler measurements, which permit angular observations from an infinite number of stations, while their orbits encode the variable gravitational signal created by a non-spherical globe. Besides atmospheric drag effects and the like, which can reasonably be allowed for, the gravitational signal is clearly also rich in information on mass variations within the Earth. Therefore, the need arises to distinguish between the geoid, which is the shape of the Earth in response to variations in gravity from place to place, and the spheroid of rotation, which is the shape to be expected from a spinning Earth in which any variations in mass distribution with depth are – as in Newton's model – radially uniform.

The term "topoid" is sometimes used for the mean physical surface to include continents as well as oceans, with hydroid as synonym for the spheroid. Some early models of the Earth, such as Green's tetrahedral theory (Steers 1945), are remarkably percipient in recognizing that the morphology of the topoid as a whole needs explaining. Thus, even after allowing for oceans and mountains, the figure is decidedly asymmetrical, both between Northern and Southern Hemispheres and antipodeally. Whether the asymmetry is significant is still not known.

The figure is modified ceaselessly by Earth tides (i.e. tidal effects in the solid Earth), ocean tides and ocean currents, as these influence with different periodicities the orientation of the axis of rotation and its rate, and thus the planet's flattening or oblateness. On longer timescales there may be contributions from the shape and position of polar and mountain icecaps, lakes and such gross geological constructs as rift valleys, mountain ranges and flood lavas. All are already increasingly susceptible to measurement, whether by direct or indirect means.

The Earth's volume is generally not considered a matter for serious investigation, even though many of the phenomena of plate tectonics are broadly consistent with a progressive increase in terrestrial radius (Carey 1976), and volumetric changes are to be expected from outgassing, internal differentiation and heat dissipation. On the whole, the notion of an expanding Earth is not in favour, but the topic may be revived by global geodesy, witness the recent claim that SLR to LAGEOS (Laser Geodynamics

Satellite: see Frontispiece) and VLBI data for stable continental regions indicate an increase of $4.15 \pm 0.27$ mm yr$^{-1}$ in terrestrial radius since the techniques came into operation (Scalera 2000).

# Orbit

Between 1965 and 1980, several important technical developments, notably in the definition of universal time (UT) and atomic time (introduced in 1955) and in the gathering of global meteorological data, proved of great value in the investigation of changes in the length of the day (LOD) and the mechanisms responsible for them (Lambeck 1980, Wahr 1988). Progress has been sustained in all areas, including the analysis of 2700 years of historical astronomy (Stephenson & Morrison 1984, Yau & Pang 1995). Reliance had to be placed almost wholly on the timing of solar and lunar eclipses (Stephenson 1978, Li 1987; Fig. 4.1a) prior to dependable telescopic observation of occultations in the late eighteenth century, when "mean time" began to be adopted widely. Artificial satellites now provide a direct measure of changes in LOD (Fig. 4.1b), and laser ranging to the Moon underpins calculations of changes in the mean angular velocity of the Moon.

# Rotation

The Earth's rate of rotation varies by up to several parts in $10^8$ over timescales ranging from days to millennia (Dickey et al. 1990). The cumulative slowing since 700 BC is 9 hours, which is substantial enough to be detected using historical data. Most of the secular decrease of 0.001–0.0025 s every century, as well as the geodetic signal in the diurnal and semi-diurnal frequency bands, is ascribed primarily to tidal dissipation (Herring & Dong 1994). Thus, discrepancies between measured changes in the Moon's mean orbital velocity and predictions based on lunar and solar tides give a measure of non-tidal effects: the numerical tidal model predicted a change of $-29.6 \pm 3.1$ arcsec per century, compared to $-26.1 \pm 2.9$ indicated by artificial satellites and $-25.1 \pm 1.2$ by LLR (Stephenson 1988b). LOD variations with a period of a few days to a few years or less and with amplitudes of up to 1 ms are influenced above all by atmospheric changes: seasonal oscillations in LOD are dominated by winds running roughly parallel to lines of latitude (Lambeck 1980). LOD data based on VLBI and LLR (Chao 1995a) can thus be corrected for the angular momentum of the atmosphere, which is calculated on a daily basis. Note that anomalous climatic years, such as those associated with the El Niño effect, can seriously upset the outcome.

Decadal fluctuations with amplitudes of 2–3 ms are generally attributed to the transfer of angular momentum between the Earth's mantle and the fluid core. The relative importance of electromagnetic as distinct from topographical effects at the core/mantle

**Figure 4.1** **(a)** Changes in length of day (LOD) in milliseconds since 700 BC; the dashed portion of the curve is based on Babylonian and Arabian solar and lunar eclipse data (simplified from Stephenson & Morrison 1984, by permission of the Royal Society). **(b)** Variations in LOD relative to the atomic time-scale (courtesy of IERS Rapid Service/Prediction Center, US Naval Observatory).

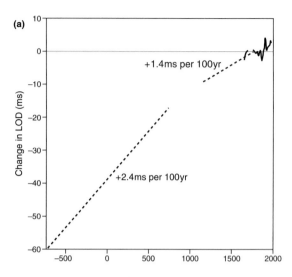

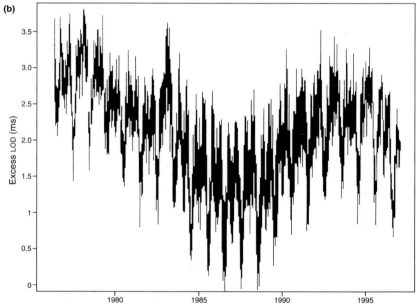

boundary (Dickey et al. 1990) will be clarified by improved mapping of its morphology from the analysis of earthquake travel times in 3-D (seismic tomography) and gravity analysis, combined with estimates of the horizontal motion beneath this boundary, based in part on secular changes in the magnetic field and judicious assumptions about the rheology of the upper and lower mantle.

Longer-term changes on century or millennial scales will in due course be measurable. The redistribution of loads produced by the rapid melting of the Pleistocene ice sheets and the associated rise in sea level has attracted the attention of many workers who see it as a route to the evaluation of mantle viscosity and structure and of the elasticity of the crust and the lithosphere as a whole (Wu & Peltier 1983). With polar icecaps at their maximum, and sea level consequently 100 m below its present global level, the Earth's rate of rotation would be 1 per cent higher than at glacial minimum (when icecaps were depleted and general sea level was some 7 m above present-day levels) and LOD would be correspondingly shorter.

If glaciation were to alternate between the polar hemispheres, the effect would be more complex; Wallace (1881) argued that the Earth's centre of gravity would shift towards the heavier pole and there would be a corresponding rise in sea level. For direct comparison to be feasible, the corresponding data for ice melting and crustal rebound will need to be disaggregated: a rise in sea level by 6 mm should increase the LOD by 0.1 ms, but in due course reduced oblateness resulting from isostatic rebound at high latitudes will increase the rate of spin.

## Polar motion

The Earth's rotation varies not only in rate but also in the orientation of its axis relative to a terrestrial frame (polar motion, PM) and to a celestial frame (precession and nutation) (Wilson 1995). PM (Fig. 4.2) is caused by a discrepancy between the axis of rotation and the polar axis of the spheroid; it amounts to irregular displacements of the former within an area 30 m in diameter. PM is caused partly by the Chandler Wobble, which has a period of about 434 days consisting of the 10-month period expected for a rigid Earth and a component attributable to non-rigidity (Wahr 1988), and which amounts to about 6 m at the North Pole. There is also an annual wobble in response to seasonal atmospheric and oceanic factors. PM, in short, is a geophysical phenomenon that depends on the deformation and shift of material within and on the planet and its interaction with the atmosphere.

## Precession

Insofar as one can make such sharp distinctions, the precession responsible for the shift in the timing of the equinoxes is an astronomical effect caused by lunisolar gravitational pull acting on an oblate Earth with an axis of rotation at 23.5° from the perpendicular, and it shifts the equinoxes along the ecliptic (the mean orbital plane of the Earth) at about 50″ a year. Less pronounced and more complicated is planetary precession driven by the major planets in the Solar System, which among other things reduces the obliquity of the ecliptic by about 0.5″ a year. The combined or general precession has a period of about 25 870 yr. Superimposed on this secular or long-term motion are shorter-term periodic changes or nutations (from the Latin, *nutare*, to nod) in the

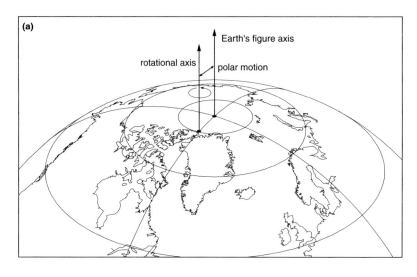

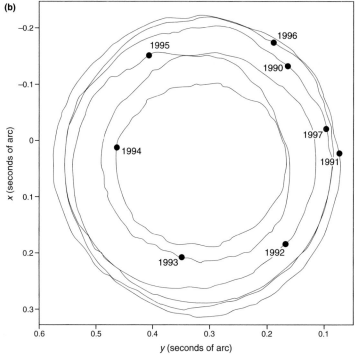

**Figure 4.2** **(a)** Definition of polar motion. **(b)** Polar motion 1990–97. **(c, opposite)** $y$ component of polar motion (courtesy of IERS Rapid Service/Prediction Center, US Naval Observatory). Note prominence of variations in the Chandler wobble.

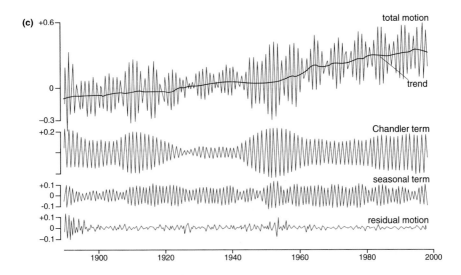

orientation of the axis of rotation. They are produced primarily by variations in the orbital elements that govern precession, and include a term with a period of 18.6 yr attributable to the precession of the Moon's orbit.

Polar motion for 1900–1992 has been computed using observations of star positions by the International Latitude Service observations for 1899–1979 recalculated (Gross & Vondrak 1999). It was recalculated in 1980 and again using the star catalogue obtained by the Hipparcos astrometric satellite, which was launched in 1989. There were additional corrections for instrumental error, plate-tectonic motion, ocean loading and tidal variations, and a set of independent space geodetic measurements (SPACE96) based on LLR, SLR, VLBI and GPS measurements.

The analysis gave a mean value for 1900–1992 of $3.51 \pm 0.01$ mas (milli-arc seconds) towards $79.2 \pm 0.2°W$. Allowing for any associated displacement of geodetic stations, plate movements are likely to have little effect, because under conditions of isostatic equilibrium excess topographical mass is cancelled out by the presence of a compensatory root (Dickman 1979). An interesting consequence of the shift in spin axis is southward displacement of land masses at 90°E at about 120 mm yr$^{-1}$, so that, despite its northward convergence with Eurasia at 38 mm yr$^{-1}$, India is moving south at 80 mm yr$^{-1}$. GPS has confirmed the prediction (Paul et al. 1995).

Of course active erosion of mountainous areas and rapid uplift or subsidence, for example over detached portions of subducted lithosphere, take place in non-isostatic conditions. It has been estimated that an area similar to that of the Himalayas and Tibet (77–95°E, 55–65°N) undergoing uplift at 5 mm yr$^{-1}$ would produce a mass displacement equivalent to a shift in the rotational axis of 2 cm on an azimuth of 97.5°W. The observed shift is 10 cm towards 75°W (Vermeersen & Vlaar 1993).

The study of nutation is best accomplished using VLBI alone; unlike SLR or LLR, it is tied to an inertial coordinate system defined by distant radio sources. By 1988 the accuracy attained using VLBI was better than 0.2 mas and by 1992 it was 0.04 mas for observational epochs of about 430 days (Matthews & Shapiro 1992). VLBI determinations on a single baseline (Robertson et al. 1985) have obtained precisions of 0.1 ms in one hour. VLBI and SLR data for polar motion are available since 1980 (Carter et al. 1986). They agree closely with each other but not with the historical series. Doppler pole positions began to be plotted from US navigation satellites in the 1960s; they secure useful results in a few hours, whereas optical determinations typically required several weeks of observation for a precision of 1.5 ms.

There is no evidence that the Chandler wobble is being damped (as one would expect from a free motion) and the problem then arises of what it is that maintains the wobble. One suggestion is seismic moment, as there appears to be a measure of association between the annual number of earthquakes above a specified magnitude, the elastic energy released by them, and fluctuations in the wobble, but there is disagreement over the moment for many large recent earthquakes, especially where there is evidence that a substantial portion of an episode of fault slip was aseismic (Lambeck 1980). Using data for 1985–95, Gross (2000) showed that two thirds of the wobble was produced by pressure changes on the ocean floor resulting from fluctuations in salinity, temperature and circulation, the remainder being attributable to atmospheric pressure.

A related effect, this time with a period of a year, is attributable to the seasonal redistribution of mass within and between the atmosphere, the oceans and the Earth. Its amplitude is 0.10″ or about 3 m on the surface of the Earth. The possibility thus arises that climatic changes can affect the Earth's tilt as well as vice versa, if at very different timescales (Rubincam 1995). Strong correlations have been recorded between atmospheric excitation functions of polar motion and the ENSO, a combination of the El Niño effect in the east tropical Pacific and the southern oscillation in pressure between Tahiti and Darwin (Kolaczek et al. 2000).

The Milankovich model of climatic change, which is widely accepted, hinges on three variables: the eccentricity of the Earth's orbit, the obliquity of the ecliptic and the precession of the equinoxes (Milankovich 1930). The corresponding periods are ~90 000–110 000, ~42 000 and ~26 000 years. The precession shifts the timing of perihelion from summer to winter and back again. Over a century ago, Wallace (1881) took for granted an astronomical explanation for the ice ages, and he used short-term changes in the extent of the snow caps of Mars to test the significance of precession on that planet at times of moderate orbital eccentricity. For example, on 23 June 1830 he observed that the southern Martian cap had a diameter of 11°30′; by 9 July it had shrunk to 5°46′.

Periodicities clearly also underpin modern tests of the Milankovich model. As sedimentation rates are often unsteady or impossible to determine, many such analyses have depended for their time calibration on orbital tuning to the astronomical timescale, that is to say, making the assumption that the sequence is indeed driven by astronomical variables. Independent dating avoids circular argument; but it sometimes leads to surprises. For example, according to the Milankovich model, the last summer insolation minimum occurred 23 000 yr ago; the corresponding glacial maximum is dated by $^{14}$C to 18 000 yr. Now if the $^{14}$C age is corrected by reference to the Th/U ages scale (p. 62), the apparent time lag between supposed cause and effect disappears (Bard et al. 1990). The age discrepancy implies enhanced cosmic-ray activity, and thus

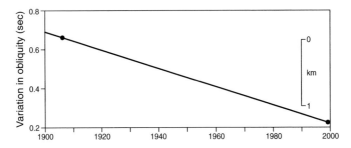

**Figure 4.3** Predicted variation in obliquity of the ecliptic in the twentieth century; dots indicate the location of the Ja-Yi monument in Taiwan and its modern replacement (after Chao 1996, ©AGU).

perhaps a magnetic field with half the present strength, an inference supported by data from lavas and deep-sea sediments (Broecker 1992). In other words, the link between orbital geometry and climate is complicated by geomagnetism, just as it appears to be with the 11 yr and the Gleissberg solar cycles.

Note that, even though this discussion bears on periods measured in thousands of years, orbital change is surprisingly rapid. The obliquity of the ecliptic is now 23°26′22″ and is decreasing by about 46.85″ (14.4 m) annually. On Taiwan a monument was erected in 1906 at latitude 23°27′4.51″N to mark the contemporaneous Tropic of Capricorn. The tropic has since moved 1.27 km south and will continue to do so for a further 93 km over the next 9300 yr before it swings north again (Fig. 4.3). As Chao (1996) puts it, the Arctic Circle and the Antarctic Circle are currently moving towards their respective poles at the same rate. The world's temperate zone is expanding at the expense of the tropical and Arctic zones at a rate of some 1500 km² yr⁻¹: this is the Milankovich cycle happening right before our eyes. Before long it should be possible to detect the associated change in solar luminosity at different latitudes, at the top of the atmosphere if not at its base.

Precession has also been invoked to date the Egyptian pyramids at Giza. Existing Old Kingdom chronologies are accurate to no better than ± 100 yr. Spence (2000) has shown that, if we assume the pyramids were aligned to north by using the two circumpolar stars ζ-Ursae Majoris and γ-Ursae Minoris, the precession of the two stars during the second half of the third millennium BC would explain differences in the alignment of the various pyramids. By assuming that the alignments were determined in the second year of the reign of the pharaoh in question, Spence could then fix the date of their reigns to ±5 yr.

# Gravity

The Earth's gravity field has been incompletely determined from terrestrial measurements, an obvious gap being oceanic coverage south of about 30°S. Earth gravitational models derived from the earliest ground-based tracking systems used for Sputnik and the Transit Navy Navigation Satellite system have evolved to models that use radar altimeter data from a variety of satellite altimetry missions including GEOS-3, Seasat, Geosat, ERS-1, TOPEX/Poseidon and ERS-2, as well as information from the GPS satellites (Vetter 1994). Tracking information may use over 30 satellites and involve Doppler, optical and satellite-to-satellite tracking, as well as SLR measurements. When it comes to airborne gravity measurements over water, land and ice, GPS techniques permit the accelerations attributable to aircraft motion to be eliminated. A recent example (Bell 1995) is a survey of the whole of Greenland with a line spacing of 25–50 km and a resolution of 4.5 mgal.

The dramatic improvements in the models benefit calculations of the satellite orbit error attributable to gravity. The root mean square combined error of orbit and altimeter for the determination of sea level relative to the Earth's centre, as we saw in Chapter 1, has fallen to <5 cm for TOPEX/Poseidon (Fu & Cheney 1995, Shum et al. 1995).

The potential for dynamic analysis of the novel data has been enhanced by improvements in spatial resolution. SLR ranging to LAGEOS demonstrated that atmospheric pressure and surface-water fluctuations are the dominant influence on seasonal variations in the Earth's gravity field (Dong et al. 1996). The gravity field is also altered by lunisolar tides, shifts in ice and snow cover and in groundwater, postglacial rebound, convection in the mantle, and the activity of the core.

The long wavelengths, that is to say the large-scale patterns (Fig. 4.4), are governed primarily by density differences in the mantle (Watts & Daly 1981). From the earliest days of oceanic gravity studies, notably those of Vening Meinesz in the 1920s, geoidal studies have been shown to bear on the dynamics of the planet, as zones of mass deficit or excess could be taken to reflect incomplete compensation and hence active tectonic regimes. For instance, there is some correlation between gravity and topographical anomalies in the North Pacific (Watts & Daly 1981), which argues for convection in the mantle (McKenzie et al. 1980), although the pattern appears to be confined to the part of the lithosphere dating from 30 to 110 Myr.

The short-wavelength measurements, after correction for track and orbit errors and the noise produced by sea-surface condition, have proved of great value in the study of the ocean circulation, but their greatest impact has been on the analysis of bathymetry, that is, seafloor topography.

There is also the suggestion that shifts in the geoid would produce local changes in sea level unrelated to any worldwide increase or decrease in oceanic volume (Mörner 1976). The proposal is especially attractive where, as off New Guinea or southern India, there are mounds or holes in the geoid of over 50 m, because a slight rearrangement of the map would readily explain fossil shorelines now standing well above the high-water mark. The difficulty lies in accounting for the requisite mass redistributions rapidly enough to match the shoreline chronologies.

Yet the idea that sea level need not shift uniformly throughout the globe, although counterintuitive, is now considered self-evident (see Ch. 6). Even when the term eustatic was taken to denote uniform worldwide oscillations in sea level, it was seen to be consistent with local divergences attributable to salinity and temperature variations and to those produced by oceanic circulation and meteorological factors. The position

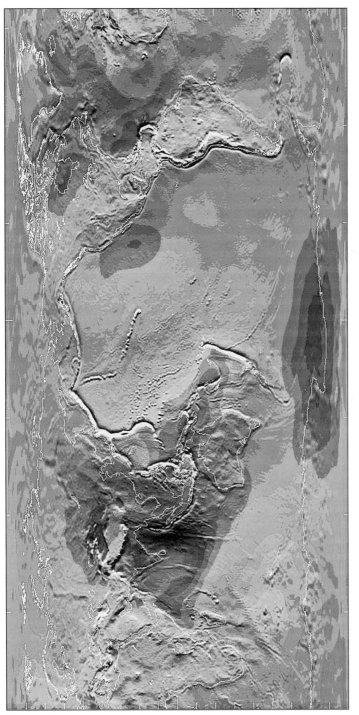

**Figure 4.4** Geoid map with contour interval of 5 m relative to the World Geodetic System 1984 reference ellipsoid; note the trenches, especially in the western Pacific Ocean (courtesy of NGS/NOAA and NASA/NIMA).

of sea level as defined by the coastline will be affected by isostatic and elastic adjustments of the land and the adjacent sea floor in response to the loading and unloading produced by the growth and melting of icecaps and glaciers (Walcott 1972). There is a third, hydrostatic, element, which amounts to the deformation of the Earth as a whole, resulting from the redistribution of mass contingent on glacial advances and retreats (Tushingham & Peltier 1991).

SLR measurements to the satellites LAGEOS I and II between 1993 and 1998 have given annual variations in the gravity field with half wavelengths of 5000 km that agree well with the predicted effects of water redistribution between the atmosphere, the oceans and the continents (Nerem et al. 2000). The dedicated satellite Gravity Recovery and Climate Experiment was designed to improve time calibration of local gravity measurements and thus its application to geophysical exploration. An example is the use of short-term changes in gravity as possible indicators of magma displacements beneath volcanoes that are about to erupt, as discussed in Chapter 7.


# Magnetism

The Earth's magnetic field is central to the present study as a guide to crustal displacements and also because it impinges on the validity of $^{14}$C dating. More profound questions about magnetism have to be shelved but cannot be totally ignored: for example, Gauss attributed secular variation – the rate of change of the internal part of the geomagnetic field (as distinct from the second derivative, or secular acceleration) – to cooling and thickening of the crust (Courtillot & Le Mouël 1988).

Perhaps the greatest impact of palaeomagnetic studies has been on the chronology and geometry of crustal displacements and deformation. The early disputes over the bearing of apparent polar wander on continental drift have yielded to increasingly fastidious reconstructions of continental and terrane displacements, and to the extension of palaeomagnetic analysis to microplates and individual structures. Rotation around a vertical axis is especially prominent in belts affected by major strike-slip movement or oblique convergence as an inevitable consequence of deformation distributed in fault sets (Nur et al. 1989) and sometimes as a secondary consequence of fault drag, as on the North Anatolian Fault (Platzman et al. 1994).

True reversals are by definition unambiguous, but the youngest, which defines the Brunhes/Matuyama boundary (Shackleton et al. 1990), dates from ~790 000 yr BP. It consisted of a westerly change in declination, while inclination progressed from reverse to normal over a period of some 4400 yr and with intensity low (Clement & Constable 1991). Excursions, which are brief departures of the geomagnetic field from the full polarity state, are potential sources of global correlation but difficult to date securely (Thompson & Berglund 1976). The youngest well attested excursion is the Laschamp event of ~42 000 yr ago, which has been reported in lavas in France and Iceland, but marine deposits are beginning to yield evidence for 14 excursions in the past 1 Myr, each lasting 2000–10 000 yr, of which 6 at least appear to be global phenomena

(Gubbins 1999). The stability of the geomagnetic field may thus be a misleading product of a defective depositional record.

The main items to be discussed here are field intensity, dip and declination, the last ranging from minor shifts in azimuth to the full-blown reversals on which seafloor chronology still heavily depends. The topics are of course inseparable. Thus, field intensity reportedly almost disappears during periods of reversal, which has encouraged speculation about the possible biological impact of the resulting nakedness to cosmic rays. (Bullard once suggested that the evidence was not sufficient to rule out the possibility that it was in fact the genetic mutations that had caused the magnetic reversals.)

The current decline in intensity is seen by some as ominous (Fig. 4.5). But the quality of the evidence is decidedly uneven. There are 180 permanent magnetic observatories, but many of the key data on the current field come from temporary stations and satellite observation, notably by MAGSAT, which operated for 7.5 months in 1979–80. The time range over which the field varies spans more than 20 orders of magnitude from over $10^3$ Hz to $> 100$ Myr (Courtillot & Le Mouël 1988). Archaeological data have been a prominent source since 1959. Pottery and bricks acquire thermoremanent magnetization after the last cooling event and can often be dated by $^{14}$C analysis of associated ashes. Inclination and declination can be derived from undisturbed hearths, inclination from bricks, and field intensity from all such sources.

The archaeomagnetic evidence allows the sequence to be extended to 1800 yr BP, and lake sediments to 10 000 BP. Geological sources include lava flows, which acquire the local field quickly on cooling; the flows cannot always be dated reliably by $^{14}$C and K/Ar, but in Hawaii $^{14}$C dating has successfully taken the sequence back to 30 000 yr BP. Sediments acquire post-depositional magnetization during de-watering and consolidation, and may be affected by bioturbation and distortion following compaction (Hagstrum &

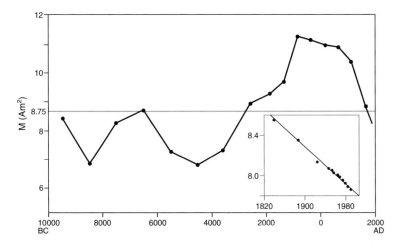

**Figure 4.5** Global mean dipole moment from archaeomagnetic data ($Y$ scale $\times 10^{22}$) (after McElhinny & Senanayake 1982, by permission of Terra Publishing (Japan)). Inset: decay of the dipole moment 1835–1985 (after Courtillot & Le Mouël 1988, by permission of the *Annual Review of Earth and Planetary Sciences*, vol. 16; © Annual Reviews Inc.).

Champion 1995), but they provide continuous records and are more easily calibrated by a few $^{14}$C dates than are lava flows.

An important source of motivation today in the study of field intensity is the search for greater reliability in radiocarbon dating. In his original formulation of the $^{14}$C method, Libby (1952) assumed that $^{14}$C levels had remained constant. We have seen that they have varied because of changes in solar activity, the cosmic-ray flux and the geomagnetic shield. Oceanic ventilation can be added to the list. One consequence has been a discrepancy between $^{14}$C and Th/U ages amounting to $2-3.5 \times 10^3$ yr during the 20 000–40 000 yr interval.

The validity of the analyses is not always self-evident. A key problem is that only thermoremanent magnetization (TRM) lends itself to palaeo-intensity analysis (Merrill & McElhinny 1983). The standard or Thellier method risks changing the magnetic mineralogy of the samples to obtain an estimate of the field in which the natural remanent magnetization was acquired (Clement & Constable 1991).

The magnetization of marine sediments, although not fully understood, appears to be linearly related to the field intensity (Tric et al. 1992). Nevertheless, the upper part of marine cores is commonly disturbed by organic activity. As they generally have a high water content, they may also be blurred by handling in the laboratory, and it is helpful to calibrate the evidence by reference to a known episode. For instance, volcanic rocks record a period of high intensity 9000 yr ago and one of low intensity 40 000 yr ago (Laj et al. 1996). For the past 15 000 yr, archaeomagnetism provides a detailed if patchy source of corroboration.

Soon after the first measurements by Gauss in 1832, the dipolar moment was seen to decrease by 5 per cent a century. Certain consistent patterns are beginning to emerge from such diverse sources as pottery and lake deposits. A compilation of 1167 palaeo-intensity measurements averaged for 500 yr intervals for the past 12 000 yr indicates an increase in dipole strength from 6000 to 3000 yr BP and a subsequent fall (McElhinny & Senanayake 1982). Marine cores from the western Mediterranean, the eastern Mediterranean and the Indian Ocean have extended the narrative back to encompass the past 80 000 yr (Tric et al. 1992). Pronounced drops to 28 per cent of the present level are reported for 39 000 and 69 000 yr ago. Nevertheless, there are discrepancies both among the cores and between them and results obtained in other parts of the world.

Where some workers detect a periodicity of ~43 000 yr in the secular palaeo-intensity, others prefer interpretations that simply concede that the dipole values are very unsteady (Merrill & McElhinny 1983). In one of the Azores cores, the inferred palaeo-intensity varied inversely with $^{10}$Be levels, which, as we have seen, are an independent measure of cosmic-ray incident flux and thus of the effectiveness of the magnetic shield. After allowing for variations in oceanic circulation, the results account for 80 per cent of the discrepancy between $^{14}$C and Th/U ages during the past 80 000 yr, and thus give added support to the contention that long-term changes in atmospheric $^{14}$C concentration are produced mainly by variations in the geomagnetic dipole moment (Laj et al. 1996) .

The thesis is also strengthened by comparison of $^{14}$C ages with those derived from dendrochronology (tree-ring analysis), which spans the past 6500 yr, on the grounds that the geomagnetic dipole moment can be calculated from the difference between the two sets of ages because $^{14}C$ production and decay are balanced. It is claimed that the radiocarbon dipole moment shows the same general trends as the global dipole moment derived from archaeomagnetic data (Merrill & McElhinny 1983), granted that some discrepancies will result from the burning of fossil fuel and other human activities.

Changes in declination and inclination have been studied since the sixteenth century. The distinction between external and internal sources of change was soon noted, even though the extent to which their timespans overlap remains in dispute. An 11 yr period related to the solar cycle, for instance, has been known since 1973 (Courtillot & Le Mouël 1988); events of internal origin 1 yr in duration have also been detected.

The position of the dipole axis has displayed a westward drift since 1600, but little change is recorded since 1850. When the account is extended by archaeomagnetism to encompass the past 2000 years, it is apparent that the north magnetic pole (NMP) has remained within 10° of the geographic pole during this period. (The NMP is obtained by averaging several virtual geographical poles, thus minimizing the effect of the non-dipole field.) The sedimentary record for the past 10000 yr (Ohno & Hamano 1992) suggests that, between 5000 and 3700 yr BP, movement was restricted to 5° of the geographical pole.

Declination in London and Paris decreased from 11°E in the late sixteenth century to 24°W in the late eighteenth century, and increased again after 1830 (Fig. 4.6). The inclination data, which are less complete, show a maximum in about 1720, decreasing to about 1860, followed by little change (Courtillot & Le Mouël 1988). The data are proving of great value in constraining models of the magnetic field. For instance, a difference of 350–400 yr in the timing of the inclination variations in southeast Europe and in Japan, similar in latitude but 110° apart in longitude, points to a westward drift averaging $0.3° \, yr^{-1}$ over the past 1400 yr; an average of $0.38° \, yr^{-1}$ was obtained for various parts of the Northern Hemisphere.

The discrepancy with the $0.2° \, yr^{-1}$ estimate for the westward drift of the non-dipole field suggests that the non-dipole field consists of a drifting component and a standing component (Merrill & McElhinny 1983). Analysis of the historical records for both declination and inclination further suggests a correlation between the rate of westward drift and latitude consistent with a rotation of the field at $0.0058 \, cm \, s^{-1}$ at the surface of the core. More generally, geomagnetic variations are useful in calculating the conductivity of the mantle, as variations that are mainly of external origin can be set against the internal variations they are suspected of inducing. The variations also contribute to discussion of competing models of fluid-core motion, and to explanations of changes in LOD and the Chandler wobble that invoke the interaction between the core and the mantle.

In 1790 John Churchman suggested that variations in declination over time might be reconstructed from records kept during early land surveys of the USA (Silverman 1998). There are doubtless other short-term changes in the physics of the Earth to be fruitfully chronicled from such sources.

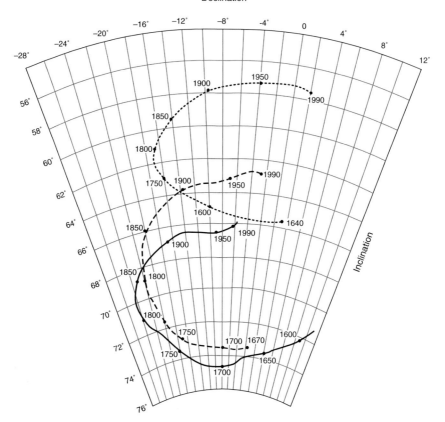

**Figure 4.6** A Bauer plot showing the inclination and declination of Earth's magnetic field for London (solid line), Paris (dashed line) and Rome (dotted line) for 1600–1990; note the steady decrease in declination to about 1800, followed by an increase (after Soare et al. 1998, by permission of the Annali di Geofisica).

# CHAPTER 5
# Shifting plates

*. . . it will shortly be possible to determine, by direct measurement over a span of 5 years or so, whether there is intercontinental plate-tectonic movement at present.*
Robbins (1980)

In the first chapter of *The origin of continents and oceans* (1929), Wegener tried to demonstrate the truth of continental drift with the help of astronomical longitude determinations. The rate he reported for North Atlantic opening was $19 \pm 3 \, \text{m yr}^{-1}$. The value accepted today is a thousand times lower, namely $19 \, \text{mm yr}^{-1}$, and Wegener stands at once vindicated and discredited (Stein 1987). He also emerges as the founder of what has come to be called tectonics in real time (Tapponnier 1991), the direct measurement of crustal deformation while it is in progress or soon after, and an early exponent of the experimental approach whereby rates inferred from the geological record are compared with instrumental data.

Thirty years later, the two central assumptions of the novel plate-tectonic model – that the plates are rigid and that their boundaries are sharp – also needed simple numerical testing. Since the 1960s, advances in marine geophysics and bathymetry, and the geodetic techniques paraded in Chapter 1, have shown many plate boundaries to be so indistinct that they occupy up to 15 per cent of the Earth's surface. Moreover, the rigidity of plate interiors is seen to be very much a relative term (Gordon 1998), as strain rates within some plates range over two orders of magnitude or more.

## Plate translation

Vine & Matthews (1963) showed that the pattern of magnetization observed in the North Atlantic was consistent with repeated reversals of the Earth's magnetic field during seafloor spreading on both sides of a mid-ocean rift. Once an appropriate sequence of lavas had been dated by radiometric methods (primarily K/Ar), the narrative gained a numerical timescale. Nevertheless, much of the ensuing discussion remained mainly descriptive and the interpretations correspondingly qualitative, especially where, as in the Mediterranean and in Southeast Asia, plate convergence has prevailed in the past few million years and thus destroyed the local magnetic record.

Even where extension has been the rule and a suitable patch of sea floor was conveniently at hand, such as the Atlantic itself, rates of plate movement were necessarily averages derived from successive dated palaeomagnetic intervals, of which, as we saw in Chapter 4, the latest spans almost 790 000 yr and many are far longer than that.

Seafloor spreading creates new oceanic crust. The question then arises of how the excess material is accommodated if the Earth's diameter is constant. The conventional answer is subduction, the process by which a plate is driven under another to be consumed by the mantle. The implication is that the global network of plates is broadly in balance, the few major exceptions being the mid-ocean ridges, where new crust is being generated, and compressional mountains, where there is too much of it.

There have been attempts to check and build on the global network of plate movements. Some attempts are simple algebraic sums of the average annual rates of separation and convergence between the major plates, usually based on palaeomagnetic data. Others, notably the NUVEL-1 scheme of DeMets et al. (1990), were elaborate analyses of plate interaction that supplemented the magnetic chronology with information on the azimuth and extent of earthquake slip. Focal-plane solutions for shallow earthquakes are especially helpful for identifying plate kinematics, whereas those for intermediate or deep earthquakes tell us more about plate dynamics by reflecting, for example, whether a subducted slab is undergoing compression or extension.

Where both palaeomagnetic and focal-plane data were available, there was often encouraging agreement in the averaged annual rate, even though the former deals in averages over $10^5$ yr or more and the latter mainly in events dating from the past few decades. The agreement supported the view that plate movement was uniform and that any jerkiness was confined to the plate margins.

Improved global syntheses, notably those referred to as PO1 and RM2, took advantage of new surveys of the ocean floor, which brought out the transform faults that appeared to define arcuate zones of differential seafloor movement transverse to the mid-ocean ridges. Earthquake focal-plane solutions, using body-wave first motions, were increasingly supplanted by more robust centroid-moment tensor (CMT) focal mechanisms, which are based on long-period body and surface waves. Moreover, where PO71 used 260 items of data and RM2 330, NUVEL-1 (DeMets et al. 1990) was based on 1122 data points: 277 spreading rates bearing on 22 plate boundaries, 121 transform-fault azimuths and 724 earthquake-slip vectors of which nearly 70 per cent were from CMT solutions.

The analysis now included areas that had previously been poorly represented, including the Arctic Ridge and the northern and southern extremities of the Mid-Atlantic Ridge. The quality, as well as the coverage, of the data had been greatly improved by side-scan and high-resolution sonar systems, including GLORIA and SEAMARC, and Seasat altimetry of the ocean surface. The orientation of transforms on the sea floor was consequently much better defined and, although the results were inevitably more uncertain than those derived from shipboard soundings, they covered vast areas and did not require interpolation between isolated readings.

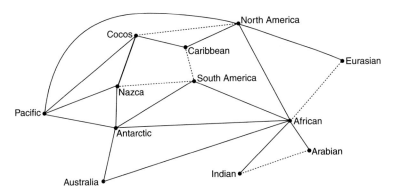

**Figure 5.1** Plate circuit for NUVEL-1 . Dotted lines signify azimuth only; solid lines represent rate as well as azimuth. (After DeMets et al. 1990, by permission of Blackwell Publishing.)

The plate model NUVEL-1 was created on four levels. First, spreading rates and transform-fault azimuths were estimated from magnetic and bathymetric data and focal-plane solutions. Secondly, best-fitting angular-velocity vectors were found for single-plate boundaries. Thirdly, circuits of three or more plates (Fig. 5.1) were used to analyze how well the plate movements fitted together (closure). Finally, the Euler (i.e. the angular-velocity) vectors were identified that best fitted the data and were also consistent with global plate circuit closure. The spreading rates still had to be derived from the magnetic record, and consequently the latter part of the narrative was perforce confined to actively spreading ridges. On occasion the sequence was completed by identifying the synthetic magnetic profile that best fitted the observed distance between the centre of anomaly 2A (~3 Myr) on both sides of a spreading centre, with the express intention of avoiding any problems caused by changes in the rate of plate motion over the past few million years.

The quotation at the head of this chapter shows that, as recently as 1980, direct measurement of plate movement was still not commonplace; indeed, some scientists were not sure that movement was currently taking place. By 1987, plate velocities determined by SLR, GPS and VLBI were sufficient in number and resolution for sensible comparison with the long-term plate model averages. Away from plate boundaries, plate motion appeared to be steady over periods of a million years (Fig. 5.2). No internal plate deformation had been reliably detected (Stein 1987). A further five years of VLBI and SLR measurements gave results very close to rates averaged over the preceding 3 Myr. So did DORIS and GPS data.

On the other hand, many changes in the rate and azimuth of plate displacement are known from the Cainozoic record. The Dead Sea transform (Fig. 5.3) reportedly reflects "continuous adjustment to small changes in the relative plate motion between Africa and Arabia" (ten Brink 1999). Accelerated extension coincided with the onset of extrusion tectonics north of the Bitlis–Zagros suture (Hempton 1987). A later plate-scale rearrangement of the stress field left its traces in the Gulf of Suez rift and in the central Red Sea, and led during the late Pleistocene to a change in extension azimuth from 045–055° to its present orientation of 010–020° (Bosworth & Taviani 1996). A similar

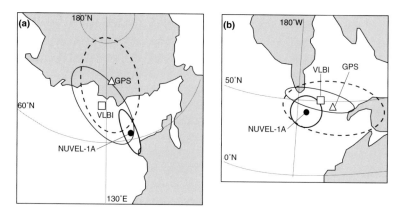

**Figure 5.2** Comparison between pole determinations by NUVEL-1A, VLBI and GPS. **(a)** Eurasia and North America, **(b)** North America and Pacific. (After Argus & Heflin 1995, © AGU.)

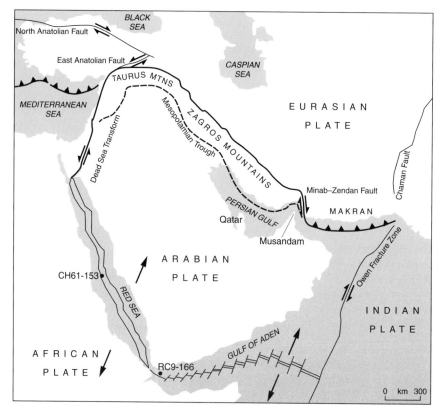

**Figure 5.3** The Arabian plate margins, showing location of features and boreholes discussed in text.

change is reported from the Kenya Rift system. GPS data collected since 1995 in north-east Asia indicate a shift in the pole of relative rotation for Eurasia and North America by 1200 km to the northwest in the past 3 Myr or so (Kogan et al. 2000), an effect already suggested by the seismic evidence (Cook et al. 1986). This amounts to an average of 400 mm yr$^{-1}$, which is comfortably within reach of modern geodetic techniques and is therefore readily testable.

Significant differences have in fact been reported between NUVEL-1 predictions of the angular velocity of the Pacific relative to the North American plate (Fig. 5.4) and VLBI measurements over 10 yr (DeMets et al. 1994). In the Gulf of California the VLBI rate was faster by $5 \pm 4$ mm yr$^{-1}$.

Some authors question the validity of GPS-derived evidence for deformation if based on GPS networks that were set up for purposes other than deformation monitoring, such as surveying (Riguzzi et al. 2001). In any case, disagreement would seem inevitable when different timescales are used. Where agreement was close, there were those who noted that the Euler vectors by which plate movements were described, and which had formerly been derived from long-term palaeomagnetic chronologies, were now based on space geodetic data in a reference frame (ITRF-94) specifically designed to agree on average with other geodetic data (Norabuena et al. 1998). At all events the reversal timescale, formerly calibrated by K/Ar ages and now tuned to the astronomical time-scale, gave plate velocities 4.38 per cent slower than those derived from K/Ar ages and used in NUVEL-1, in excellent agreement with 148 geodetic measurements by VLBI and SLR and with ages obtained with the $^{40}$Ar/$^{39}$Ar method.

A revised plate model NUVEL-1A, was the outcome. It soon proved its worth. In the Pacific sector, for example, permanent GPS stations have been in operation at five sites in Australia since 1990, at two sites on the Pacific plate since 1987 (Hawaii) and 1992

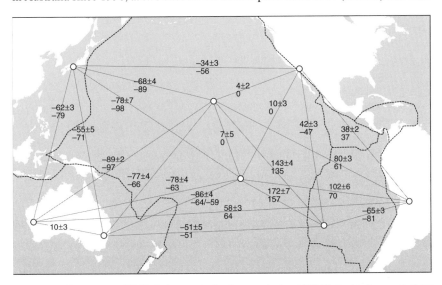

**Figure 5.4** Comparison of VLBI displacement rates (upper value) and NUVEL-1 rates (lower value) for the Pacific Basin (after Dunn et al. 1989, with permission).

(French Polynesia), and at one site in Antarctica (McMurdo) since 1992. Measurements over a period of three years supplemented by the permanent International Global Positioning System and Geodynamics Service, first tested in 1992 (Puntodewo et al. 1994, Larson & Freymuller 1995), gave Euler vectors for Australia–Antarctica and Pacific plate–Antarctica that agreed with NUVEL-1A within one standard deviation.

Elsewhere, however, VLBI data agreed better with NUVEL-1 than with NUVEL-1A predictions. DORIS data for 1993–6 for 28 sites away from deforming plate boundaries gave a good match with GPS, SLR and VLBI networks, but as regards poles of rotation (Crétaux et al. 1998) there was better agreement with NUVEL-1 predictions for the Eurasian, Pacific, African and South American plates, and with NUVEL-1A for the Australian, Nazca, Antarctica and North American plates.

Granted that coverage for the different plates ranged widely in history and quality, the differences cannot be ignored. Note also that variations at individual stations over time are probably real (Crétaux et al. 1998), as they persist even though the DORIS data have been corrected for geopotential, lunisolar and planetary accelerations, atmospheric drag, solid Earth and ocean tides, direct and Earth-reflected radiation pressure, and relativistic acceleration.

## Plate interaction

Thus, whereas modern geodesy began by confirming the essential validity of geological estimates of plate motion, it can now be deployed to search for local departures in rate or azimuth from the mean, essential material for any full account of the forces responsible for the motion and its bearing on Earth history. A fruitful approach is to combine geodetic observations with predictions deriving from modelling of plate interaction. The setting that has received the most attention, understandably in view of its potential for destructive earthquakes, has been coastal subduction.

In general the strategy is to compare the measured average rates with the long-term rate of deformation supplied by a plate model such as NUVEL-1A in order to identify variations along and across strike. Detailed analysis of the interplate zone requires many judiciously placed geodetic stations and is therefore currently ruled out when it is not on land.

A study of motion of the Philippine Sea plate (Matsuzaka et al. 1991) was the first to use a mobile VLBI system to this end, following a trial run in 1984 that showed it could detect changes of a few centimetres in as little as one or two years (Fig. 5.5). Unlike some American systems, the device is not entirely portable, as the 5 m antenna has to be bolted down to a fixed concrete base with a brass mark, but this permits positioning to better than 3 mm in the horizontal direction and 5 mm in the vertical.

In November 1987 and November–December 1989, two sessions separated by a week were held in Chichijima (Philippine plate, PHS) and Kashima (North America plate, NOAM). The result was found to be 74 mm yr$^{-1}$ on an azimuth of 293°. Seno (1977) had computed a Euler vector for PHS relative to the Eurasian plate (EUR) which, when

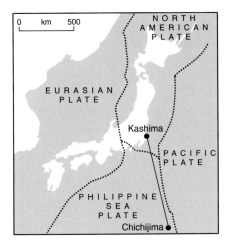
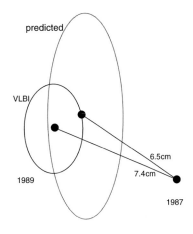

**Figure 5.5** Comparison between predicted displacement between Eurasian and Pacific plates and VLBI stations at Chichijima and Kashima 1987–9 (after Matsuzaka et al. 1991, © AGU).

combined with the NUVEL-1 vector for EUR–North America (NOAM), gave a PHS–NOAM vector of 40 mm yr$^{-1}$ at 305°. Now Kashima itself is known to be undergoing displacement relative to NOAM of 7.9 mm yr$^{-1}$ at 357°. Vector addition gave the final displacement of the Chichijima VLBI site with respect to Kashima as 65 mm yr$^{-1}$ on an azimuth of 304°, in reassuring if unexciting agreement with the measured shift within the 2 s.d. error ellipses

The more portable GPS approach is evidently better suited to complex physical and political terrain, such as that of the eastern Mediterranean. The classic formulation by McKenzie (1972) for the plate-tectonic framework of the Mediterranean postulated, among other things, that convergence between Arabia and Eurasia in eastern Turkey led to westward movement of a Turkish plate separated from an Aegean plate in the west by a zone of north–south extension.

An international GPS survey in 1988–92 gave general support to this tectonic pattern but also suggested that Turkey and the southern Aegean were moving as a single unit provisionally termed the Anatolian plate (Oral et al. 1995). It recorded some crustal extension in the southern Aegean and western Turkey, but at a rate of 10 mm yr$^{-1}$, which is substantially less than indicated by earthquake data; and by shifting the Euler pole for Turkey about 12° to the north it indicated more rotation (as distinct from translation) in the movement of Anatolia relative to Eurasia.

These findings may disagree with the plate map derived from earthquake evidence simply because they only refer to a four-year period and, what is more, a particular four-year period; and they bear mainly on plate kinematics. But the potential for dynamic discussion of plate translation is illustrated by a later study of the same area (McClusky et al. 2000), which used additional data from 1988–97 at 189 sites. One of its conclusions, based on variations in the rate of deformation, was that the continental lithosphere of eastern Turkey and the Caucasus was being deflected to the east by the strong oceanic

71

lithosphere of the Black and Caspian seas. The inference is still largely descriptive, but, by identifying variations in movement resulting from plate interaction, it is in the spirit of geodynamic analysis in focusing on response to stress rather than simply comparing velocities on a sphere.

An analysis in Central America based on GPS data collected in 1988 and 1991 went further. It showed that the islands of Cocos and San Andres, over 400 km from the Middle America trench, had velocities to within 2 s.d. of the value predicted by the NUVEL-1 model (88 mm yr$^{-1}$ at 202°), whereas Liberia, 120 km from the trench, gave a velocity with the predicted azimuth at 1 s.d. but substantially slower than that of NUVEL-1 (70±5 instead of 85±6 mm yr$^{-1}$, errors again at 2 s.d.). In the absence of any evidence for active crustal shortening in the order of 15 mm yr$^{-1}$, the discrepancy could be explained by the accumulation of elastic strain because the Pacific and North American plates were locked together rather than sliding past each other (Dixon 1993). This agrees well with a model proposed ten years earlier, which on the basis of the sparse seismic evidence postulated that strain was indeed accumulating above a locked subduction zone (Savage 1983). We now have an estimate of the strain and are thus well on the way to evaluating the stored seismic energy it represents, although not yet how and when it will be released.

The same dislocation model was used with SLR and VLBI data to investigate strain along a transform plate boundary, the San Andreas Fault. Taking eight VLBI stations on the Pacific side and five on the North American, station velocity towards the northwest or southeast was compared with plate velocity as indicated by the revised NUVEL-1 model (Robaudo & Harrison 1993). The data fell close to the curve derived from the dislocation model. This time the locking depth was set at 23 km, and the values governing the curve also differed from those for subduction where the subducted plate is old, as with the Pacific, and where it is young, as with the Nazca or Philippine plates. More important, however, is the implication that the model is valid for two very different tectonic settings and that geodetic data can be used to establish the key controlling variable of locking depth.

Subduction modelling may also provide an estimate of the energy release accounted for by recorded seismicity. Where the Nazca and South America plates meet, the boundary zone is 500–1000 km wide. Here too, shortening is thought to occur by elastic deformation on locked parts of the plate interface at the trench, to be released subsequently by large thrust earthquakes and possibly also by aseismic sliding, by permanent crustal thickening in the Andes, by thrust faulting and folding in the foreland belt east of the Andes and, as convergence is oblique, by strike-slip motion in the fore-arc (Norabuena et al. 1998).

Measurements were made during 1994–6 by GPS, SLR and DORIS. All three had given values for convergence at the trench of 68 mm yr$^{-1}$ at N76°E, not very different from the NUVEL-1A prediction of 77 mm yr$^{-1}$ at N79°E. The proportion of the shortening taken up as locked strain at the trench was modelled on the basis of geometries for the plate interface derived from seismic data. Two profiles could be identified. In the northern, the best fit between modelled velocity and GPS observations indicated 30 mm yr$^{-1}$ of slip accumulating on the plate interface and 15 mm yr$^{-1}$ of shortening on reverse faults in the foreland belt in the east. The corresponding figures for the south were 38 mm yr$^{-1}$ and 12 mm yr$^{-1}$.

According to whether we use geodetic data or NUVEL-1A, seismicity fails to account for 34–42 per cent of the convergence in the north and 26–35 per cent in the south. Trench parallel movement is too slight (c. 8 mm yr$^{-1}$) to plug the gap. The most popular explanation, granted that the earthquake component has been underestimated by inadequate historical and instrumental records, is that the deficit lies in plate motion by aseismic stable sliding (Norabuena et al. 1998; see also Ch. 8).

Until recently, geodesy could not discriminate between a defective seismic record and aseismic interplate slip, especially where deformation is widely distributed and much of it is in the subsurface or beneath the sea. Precise positioning of seafloor reference points, using a combination of GPS measurements on ships or buoys (i.e. in the absence of islands) and underwater acoustic methods, promises to reduce the problem at least for horizontal motion (Spiess et al. 1998). On land, deformation ascribed to subsurface creep has now been detected, after eight years of observation by radar interferometry, in a part of southern California where it was long assumed that there was steady creep on two faults at right angles to one another, the Blackwater Little Lake Fault and the Garlock Fault. Interferometry indicates that more than half of the right-lateral motion of the eastern California shear zone is concentrated along the Blackwater fault system, and that it is building up stress in the shallow crust at a rate three times faster than the rate inferred from geological observations. Peltzer et al. (2001) suggest this may represent stress transfer between the Garlock Fault and other faults in the Mojave area, in particular those that produced the 1992 Landers earthquake and the 1872 Owens Valley earthquake.

Similarly, geodetic techniques have shown that the contact between the Juan de Fuca and North America plates on the Cascadia coast, down dip from the seismogenic part of the fault, had slipped aseismically by about 2 cm over a fault surface measuring 50 km by 300 km and equivalent to an earthquake of $M_W = 6.7$ (Dragert et al. 2001; Fig. 5.6). To seismologists this was especially interesting as an example of discontinuous movement in the plastic portion of the plate interface and as a possible example of the kind of slip event thought to have propagated up dip to trigger the 1960 (Chilean) $M_W = 9.5$ and other great subduction earthquakes. In the present context, the report nicely illustrates the elusive nature of some major geological structures. For, without the continuous monitoring of 14 permanent GPS stations, the movement was unlikely to emerge, especially as it amounted to a temporary and localized reversal of the long-term trend attributable to plate convergence and would thus have been swallowed up in the average rates yielded by pre-satellite geodetic methods.

However, any full analysis of crustal rheology requires data on strain rather than simply on net displacement. The Australia/Pacific plate boundary in South Island, New Zealand (Fig. 5.7), illustrates what can be done by combining traditional first-order triangulation and trilateration networks (here dating from 1978) with GPS observations. The NUVEL-1A velocity of the Pacific plate relative to the Australian plate is 38 mm yr$^{-1}$ on an azimuth of 253°, implying mainly dextral strike-slip movement (with some secondary compression) on the Alpine Fault and almost pure strike-slip motion on the

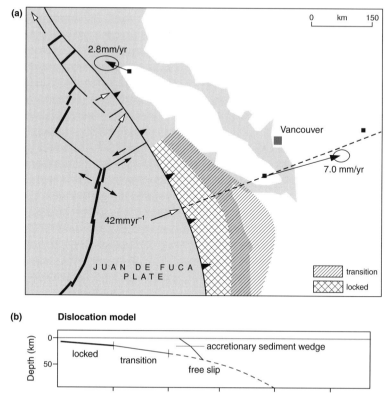

**Figure 5.6**  Northern Cascadia margin. **(a)** Dashed line = plate convergence at 42 mm yr⁻¹; filled squares are GPS stations (after DeMets et al. 1990, © AGU). **(b)** Model showing sections of the subduction zone (after Dragert & Hyndman 1995, © AGU).

Marlborough Faults to the northeast. There is disagreement over the proportion of the relative plate motion accommodated by the Alpine Fault, with authoritative estimates ranging between 25 and 100 per cent. Historical seismicity is concentrated in the Marlborough faults, and the last major breaks on the Alpine Fault date from 550 yr ago in the central part and 300–350 yr ago in the south.

The observations can be discussed as strain rates rather than as velocity or displacement vectors, because they are independent of origin and thus do not call for a stable reference point on the plates (Pearson et al. 1995). Integrating the strain across the island, on the assumption that shortening is taken up perpendicularly to the Alpine Fault, gives a relative velocity of $34 \pm 7$ mm yr⁻¹ on an azimuth of $256 \pm 7°$ across the network, implying (at 95% confidence) that most of the plate-boundary deformation hereabouts occurs on land. The highest strain rate ($>0.4\,\mu\text{rad yr}^{-1}$) occurs in the Southern Alps, near the Alpine Fault and on the western coastal plain, and amounts to 75 per cent of the rate predicted by NUVEL-1A. Dislocation modelling shows that the observations are consistent with a fault dipping 50° and locked to a depth of 12 km, the implication

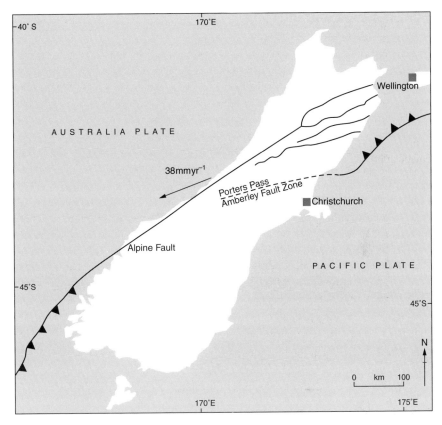

**Figure 5.7**   Plate setting of New Zealand (after Pearson et al. 1995, © AGU).

being that, as on the San Andreas Fault, the upper part of the crust (here to a depth of 12 km) is storing the right-lateral shear component of relative plate motion as elastic energy, whereas the deeper portions slip freely.

By the same token, detailed geodetic analysis may reveal the effects of inherited strain. In the Kenai Peninsula of Alaska, GPS measurements between 1993 and 1997 indicate two patterns of motion (Freymuller et al. 2000). On the eastern side (and on western Prince William Sound), sites moved in the direction of plate convergence at rates that ranged from almost the full plate NUVEL-1A rate of 55 mm yr$^{-1}$ to a mere 5 mm yr$^{-1}$. On the western side the sites moved towards the trench at about 20 mm yr$^{-1}$. Modelling suggested that any uplift resulting from deglaciation would amount at most to a few millimetres a year. The eastern pattern could be explained by a locked plate interface and consequent rapid motion in the overriding plate, the western by continuing post-seismic response to the Prince William Sound earthquake of 1964 ($M_W = 9.2$). Quite apart from the details of the trenchward mechanism, and of the boundary between the two deforming zones, the evidence for significant post-seismic effects 30 yr after a great earthquake is sobering to the student of geological change in near real time.

75

# Plate deformation: interiors

In the pioneering analysis of Alpine deformation by Argand (1924), the irregular margin of Africa drives into southern Europe to produce a sinuous mountainous belt. Wegener (1929) likewise explained the mountains of southwest Persia by the intrusion of the Omani spur. The modern indenter model generalizes the process as a rigid block being driven into a plastic mass, but one specific instance continues to attract attention: the collision between India and Eurasia. The reasons include its probable impact on many aspects of global climate and the intriguing suggestion, stemming from a kinematic approach to the deformation, that much of the convergence is taken up by slip on a few faults bounding crustal blocks, leading among other things to substantial crustal extrusion southeastwards (Molnar & Tapponnier 1975).

The contribution to shortening by crustal thickening in the Himalayas and Tibet remains in dispute, as its testing currently hinges mainly on the often ambiguous data of gravity and seismology. Extrusion is eminently testable, and evidence for significant slip along the 2000 km-long Altyn Tagh Fault at first appeared to endorse it (Molnar et al. 1987). However, geodetic data between 86°E and 92°E show that the Altyn Tagh Fault is experiencing a left-lateral slip rate of $9 \pm 5$ mm yr$^{-1}$, two to four times lower than the rates derived from displaced Holocene features, and contraction normal to the fault at $3 \pm 1$ mm yr$^{-1}$, less than a tenth rather than a third of the total Indo-Asian convergence (Bendick et al. 2000). Although the discrepancy in geodetic and geological rates could indicate a deceleration in slip rate, or merely a temporary lull, it could just as well indicate that Tibet is not now being rapidly extruded southeastwards, or that some of the observed strike-slip movement may stem from relatively local block rotation (England & Molnar 1990).

Three years of GPS data from Mongolia point to crustal thickening rather than lateral extrusion; and, as the measured rates are faster than is to be expected from the India/Eurasia collision, they suggest that other agencies, such as subduction at the Pacific and gravitational forces, may play a role in the deformation (Calais & Amarjargal 2000). The broad belt of deformation at issue also serves as a reminder that the definition of a plate interior is arbitrary; to identify it as a zone not affected by processes that are directly the product of interaction between plates is to jump the gun.

Consider the prolonged speculation about the extent to which the Indian plate itself has undergone internal deformation consequent on its collision with Eurasia. The accumulation of strain is implicit in the occasional release of substantial intraplate earthquakes, witness the recent reverse-fault earthquakes at Jabalpur (21 May 1997, $M_W = 5.8$) and Latur (29 September 1993, $M_W = 6.2$), both of which are suspected of representing fault reactivation in the basement (Ramesh & Estabrook 1998). Circumstantial but impressive evidence for buckling at the latitude of Mangalore (Subrahmanya 1996) includes a major east–west drainage divide associated with channel migration away from the inferred uplift axis, coastal progradation and tide-gauge evidence for emergence since 1955 on both coasts, a positive gravity anomaly, and a belt of low to moderate seismicity (i.e. with magnitudes between 2 and 5).

The geodetic data do not yet provide any kind of verdict: GPS measurements made in 1991–6 between Bangalore in southern India and Nepal show that any deformation of the Indian plate proper resulting from its collision with Eurasia is 0–3 mm yr$^{-1}$ (Bilham et al. 1998). But additional tide-gauge data indicate relative subsidence at Cochin at 3 mm yr$^{-1}$ (Bendick & Bilham 1999), consistent with continued buckling (Fig. 5.8).

A similar problem arises with regard to the 1811–12 New Madrid (Missouri) earthquakes. Once again, there are indications that reactivation of basement faults in response to compression (this time east–west) was responsible. But the surface manifestation of this activity remains in dispute. According to one study, three of the original earthquakes were of $M_S > 8$. The palaeoseismic data appeared to indicate recurrence intervals of 400–1000 yr in the northern New Madrid seismic zone and a seismic hiatus of 5000–10 000 yr prior to the 1811–12 events in the south. These magnitudes and recurrences imply a level of seismic hazard that in some respects exceeds California's. An alternative interpretation puts the recurrence of $M = 7$ earthquakes at $1400 \pm 600$ and for $M = 8$ at $14 000 \pm 7000$ yr.

A GPS survey was set up to include the seismic zone and sites beyond the area deformed in 1811–12. A total of 24 monuments were used and the observations lasted about 10 hours for at least 5 consecutive days in November 1991 and October 1993. The

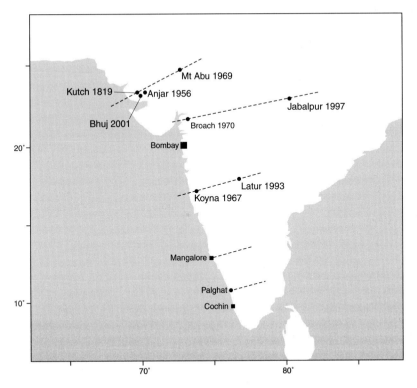

**Figure 5.8**  Major recent earthquakes in peninsular India and proposed relationship to pattern of lithospheric buckling indicated by dashed lines (after Vita-Finzi 2002).

survey was later extended to 1997 (Weber et al. 1998, Newman et al. 1999). As strains were likely to be small, velocities were investigated along and across the main seismogenic (strike-slip) faults, within a series of subnetworks, and by comparing linear strain rates with the rates predicted by earlier surveys. It still proved impossible to demonstrate deformation; there was a hint of strain accumulation across the southern seismic zone at $3-5\,\mathrm{mm\,yr^{-1}}$; but this was conceivably a post-seismic effect of the 1811–12 events.

The period of observation will doubtless yield persuasive results in due course. Where the key structures are not known and the probable geometry of deformation is not so well understood, sustained measurement over large areas would generally be too costly. For the Indian plate an alternative approach might be to concentrate geodetic measurements on the zones for which there is indirect evidence of buckling and thus of strain accumulation on underlying reverse faults. A map of well documented recent earthquakes, including the Jabalpur and Latur events, is consistent with a series of zones running west-southwest–east-northeast and crossing the west coast of the peninsula roughly at 10°, 13°, 17°, 21° and 24° N (Vita-Finzi 2002), the second of them corresponding with the zone of uplift identified by Subrahmanya (1996). If the earthquakes are indeed the products of buckling, they could well yield evidence of tilting before any shortening is unambiguously detected and, quite apart from its geodynamic interest, the outcome would emerge as a useful tool in the hunt for premonitory strain accumulation and for a scheme that will permit the focusing of emergency resources and the rational allocation of earthquake-resistant housing.

Here, seismicity appears to endorse a scheme of plate deformation. Elsewhere it reverts to its original role as the basis for drawing plate boundaries by inviting plate subdivision. For example, the Indo–Australian plate is a unit that meshes well with other major structures in the region, not least when comparing oblique convergence off Sumatra with normal convergence with the Makran; but fitting seismic data along the three mid-oceanic ridge systems that meet at the Rodrigues triple junction presents difficulties best resolved by detaching a Capricorn plate from the Indo–Australian plate (Royer & Gordon 1997). The case brings two interesting implications. First, drawing plate boundaries depends on the aims of the enquiry as much as on the quality of the data; and, secondly, oceanic boundaries, at any rate if based on earthquake distribution, can be just as diffuse and broad as many of those on land.

The agreement between short-term geodetic and long-term rates at plate interiors, compared with lower and sometimes spasmodic movement in the boundary zone, leads to the simple conclusion that, although body forces move the plates uniformly, their displacement at the margins is distorted by elastic stress accumulation (Bott & Dean 1973). On occasion, spasmodic boundary forces may initiate movement that diffuses into the bulk of the plate. GPS observations in northeast Iceland between 1897 and 1990, about 10 yr after an episodic divergent movement between the North American and Eurasian plates during 1975–81, suggest that the horizontal displacement field fits a two-dimensional model of post-rupture stress relaxation that assumed a thin elastic layer overlying a viscous layer (Heki et al. 1993).

In this scheme, plate motion is the sum of many displacements that have diffused from boundaries where episodic displacements occur periodically. The width of the boundary zone depends both on the geological conditions that control stress diffusivity and on the frequency of the episodic movement, but is generally of the order of 100 km. The Arabian case study discussed below raises the possibility that edge effects can penetrate more deeply into the plate.

# Movement, mechanism and forces

A key issue still to be resolved in geophysics is what drives the lithospheric plates. In very broad terms the answer is well known. Heat energy from the Earth's interior, supplied primarily by radioactive decay, is transferred to the plates by ridge push at ocean ridges, slab pull at ocean trenches, and drag at the base of the plate by convection in the mantle. Other energy sources may be shortlived but locally influential: large meteoritic impacts, for example, may help to explain sudden changes in the rate or direction of plate movement (Price 2001). To go beyond this level of explanation requires information on the angular velocities of the plates relative to some reference (generally hotspots), the orientation of stress measurements within plates, and strain rates. Of these, as Gordon (2000) notes, only strain rates are sensitive to the rheology of the lithosphere, and thus are geologically realistic.

As we have seen, strain rates within plate interiors are generally too low for direct monitoring with existing techniques; indeed, the fact that strain rates across narrow plate boundaries can be $10^9$ greater than the minimum for plate interiors is a major obstacle to reconciling plate tectonics with mantle convection (Gordon 2000). But, in any case viscous drag at the base of the lithosphere is seen by many workers as implausible on the grounds that the plates are not coupled to the mantle.

That leaves the two forces acting at the trenches and ridges. Trench pull has proved the easier of the two to evaluate, even when, as in a study of the Philippine Sea plate (Pacanovsky et al. 1999), much of the plate is under water, there are few midplate borehole stress measurements, and intraplate seismicity is also limited, and the analysis hinged on a finite-element model invoking a spherical elastic shell. It turns out that, away from the plate margins near Taiwan and the Izu Peninsula of Japan, where collisional forces dominate the stress field, trench-pull forces can explain the bulk of the plate's motion and deformation, and yield a pole of rotation very similar to that derived from NUVEL-1.

Nevertheless, once a plate has attained a terminal velocity, slab pull may be balanced by viscous and frictional forces, both at the base of the plate and, to judge from the slowness with which detached portions of slab appear to be moving through the mantle, in the vicinity of the descending portion of the plate (Price et al. 1988).

Hence, despite the claim that ridge push is ten times less effective, it remains the only candidate to explain the widespread intraplate stresses. The injection of new seafloor material at ridges would seem to be an inadequate mechanism, and transmission of the stress across hundreds or thousands of kilometres of lithosphere improbable. On the other hand, an early version of ridge push in its broadest sense, gravity glide (Price et al. 1988), provides a plausible source of energy as it invokes the gravitational energy of a lithospheric slab over the asthenosphere solely as a result of its differential uplift by mantle upwelling at the ridge.

The proposal can be evaluated most readily at the Arabian plate. The regional kinematic picture is complex: the evolution of the Red Sea, for example, has been influenced by the motion of the Indian Ocean and of Africa west of the Rift (Somalian subplate), as well as Arabia and the Nubian subplate. Nevertheless, translation of the Arabian plate itself can to some extent be disengaged from the jigsaw. Its northeastward movement is usually linked to displacement along the Dead Sea transform (Searle 1994). Shortening in the Zagros is about the same as the separation between Arabia and Africa during development of the Red Sea axial trough (Falcon 1974), and conversion of Holocene folding rates to shortening in the Zagros (Vita-Finzi 2001) gives a convergence rate ($29\,\mathrm{mm\,yr^{-1}}$) that is very similar to the average opening rate for the Red Sea.

The seismic evidence shows that there is no subduction at the leading edge of the Arabian plate along the Zagros. The present consensus is that the basement is taking up convergence mainly by thickening associated with the reactivation of normal faults as reverse faults (Falcon 1969, Jackson 1980); detachment between the sedimentary cover and the faulted basement is promoted by salt. Some version of gravity spreading from the Red Sea Rift has been shown to be plausible (Bird 1978); uplift at the Red Sea provides circumstances propitious for gravity glide. There is prima facie evidence for the requisite gravitational gradient in a seismic refraction profile (Mooney et al. 1985), which shows a northeastward deepening of the base of the crust abruptly from $18\,\mathrm{km}$ beneath the coastal plain to $38\,\mathrm{km}$ at the Red Sea escarpment and then gradually down to $45 \pm 5\,\mathrm{km}$ under the Zagros.

The real test of the model is its success in explaining current deformation of the mountain range at the leading edge of the plate. This time, variations in rheology, known or suspected from lithology and structure, hinder any attempt to assess the force required to deform a fold belt (McClusky et al. 2000). A provisional stratagem for the Zagros is to evaluate the work that had to be done against gravity to sustain the Zagros folds, in the knowledge that the answer would be a minimum and omitting from consideration the folding itself and any associated faulting and uplift (Mann & Vita-Finzi 1988). The answer is $0.145\,\mathrm{kbar}$ for folds sliding over a décollement or detachment surface, and $0.134\,\mathrm{kbar}$ for folds not thus constrained.

The force created by gravitational spreading of the Red Sea Rift is estimated to be about $0.28\,\mathrm{kbar}$ (Bird 1978); ridge push amounts to $0.2$–$0.3\,\mathrm{kbar}$ (Kusznir & Park 1984). Both are well in excess of the minimum required to keep the Zagros Mountains up. To determine whether this force could induce fault reversal and surface folding will require information on how far they vary over time. The present phase of Red Sea spreading dates from only $4$–$5\,\mathrm{Myr}$ ago, when the spreading rate dropped from $13\,\mathrm{mm\,yr^{-1}}$ to $9\,\mathrm{mm\,yr^{-1}}$ (Girdler & Styles 1974), and the higher rate may have sufficed to initiate at least localized buckling. But even the lower average rate of plate translation conceals coseismic peak values that, as in the Golbaf earthquake ($M_{\mathrm{S}} = 5.7$) of 20 November

1989 (Berberian & Qorashi 1994), can bring new surface folds into existence.

Convergence significantly exceeds the measured or modelled deformation, but there is no surface evidence for creep (Tchalenko 1975). At Tujak, east of Musandam (see Fig. 5.3), a sequence of Holocene marine terraces rising to 28.6 m above present sea level is best explained by rare but substantial uplift. Abrupt uplift is indicated by the presence of undisturbed mollusc assemblages (including oyster banks) on the terraces. The available [14]C ages suggest that the most recent such event raised the lowest terrace by some 1.4 m and that there has been a tectonic hiatus during the past 1000 yr (Vita-Finzi 2001). This would help to explain the apparent discrepancy between seismicity and the predicted rate of convergence, if only by showing that the instrumental record is at least 1000 yr too short for tectonic analysis and adequate assessment of the earthquake hazard.

All the proposed plate-moving mechanisms may turn out to be effective according to local circumstances, in which case the question will become that of evaluating their relative importance at the site in question – unless, as in the Zagros, one of them can be excluded by independent evidence. More probably the issue will need to be recast into something a little more subtle. After all, ridge push, gravity glide and slab pull are parts of a continuum, and the boundary between heat and gravity is equally blurred. The need for local measurements of velocity and azimuth will then be all the more pressing.

CHAPTER 6
# Ice and water bodies

*The surface of the sea stretched as flat as a rooftop.*
From *The epic of Gilgamesh*

As the Earth swung repeatedly from glacial to interglacial conditions in the course of the past 2.5 Myr, the fluctuations of its icecaps and glaciers impinged (as we saw in Ch. 4) on the globe's angular momentum, both directly and through the agency of ocean volume. Yearly and century-scale changes in terrestrial ice and water bodies have doubtless also influenced planetary dynamics, but they are of more obvious concern as indicators and, in favourable settings, as agents of climatic change and crustal deformation.

Dependable records bearing on the changing extent of Alpine glaciers go back at least to the fourteenth century AD (Grove & Rackham 2001), but the current emphasis is very much a creature of topical concerns and technical advances. The dispute over how far human activity has accelerated the atmospheric greenhouse effect calls for detailed information on the status of icecaps and glaciers, and on direct measurement of sea level. Interest in rates of change and net advances and retreats is fuelled by the realization that there have been intervals in the past 20 000 yr when sea level rose at rates in excess of $60 \, mm \, yr^{-1}$, compared to the mere $1$–$2 \, mm \, yr^{-1}$ of the past four millennia (Bindschadler 1998) and that rapid deglaciation and therefore accelerated submergence could return. By good fortune, although not entirely fortuitously – since much of the pressure for the release of classified data and the development of appropriate software comes from advisers to submariners and the managers of snow-fed hydroelectric installations – the requisite improvements in ground- and space-based geodesy make it increasingly possible to satisfy these needs.

## Glaciers

The presence of large glaciers in the heart of Europe and in well trodden parts of North America ensured that any change in the shape and position of their snouts would be well recorded. The acceptance of a Little Ice Age in about 1550–1850 initially owed much to engravings of Swiss settlements overwhelmed by glaciers, evocative if not faithful echoes of a former grander ice age. Yet what the advances and later retreats signified was long to remain in dispute, even after the basic physics of ice movement had been worked out and the difference between flow by deformation and bodily sliding recognized. Advances might reflect excess snow accumulation up valley and thus some sort of cooling; yet rapid flow, or surging, could be promoted by the presence of lubricating meltwater at the glacier bed and therefore signal a phase of warming rather than increased snowfall (Dowdeswell et al. 1991). Moreover, the freshwater input from melting glaciers further influences the global climate through its effect on oceanic circulation.

But before glacier retreat can be confidently added to the evidence for global warming, we need to know whether it is widespread and synchronous and how far it is matched by the behaviour of continental ice sheets. Synchroneity cannot be assumed, even within the same hemisphere. During the most recent glacial period, for example, maximum mountain glaciation was sometimes out of phase with ice-sheet advances (Gillespie & Molnar 1995), perhaps because glacier growth is as dependent on adequate precipitation as on low temperature. In any case it responds more promptly to short-term changes than do massive ice sheets.

Many mountain areas, especially in the tropics, have been documented only recently, so that much climatic analysis has been lopsidedly focused on temperate latitudes. The Qori Kalis glacier, an outlet glacier of the Quelccaya icecap (14°S, 71°W), 5200 m above sea level in the Peruvian Andes, has been surveyed since 1963, once by aerial photogrammetry and three times by terrestrial photogrammetry (Brecher & Thompson 1993). The glacier retreated almost three times as fast between 1983 and 1991 as it did between 1963 and 1978, and the rate at which it lost volume was over seven times as great. Both retreat rate and volume loss are accelerating. The surveys were coupled with coring into the ice, the first time in 1983 and the second in 1991, and the latter indicated 1°C of warming between the 1970s and 1980s at a time when precipitation was average or higher.

Recent glacier retreat in other tropical glaciers – in the Ruwenzori Mountains, on Mount Kenya, and New Guinea (Brecher & Thompson 1993) – supports the conclusion that global warming is to blame. But, whereas in the 1950s–1980s about 73 per cent of glaciers in Central Asia were retreating, 15 per cent are advancing and 12 per cent are stable. In New Zealand, glacier retreat in the twentieth century has reversed since 1983. In Patagonia the icefield has shrunk, yet the Pio XI glacier is larger than at any time in the past 6000 yr (Fitzharris et al. 1995). In the Alps the glacial area has fallen by 30–40 per cent since about 1850, but the Grosse Aletsch is growing.

Glaciers that serve as outlets to icecaps or sheets benefit from an assured ice supply, but they too can display major fluctuations in response to local controls. Jakobshavns Isbrae, on the west coast of Greenland at 69°10'N, is the fastest glacier in the world. The weight of the evidence – calculations of the mass balance based on snow supply and meltwater flow, and glacier movement – suggests that it is almost in equilibrium (Pelto et al. 1989). Now, whereas between 1964 and 1986 it was advancing at an average of nearly 21 m per day, the rate varying by less than 1 m day$^{-1}$ from one year to the next, between 1850 and 1964 its front retreated at 240 m yr$^{-1}$ (a total of 27 km), and between 1964 and 1986 at 50 m yr$^{-1}$. Part of the answer lies in calving, of which a single instance can lead to 1000 m of retreat, and hence in the waves, tides and sea-level changes that bring it about; but fluctuations in ice supply are not thereby excluded.

The pattern of flow is an obvious starting point in any attempt to determine the budget of glaciers of any kind. Where access is not problematic, the classical method is to drive stakes on the glacier surface in a grid and return some months later to measure their displacement. On Byrd Glacier (80°S, 160°E) a photogrammetric survey in 1978–9 exploited the many natural features on the surface and yielded coordinates for 1467 terrain points. Comparison with maps derived from aerial photographs dating from 1960–62 indicated lowering by 50–150 m over a 60 km stretch. The discrepancy could not be accepted without further checks, as this is a major outlet glacier for the East Antarctic ice sheet, and such a dramatic lowering would have serious implications; photogrammetric strip triangulation of aerial photographs taken in 1960 and 1963 in fact showed that there had been no appreciable lowering (Brecher 1982). The need for less laborious and readily replicated measurements was clear. Satellite interferometry using synthetic aperture radar (InSAR) is increasingly being deployed for the purpose.

Rapid flow (as on Jakobshavns Isbrae) evidently requires that successive satellite passes should be close in time and in space. ERS-1 met both requirements between 28 December 1991 and 3 March 1992, and between 24 December 1993 and 10 April 1994, when it passed over a given location every three days and with small orbital separations at high latitudes (Massonnet & Feigl 1998). But ground conditions must also be suitable. In a survey conducted in Spitsbergen in 1993, few of the summer scenes were usable as the glacier surfaces were dark, possibly because of surface melting. The ice of early autumn, however, is often highly reflective, and mapping was successful when coherence persisted for the 25 days required for a repeat cycle by RADARSAT or the 35 days required for ERS (Massonnet & Feigl 1998). In western Greenland, interferograms produced from the ERS-1 satellite have allowed glacial motion to be detected at millimetre scale across a complete range of snow accumulation regimes and therefore despite great variations in radar scattering. Ice velocities estimated from the inferred flow directions and displacements (Rignot et al. 1995) agreed to within 6 per cent of *in situ* measurements along a 40 km survey line.

Besides a plan view of velocity variations, the assessment of flow volumes calls for information on vertical change, which traditional methods could supply laboriously by levelling or by gravity or seismic profiling. An interferometric survey of the Rutford ice stream in Antarctica (Fig. 6.1) has now yielded detection limits of 1.5 mm for vertical motions and 4 mm for horizontal motions (Goldstein et al. 1993). Interpretation of the interference pattern was helped by the brevity of the interval (six days) between the images, as this minimized the possibility that phase changes were the product of surface alteration by freeze, thaw or snowfall rather than genuine deformation (Fig. 6.2), and by the excellent match between successive viewpoints, which eliminated the need to correct the interferogram for any stereoscopic effect. The study produced 94 fringes between bedrock and the middle of the ice stream, each of them equivalent to 68 mm of displacement over the six days, or 390 m yr$^{-1}$, within 10 m yr$^{-1}$ of the result obtained

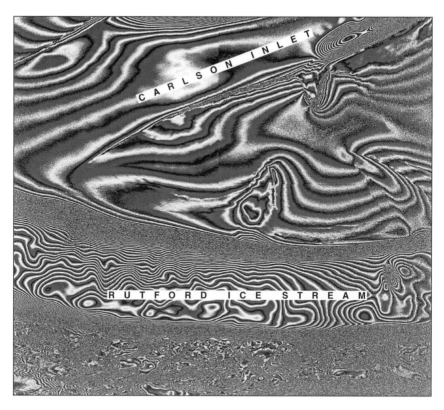

**Figure 6.1** Interferogram for Rutford ice stream, Antarctica, generated from ERS-1 SAR images. It confirmed (among other things) that the ice in the upper Carlson Inlet flows at less than a tenth of the speed of the Rutford ice stream. (After Fröhlich & Doake 1998, by permission of the International Glaciological Society.)

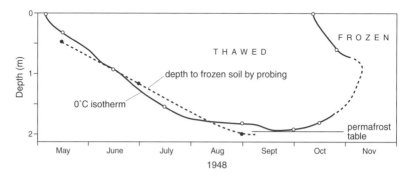

**Figure 6.2** Ground temperatures at Fairbanks (Alaska), showing upward freezing from permafrost in October (after Washburn 1973, with permission).

by ground measurement a decade earlier. The interferogram also indicated 2 m of vertical displacement at a location where the ice was floating and hence was subject to the tides, in good agreement with a calculated tidal amplitude of $2.1 \pm 0.2$ m. In short, the images not only confirmed the maximum rate of flow but also showed the location of the zone where the ice lost contact with the bedrock and consequently accelerated, a valuable item of information when the possible effects of sea-level rise are under consideration.

Where flow is confined between steep mountain walls, interferometry may be able to distinguish between surges and steady flow by the construction of digital elevation models (or DEMs). But something closer to three-dimensional flow can be obtained from pairs taken from the ERS-1 and ERS-2 satellites on ascending and descending (respectively south–north and north–south) orbits, with the pairs separated by one day, as the different view angles allow full 3-D flow patterns to be mapped (Mohr et al. 1998). The method has been tried on the Storstrømmen, an outlet glacier in north Greenland (first visited in 1908 by an expedition that included Alfred Wegener) which surged during 1978–84.

The results confirm the importance of measuring independently both the direction of flow and its magnitude. The resulting flow deviated from what might have been expected from the topographical gradient: one branch of the glacier system, which according to height contours should have received some 25 per cent of the total ice flux, was found to be almost stagnant. Again, the flow slowed down near the glacier terminus, contrary to normal glacier behaviour but consistent with post-surge conditions. The surface velocities were in good agreement with GPS measurements on stakes in the ice. Accuracies of $1–2\,\mathrm{m\,yr^{-1}}$ will be attainable once ice thickness is known, as it will then not be necessary to assume that ice flow is parallel to the ground surface. Beneficiaries of this kind of work include those engaged in interpolating between age determinations in cores drilled into icecaps and glaciers for palaeoclimatic purposes.

# Ice sheets

The prediction of changes in the mass balance of ice sheets, which make up 5 per cent of the Earth's surface (and 99% of its fresh water), would seem more important than the vicissitudes of individual glaciers if global sea level is at issue. Yet our ignorance about current trends extends to such massive features as the ice sheets of Greenland and Antarctica. It is not solely a matter of scanty data: the calculation is highly complex.

Radar altimetry would seem to be the obvious technique for monitoring short-term changes in the topography and hence to some extent the volume of ice bodies, and it is at present the main source of topographical data over the Antarctic and Greenland ice sheets (there is one optical levelling profile across Greenland and none for Antarctica), even though horizontal resolution is poor and the method can be used only when the surface has a slope of less than 1°. Measurement accuracies better than 20 cm are claimed (Krabill et al. 1995). The aircraft's position is determined after the flight to within 10 cm

**Figure 6.3** Changes in ice depth in Greenland determined by laser altimetry between 1993 and 1999 (courtesy of NASA/Goddard Space Flight Center).

by using GPS. Although the aircraft can be navigated within tens of metres of the prescribed route, a conically scanning laser (the Airborne Oceanographic Unit), with a ranging accuracy of 5 cm, can be employed to ensure that exactly the same tract is resurveyed. Errors in aircraft altitude relative to the Earth ellipsoid are estimated to be at the 10 cm level.

Measurements made in 1980–81 and 1993 suggested that the western Greenland ice sheet (Fig. 6.3) had been thickened by up to 2 m during this interval, but it was not clear whether this represented long-term change rather than the cumulative effect of annual variations in the quantity or density of the snowfall (Krabill et al. 1995). As with glaciers, satellite radar interferometry is brought in to clarify the dynamics of flow, although mainly near the surface. A trial in Greenland using ERS-1 data yielded maps with a horizontal resolution of 80 m, and comparison with laser altimetry suggests the vertical relative accuracy was 2.5 m along the profile (Joughin et al. 1996).

Simulation of the surface mass balance of the Greenland and the Antarctic ice sheets with two 5 yr integrations for the present and doubled $CO_2$ conditions showed a slight decrease in accumulation and a substantial increase in melt over Greenland, and predicted a large increase in accumulation without melting over Antarctica. The Greenland discharge would be equivalent to a sea-level rise of 1.1 mm yr$^{-1}$. But the measurements for 1994–9 (Krabill et al. 2000) indicated equilibrium above 2000 m, albeit with some localized thinning or thickening, and thinning by up to 1 m near the coast, resulting in a total loss of 51 km$^3$, equivalent to a sea-level rise of only 0.13 mm yr$^{-1}$.

Now consider the Antarctic ice sheet (Fig. 6.4), which contains 24–29 million km$^3$ of ice, equivalent to a potential eustatic sea-level change of 60–72 m. The annual surface accumulation is estimated to be $2200 \times 10^9$ metric tons, equivalent to a sea-level change of 6 mm yr$^{-1}$. About 25 per cent of this snowfall occurs in the Antarctic Peninsula, which occupies a mere 7 per cent of the continent. It is a mountainous area containing icecaps, outlet glaciers, valley glaciers and ice shelves, and thus a variety of climatic regimes in no way subject to simple relationships between surface air temperature and snow accumulation. It has been estimated by Drewry & Morris (1992) that, for a 2°C rise in mean annual surface temperature over 40 yr, ablation in the Antarctic Peninsula region alone would contribute at least 1.0 mm to sea-level rise.

Additional sources are required to refine ice-balance estimates. One possibility is the measurement of ice ablation by cosmogenic $^{14}$C, which is produced *in situ* mainly by nuclear spallations of oxygen in the ice. Concentrations have been observed of $1–3 \times 10^3$ atoms per gram of ice, three orders of magnitude higher than would be expected from trapped $CO_2$ (Lal et al. 1990); as expected, the concentration falls off with depth. Moreover, the $^{14}$C that formed *in situ* is distinctive in that 60 per cent is in $^{14}$CO and the rest in $^{14}$CO$_2$. This approach was used to evaluate ablation at two sites in the Allan Hills of Antarctica. The ablation rates indicated by the $^{14}$C measurements were $5.8 \pm 0.7$ and $7.6 \pm 0.8$ cm yr$^{-1}$, in good agreement with the rates of 3–9 cm yr$^{-1}$ obtained using stakes (Lal 1991). The method should work in accumulating ice too. The $^{14}$C *in situ* (Lal et al. 1990) can be calculated from the accumulation rate for that particular location; and as 60 per cent of the $^{14}$CO$_2$ is converted to $^{14}$CO, accumulation rates of up to 50 cm yr$^{-1}$ can be derived from a 3–5 kg sample of ice.

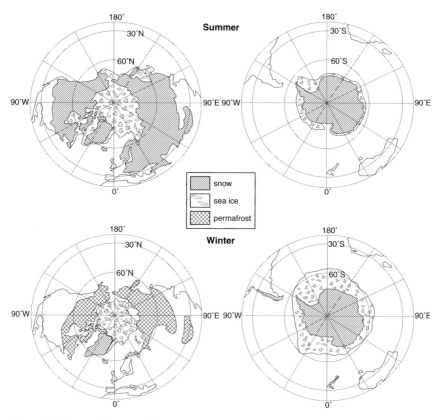

**Figure 6.4** Seasonal ice cover (including sea ice): **(left)** around the North Pole and **(right)** around the South Pole (after Peixoto & Oort 1992, by permission of Springer Verlag GmbH).

Two other isotopes promise to help in testing hydrodynamic models of ice flow. The atmospheric component of [10]Be greatly exceeds that produced *in situ*, and variations down core in the icecaps are probably inversely related to precipitation. Atmospheric [3]H will decay in ablating ice, so that its content relative to the *in situ* component is a guide to mean ablation rates (Lal et al. 1987).

Several types of remote sensing are also coming into their own in studies of ice cover. The advanced very high resolution radiometer (AVHRR) instruments on the NOAA space-craft, for example, had the stated aim of monitoring cloud cover, but have also produced images with a resolution of 1–2.5 km that have proved of great value in mapping the morphology of the ice sheets and the movement of icebergs. What is more, their thermal channel (like the thermal infrared channel on Landsat spacecraft) yields surface tem-peratures. Another source of surface-temperature data is provided by passive micro-wave emissions, which have been recorded over the globe every two days since 1973 at a resolution of about 25 km. AVHRR data can also be made to yield information on the presence of hoar frost and, in combination with TM imagery, even on the size of snow grains at the surface (Binschadler 1998).

Direct measurements on the ground retain their value despite the vastness of the task and the need for continual – and eventually continuous – updates. The need is for confirmation of forecast data, which are used to constrain mass-balance models of the Greenland ice sheet. In a recent validation exercise by ground stations – which included surface air pressure and temperature, precipitation, cloud cover, total radiation and shortwave radiation, and wind speed and direction – the forecasts were found to depict a Greenland ice-sheet margin that was on average 4°C too cold and with precipitation on average 136 per cent of the field measurements; forecast wind speeds were 66 per cent of those measured (Hanna & Valdes 2001). It is perhaps to be expected that the regions most in need of "ground truthing" are generally those least suitable for the task.

## Sea ice

The extent of sea ice varies greatly with the seasons, in the Arctic between 14–16 and 7–9 million km$^2$ and in the Antarctic between 17–20 and 3–4 million km$^2$ (NASA 2001), that is roughly 2:1 and 5:1 respectively. Cloud cover was an obstacle to remote sensing until the first launch of microwave satellites in 1972. The scanning multi-channel microwave radiometer (SMMR) was launched on the Nimbus 7 spacecraft in 1978; others have followed.

The SMMR data suggest that, between 1978 and 2000, Arctic sea ice shrank by about 3 per cent (Fig. 6.5), whereas it grew at about 0.1 per cent per year in the Antarctic (Cavalieri et al. 1997). The contrast between the two polar regions is of value in testing competing general-circulation models. For example, it is consistent with a general-circulation model in which CO$_2$ levels are increased gradually, as this might lead to such hemispheric asymmetry.

Sea ice insulates the oceans from low ambient temperatures, which has an impact on

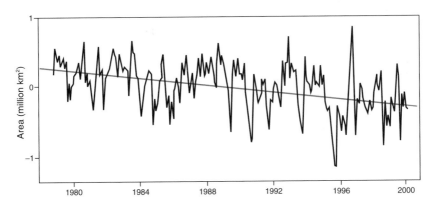

**Figure 6.5**  Extent of sea ice in the Northern Hemisphere indicated by the scanning multichannel micro-wave radiometer and special sensor microwave imager (SMMR/SSMI) launched in 1978 and 1987 respectively. It shows a 2.9 per cent decrease in the Arctic since 1978. (Courtesy of NASA.)

91

oceanic circulation; its high albedo means that 50–70 per cent of incoming solar radiation is reflected, hence the need to supplement mapping of sea ice with optical sensors such as the AHVRR and Landsat Thematic Mapper (TM), and with information on its thickness below sea level or draught.

Draught measurements by submarines using sonar have been collected within a circle with a 150 km radius from the North Pole, and supplemented by drifting buoy data for 1979–92. They show marked annual variability, with draughts ranging from a little over 2 m to over 5 m, but there was a reduction in draught between 1958 and 1997 by an average of 1.3 m (40%) in six regions covering much of the deepwater part of the Arctic Ocean (Rothrock 1999). The variations bore no relation to the source of the ice within the Arctic Ocean, but they owed something to the path it followed and the extent to which the ice converged (or diverged) for the 1–2 weeks before the submarine cruise. Even so, they conform to the microwave data for a 3 per cent reduction in the extent of the sea ice per decade since 1978, which was especially pronounced (7%) in perennial (multi-year) sea ice. The possible role of the North Atlantic oscillation, which brings warm air into the Arctic, has been assessed at 25 per cent of the sea-ice variability in the 1990s (Levi 2000).

## Sea level

Given enough case studies, we can begin to compute the net effect of glacier melting, which evidently depends on temperature change and the time over which the various glaciers respond (Wigley & Raper 1995). The bulk of the contribution at present is thought to come from central Asia and northwestern North America; glaciers in total have contributed 2–5 cm to the global rise of 10–25 cm in the past century (Dyurgerov & Meier 1997), on a par with the estimated contribution by thermal expansion of ocean water brought about by global warming.

Detecting the shape and position of the ocean surface was a key motive for the development of satellite altimetry from the outset: oceanography requires worldwide and frequently updated information on wave height and speed, ocean tides and the nature of the oceanic circulation; geodesy demands a detailed description of the geoid; even such long-established topics as the analysis of lunar tides are hungry for more and better data. Until 1974, when the first altimeter operated on Skylab, reliance for all these purposes had to be placed principally on tide gauges, which document local sea level in relation to what may be a shifting landmass, on ship-borne equipment or buoys, which reveal the properties of ocean currents but not their three-dimensional geometry, and on aerial photography, which provides occasional snapshots of surface conditions. Satellite technology brought with it the bonus of removing the need to rely on the land as datum.

Although no single sea-level history of worldwide validity is attainable (Fig. 6.6), an idealized eustatic curve remains useful as a standard against which local deviations can be measured. Short-term changes in the volume and shape of the ocean basins are less important sources of sea-level rise or fall than those attributable to thermal effects, fluctuations in salinity and ice melting, although great subduction earthquakes such as those in Chile in 1960 and Alaska in 1964 are thought to have raised sea level globally, if temporarily, by something in the region of 1 mm (Bilham 1991).

The net rise in sea level over the past century is estimated to have been about 10 cm. Departures from the general trend can be subdivided into geological and oceanographic categories. Variations in the Earth's response to deglaciation are responsible for a broad distinction into coasts still undergoing isostatic rebound at a rate outpacing glacial meltwater inputs, coasts where initial submergence has given way to emergence, and a third group too far from glacial centres to experience anything other than gradual submergence. This crude subdivision is subject to increasing refinement, generally with the aim of improving our understanding of mantle viscosities, crustal elastic response and other variables of interest to the geophysical community as a whole. The exercise has tended to focus on coastal sequences well calibrated with $^{14}$C ages, but many of the data points are poorly documented and they are necessarily confined to coasts. Tide-gauge sequences allow the records to be traced into recent decades. Parts of the east coast of North America display rates of postglacial sea-level rise that are anomalously high, and this can be explained by the collapse of the fore-bulge that had been produced by the Laurentide ice sheet. Put another way, it is possible to "decontaminate" the tide-gauge evidence of the continuing influence of postglacial isostatic adjustment so that it can be exploited for palaeoclimatic studies (Peltier 1996).

GPS is also a source of data for isostatic studies: a mere 2.5 yr of measurement in Fennoscandia shows good agreement with the pattern of uplift predicted by realistic

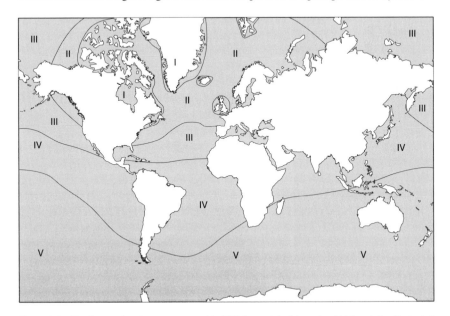

**Figure 6.6** The five sea-level zones proposed in 1978 for postglacial sea-level history (after Clark et al. 1978, by permission of Elsevier Science).

models for local deglaciation history and Earth structure (Segall & Davis 1997).

Glacial history impinges on sea level more deviously. Its effects on the volume of ocean water and on isostatic deformation are not independent, as surface loading by continental ice sheets displaces the rotation pole, which in turn leads to significant shifts of relative sea level still in progress today. Assuming a rigid Earth as a first approximation (polar motion is sensitive to the viscosity structure postulated for the Earth model but the resulting sea-level effect is not), melting of the Laurentide ice sheet (60°N 70°W, $2 \times 10^{19}$ kg of ice) displaces the excitation pole by 0.076°, and the peak sea-level signal along the great circle containing the path of the pole is $\pm 14.6$ m (at 45°N in East Asia and 45°S in South America), compared to the 55.2 m that results from the addition of meltwater to the world ocean for a rigid Earth model. The present secular drift of the rotation pole produces peak-to-peak contributions calculated to be a substantial 0.36 mm yr$^{-1}$ (Bills & James 1996).

Isolating the postglacial isostatic and eustatic component from other changes in relative sea level is equally significant in seismology, where understanding the relative contribution of coseismic and interseismic movements will be of help in interpreting precursory movements, the palaeoseismic record and the earthquake mechanism itself. On the south coast of Alaska, the tectonic impact of the 28 March 1964 earthquake ($M_W = 9.2$) could be assessed only after the tide-gauge record had been scrutinized for both antecedent trends and local effects, with the residuals from linear fits to individual tide records taken to represent short-term fluctuations caused by oceanographic factors (Plafker & Rubin 1967, Savage & Plafker 1991). The corrected data, once adjusted for global eustatic change and for the local isostatic effect to reveal local coseismic and post-seismic movement, could be exploited for modelling the earthquake.

Away from the coast a key concern is to improve mapping of the oceanic circulation. The requisite altimetric accuracy is less than 15 cm, and, as we have seen, the TOPEX/ Poseidon mission achieved this comfortably. By 1994, maps of the global 1 yr mean topography using TOPEX/Poseidon data indicated that the largest error in the dynamic ocean topography was the uncertainty in the geoid (Tapley et al. 1994). The spatially smoothed maps of the annual sea-surface topography showed many expected features, such as the known annual hemispherical sea-surface rise and fall, and the seasonal variability attributable to monsoon influences in the Indian Ocean. Also, a sequence of ten-day topography maps showed the development of an equatorial Kelvin wave in the Pacific, beginning in December 1992, with a propagation velocity of about 3 m s$^{-1}$.

The observations tallied with observed changes in the equatorial trade winds and with tide-gauge and other *in situ* observations of the strengthening of the 1992 El Niño, and the sea-surface height showed agreement with oceanic tide gauges over the tropical Pacific to a root mean square level of 4 cm. According to the investigators, the TOPEX altimeter data set could be used to map the ocean surface with a temporal resolution of ten days and an accuracy consistent with traditional *in situ* methods for the determination of sea-level variations. They might have added that telemetered spacecraft data could be analyzed by numerical and graphic methods without the bureaucratic and political hurdles of many traditional tidal surveys.

During 2.5 yr of satellite altimetry the global mean sea-level variations measured by

TOPEX/Poseidon every ten days had a root mean square error of 6 mm (4 mm after detrending), some of which could be correlated with sea-surface temperature variations. The rate of change of global mean sea level was +5.8±0.7 mm yr$^{-1}$. Little is known about the long-term behaviour of the measurement errors at the millimetre level, and there is evidence from the sea-surface temperature record for interannual variation unrelated to the long-term signal expected from global warming. Nevertheless, TOPEX/Poseidon (Nerem 1995) was soon achieving the repeatability required to measure global sea-level variations caused by climate.

More dramatic still was the seafloor morphology revealed by satellite altimetry. In 1987 the first gravity maps appeared, based on the Seasat satellite, which operated for a mere three months (Kunzig 1999). In 1996 the US Defense Department made available the Geosat data. Geosat had been launched in 1985 by the US Navy to provide submarine commanders with information on water masses derived from variations in the elevation of the sea. It would have cost at least $5 billion and taken a century of ship time to secure seafloor maps as detailed as those made by Geosat in 18 months for $80 million (McNutt 1996).

The resolution and accuracy of individual satellite altimetry profiles is still not as good as the output from the best ship-based equipment, for a variety of reasons to do with location, time of year and the satellite system itself. Thus, rough seas lead to a greater scattering of the radar pulse and less accurate tracking of the pulse than would otherwise be the case, and deep water reduces the amplitude of the vertical deflection at the surface (by a factor of 0.2 if the depth is 5 km and the wavelength 20 km). These effects can be reduced by averaging (stacking) repeat versions of individual profiles. Geographical disparities persist: high latitudes are at a disadvantage from having a relative paucity of orbits and from their greater propensity to choppy water. The latest versions, which yield maps with horizontal resolutions of 1–12 km, combine gravity data from satellites (including Geosat and ERS-1) with high-quality ship-borne bathymetry, so that the transfer function that links topography to gravity can be corrected for such local effects as sedimentation and variations in crustal thickness (Smith & Sandwell 1997).

# Loading by ice and water

Shifts in the Earth's water load presumably elicit some kind of response in the lithosphere; as with the melting of small glaciers, it is tempting to use the response as a check on mass-balance estimates. If our assumptions about the Earth's internal constitution and mechanical behaviour are reasonable, a reduction in the size of the icecaps on Greenland or Antarctica will lead to rebound that is fast enough to be detected by geodetic measurements. By recording vertical motion and gravitational changes simultaneously, it is possible to correct for the effects of ice thinning (and thickening) over several thousand years (Wahr et al. 1995); the residual uplift has been found to be proportional to current fluctuations in the ice load, and is estimated to be several millimetres per year around Antarctica and up to $10-15\,\mathrm{mm\,yr^{-1}}$ around Greenland.

Do the small rises in sea level occasioned by recent melting have any measurable effect on the Earth's rate of rotation? Mass-balance data for 85 glaciers in 13 mountain glacier systems suggest that, during the period 1965–84, the glaciers of the coast ranges of Alaska and British Columbia accounted for 82 per cent of the interannual variability in meltwater production, whereas Svalbard (Spitsbergen) dominated the secular trend (Trupin et al. 1992). On this basis, glacier melting contributed less than 0.7 per cent to the 2 ms observed change in LOD. This was not surprising, as the bulk of the LOD changes are attributed not to mass redistribution but to core–mantle coupling at decadal timescales and to atmospheric effects in the shorter term (p. 53). On the other hand, the 20 yr glacial melt signal contributes 1 mm to the displacement of the centre of mass of the solid Earth. More significant, glacial melt may account for close to 10 per cent of the observed interannual excitation of polar motion and 25 per cent of the secular trend (Trupin et al. 1992), and is thus already within the range of detection by astronomical and geodetic methods.

The shift in load resulting from the movement of individual glaciers (as distinct from shifts in load occasioned by melting or glacial growth) impinges on other aspects of the Earth system, notably the terms used to calculate the Earth's local viscoelastic response to unloading and the effect of changes in vertical stress on seismicity. In southern Alaska, where glacier retreat has predominated in the twentieth century, the Bering Glacier – the largest in North America, 191 km long and in places > 800 m thick – has surged at least six times for reasons that remain obscure (Molnia 1995). Between a surge in 1967 and one in 1993 the terminus receded by 10 km and thinned by as much as 180 m. The 1993 surge began in the spring and led to an advance of 5 km by late August 1999; the ensuing four years saw thinning of the ice and a retreat of the terminus by up to $1.0\,\mathrm{km\,yr^{-1}}$. The shifts in load were expected to produce elastic subsidence in the lithosphere at the receiving end and uplift in the Bagley Icefield (Fig. 6.7), which flows mainly to the glacier (Sauber et al. 2000).

At the three sites nearest to the area of surge, the elastic deformation that was measured by GPS in 1993–5 matched the predicted uplift with an uncertainty of 10 cm. The long-term viscoelastic response would appear to lie beyond the reach of current instrumental analysis, the one possible exception being in the ablation zone (near Icy Bay): here the predicted uplift best fits the uplift measured by GPS when the model (Sauber et al. 1995, 2000) adopts an asthenospheric viscosity of $5\times10^{19}\,\mathrm{Pa\,s^{-1}}$, compared with values of $10^{20}-10^{21}\,\mathrm{Pa\,s^{-1}}$ used in many glacial uplift models. The evidence also bears on seismicity: for example, there was an increased level of small ($M_L \leq 4.0$) earthquakes under the zone of greatest ice thinning during the surge, consistent with the idea that a reduction in the load may promote failure in shallow-thrust earthquakes, a reduction in thickness by 50 m being equivalent to a drop of 0.5 MPa.

Both net uplift and the vertical correction for the gravity measurements are determined relative to sea level, whose concurrent displacement must therefore be known. Yet, despite its central role in many branches of Earth science and its significance to the wellbeing of many nations, sea level remains an elusive item to monitor with confidence. It is not solely because the land, against which sea level has traditionally

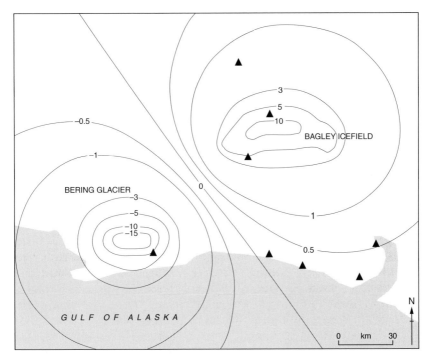

**Figure 6.7** Predicted vertical displacement (in cm) associated with surging by the Bering Glacier, on the coast of Alaska, with up to 1 cm of subsidence near its snout and 10 cm of uplift in the Bagley Icefield, which supplies it. Triangles show GPS stations. (After Sauber et al. 1995, © AGU.)

been measured, is itself subject to irregular vertical movements. The ocean has its own topography with periods from seconds to millennia and wavelengths from millimetres to thousands of kilometres (Bilham 1991). Besides its constant disruption by tides, currents and waves, the ocean surface thus departs from the idealized form of the spheroid of rotation, and the extent to which it does so is subject to ceaseless modification through shifting gravitational forces on the sea floor and within the Earth.

Satellite altimetry suggests that the Greenland ice sheet has recently risen at $28\,\mathrm{cm\,yr^{-1}}$; but there is conflicting evidence of a rise in sea level near Greenland by 50 cm and a *reduction* in the elevation of the ice. This latter interpretation is consistent with changes in polar location indicated by VLBI and SLR (Bilham 1991), which imply a redistribution of mass attributable to ice melting, with Greenland as the major source.

In favourable circumstances the lithospheric and gravitational response to changes in the ice itself can also now be calculated. In Antarctica, present-day changes in ice mass are estimated to produce, through elastic crustal response, typical uplift rates of $5\,\mathrm{mm\,yr^{-1}}$, horizontal motion rates of $1\,\mathrm{mm\,yr^{-1}}$ and solid-surface gravity rates of $1\,\mu\mathrm{gal\,yr^{-1}}$ (James & Ivins 1998). The signal may retain a viscoelastic (isostatic) memory of a more extensive ice-sheet dating from the most recent glacial maximum; the estimate will depend to a significant extent on deglaciation history.

Continuous GPS measurements of uplift in east Antarctica combined with a detailed glacial history based on exposure ages will allow the model to be tested (Zwartz et al. 1999). It may eventually prove possible to separate the viscoelastic (glacial) and elastic (present-day) signal if, besides long-term movement, the gravitational contribution of changes in local ice thickness can be evaluated. All these refinements stand to benefit estimates of the Antarctic ice-mass balance by identifying the relative importance of the many contributory factors.

On the coast the most promising procedure thus seems to be to derive sea-level history from TOPEX/Poseidon data corrected by tide-gauge time series (see Fig. 1.5) and then to check the results against DORIS determinations of vertical movement (Cazenave et al. 1999). Inland, the monitoring of changes in water loading in lakes is well suited to satellite altimetry, as analysis is not complicated by extreme tides or currents, but large enclosed water bodies can be thermally unstable, and some are subject to seasonal extremes of level. The difficulties can be seen as an additional incentive for the development of rapid systems of height determination, which will reveal rather than suffer from such variability. The Great Lakes of North America appear well suited to such a project. Data gathered during the first two years of the US Navy's Geosat Exact Repeat Mission (November 1986 to November 1988) were compared to the lake-level data collected by NOAA and found to reproduce level variations in the five major lakes with a root mean square error of 9.4–13.8 cm (combined average 11.1 cm). Geosat data for the smaller Lake St Clair had an error of 17.0 cm (Morris & Gill 1994).

Again, although shoreline and depositional correlation across lake basins should be less problematic than in moving bodies of water, one should not assume that successive strandlines will remain parallel. The palaeoshores of fossil Lake Bonneville were shown by G. K. Gilbert (1890), in his pioneering study of isostasy, to be warped by uplift proportional to the former water load and also disrupted by at least one fault. Lake Minchin, in the central Andes, combines hydro-isostatic deflection with tectonic tilting (Bills et al. 1994). At its maximum, the basin, which contains modern Lake Poopó and the playas of Uyuni, Coipasa and Empexa, was up to 140 m deep, 400 km long and 200 km wide. Fossil shorelines have been mapped using differential GPS with accuracies (relative to a base receiver) of 30 cm horizontally and 70 mm vertically. The highest fossil shoreline dates from approximately 17 000 yr ago and incorporates $27 \pm 1$ m of hydro-isostatic deflection. But the lake also displays planar tilts of 6.8 cm km$^{-1}$ up to the east and 5.3 cm km$^{-1}$ down to the north, to a total of nearly 35 m. Although it has yet to be explained (and at least six climatic or tectonic mechanisms have been proposed for it), the tilting would not have emerged without adequate forethought.

At Lake Mead such ambiguity could be avoided because the deformation produced by filling the reservoir was monitored from the outset, although the short timescales involved mean that the mechanism is dominated by elastic (rather than isostatic) processes. Subsidence over 15 years was found to be 17 cm, close to that predicted by theory (Crittenden 1967). Any further opportunity for such experiments cannot be missed, especially where, as at Koyna in India, dam construction has long been suspected of triggering, or at any rate promoting, earthquake activity.

# CHAPTER 7

# Mountains, peaks and ridges

*Men trip not on mountains, they stumble on stones.*
Hindustani proverb

The reasons for wishing to monitor an Andean volcano will usually differ from those that motivate a study of faulting in the Mid-Atlantic Ridge or of coseismic folding in North Africa. But all such investigations stand to benefit from measurements of current deformation (or the lack of it). The present chapter therefore focuses on how the measurements may be made without paying much attention to differences in the origin and evolution of the feature in question.

Planetary geologists are used to operating in this way, as they often begin by identifying on their remotely sensed images any areas that appear to have some internal homogeneity, in the hope that this reflects uniformity of age or origin or both. The Moon's surface was soon divided into terrae and maria, subdivisions still found useful, even though we no longer equate them with lands and seas. Venus displays a series of topographies that some take to represent distinctive episodes in Venusian history and others see as recurring themes. Miranda is a mosaic of discordant morphologies thrown together.

On Earth the procedure seems naïve, as it apparently disregards the detail accumulated during centuries of fieldwork and laboratory analyses. But it proved its worth in the hands of geodynamics pioneers such as Argand and Holmes, and even more in the development of plate-tectonic theory, when the protagonists boldly cut across the detail to identify crucial interplate boundaries. It remains a valuable approach for temporarily disengaging dynamic issues from those of stratigraphy. The Alpine–Himalayan system, for example, embraces a wealth of rock types and folding ages, but its relationship to the stable areas north and south benefits, at least initially, from unitary treatment.

## Volcanoes

Although volcanoes are major constituents of certain types of mountain chain, notably those at the rear of ocean trenches, their composition and genesis set them apart from the products of compression or extension. They are included in the present chapter because they present problems of access and analysis similar to those of other mountains.

Monitoring active or dormant volcanoes requires little justification, as they present a hazard that, even in the most catastrophic instance, will be reduced by advance warning and where advance warning is improved by an understanding of the underlying processes. The two mainstays of traditional volcano monitoring are ground deformation and seismicity (McGuire et al. 1995). Centuries of anecdotal observations on the movements that preceded and accompanied eruptions, notably in Italy, on Vesuvius and Etna, gradually yielded to measurement.

Spirit levelling remains an important part of such surveys, not least because it can be implemented at short notice and low cost. For instance, resurvey in 1994 of a first-order line originally measured in 1951 on the Alban Hills volcano south of Rome revealed 30 cm of uplift (equivalent to $7\,mm\,yr^{-1}$) in an area visited by earthquake swarms with recorded magnitudes no greater than $M_L = 4.2$ and close to benchmarks indicating little deformation in the preceding half century. The measurements prompted the suspicion that magma injection had been taking place in the upper crust (Amato & Chiarabba 1995).

Magma injection is of course a mechanism that encourages the search for advance warning of eruptions. There is a long tradition of levelling work on Etna directed at detecting precursory deformation. Yet, repeated levelling over an 11 km traverse between 1975 and 1980, combined with optical tilt data, helped to show that many superficial movements resulted from lava compaction and sliding. Unlike Hawaii, Etna does not display a broad pattern of inflation and deflation before and after eruptions, and what deformation does occur is far too small to account for the volume of erupted material, both observations being consistent with the view that the magma source is deep (Murray & Guest 1982).

New ground-based and space-based techniques allow these procedures to be practised more quickly and cheaply but also more selectively (Fig. 7.1). With GPS, angular measurement no longer requires intervisibility of stations (something that may change between eruptions) and can be carried out as frequently as the problem requires. Without the need for closure, only those sites that are of interest (and safe) need be re-surveyed. A permanent receiver installed in Long Valley caldera (in California) demonstrated in 1993 the advantages of near-continuous observation. Levelling surveys between 1988 and 1992 suggested uplift at $30\,mm\,yr^{-1}$; a laser geodimeter survey suggested $40\,mm\,yr^{-1}$ in 1989–91. The GPS data indicated uplift at $25 \pm 11\,mm\,yr^{-1}$ over a 500-day period after January 1993. Besides its potential for monitoring (the receiver was remotely controlled), the GPS survey made it possible to eliminate any signals related to Earth tides, which would have given a spectral peak at a period of 14.7 days (Webb et al. 1995).

Telemetered tilt measurements offer some of the same advantages. Eruptive activity began on Soufrière Hills volcano (Montserrat) in July 1995 following a 300 yr hiatus. Initial estimates of magma production and of the development of a lava dome depended on compass and Abney level surveys, photography from fixed locations, laser-ranging

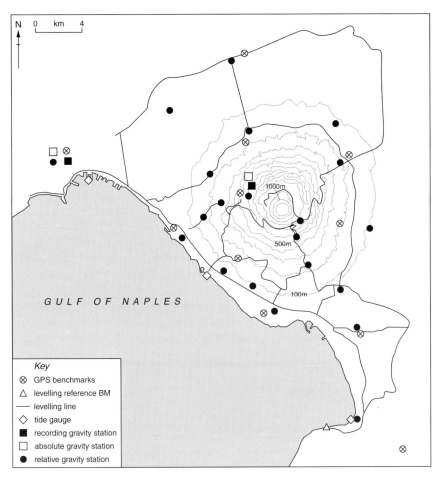

**Figure 7.1** Monitoring of Mt Vesuvius by tide gauge, gravity, levelling and GPS (after Institut de Physique du Globe website).

binoculars from a helicopter located by GPS, and photography from the helicopter (Sparks et al. 1998). GPS and EDM measurements suffered from the lack of pre-eruption data against which to set the observations. On the other hand, telemetered tiltmeters with a resolution of 0.1 µrad (i.e. 1 mm over a distance of 10 km) soon displayed cyclic variations with a period of 6–14 h. The tilt data for individual inflations indicated a source depth of 700–800 m, although if in the shape of a cylinder the top of the conduit could have been even shallower. The cycles were matched with earthquake amplitude and frequency, explosions within the volcano and pyroclastic-flow activity, and were therefore found valuable in the forecasting of increased hazard (Voight et al. 1998).

When the meters were destroyed by an explosion, reliance had to be placed solely on the seismic data. Tilt, seismicity and volcanic activity have also proved valuable predictive tools in Hawaii, where inflation (recorded as tilt near the summit) over weeks or years tends to be followed by sudden deflation before the eruption. In the early stages, when the rising magma is penetrating or creating fractures, the earth tremors that are recorded are of short period and high frequency; once the magma can move freely, the tremors are longer in period and of lower frequency (McGuire et al. 1995). As early as 1969 (Decker & Kinoshita 1971) the Hawaiian Volcano Observatory routinely conducted surveys of altitude on a continuous levelling profile measuring 35 km, including two loops 3 km long, with closure errors of less than 6 mm; ground tilt using long-base and short-base water-tube tiltmeters and continuously recording tiltmeters (accuracy $2 \times 10^{-7}$ rad, $1 \times 10^{-6}$ rad and $3 \times 10^{-8}$ rad respectively); and change in horizontal distance using a geodimeter with an accuracy of 3 mm km$^{-1}$.

Remote sensing of changes in volcano morphology is the obvious way forwards (Fig. 7.2). Laser or radar altimetry is one possibility. A laser altimeter from an aircraft typically has a footprint 1 m in diameter and, by horizontal sampling a 1–2 m intervals, can secure contiguous footprint profiling. Vertical precision is 5 cm but, as over ice, motion of the aircraft detracts from pointing information, and the errors for volcano profiling are estimated to be 1 m vertically and better than 10 m horizontally (Garvin 1996).

Surveying and seismology are increasingly complemented by other geophysical methods, including magnetic, gravity and electrical surveys, for assessing the risk of eruption and interpreting the underlying processes. By 1970, gravimeters deployed on Hawaii already had a sensitivity of 0.001 mgal, which (see p. 12) should have permitted the detection of elevation changes smaller than 5 mm, but sensitivity to temperature, tilt

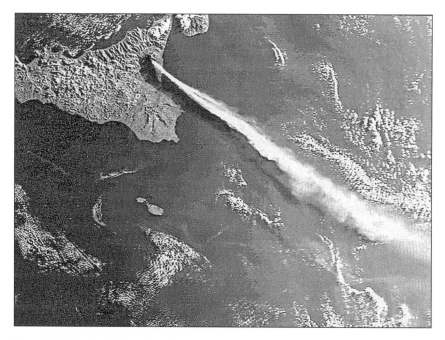

**Figure 7.2** Eruption of Etna volcano (Italy) on 22 July 2001 (see p. 143); the scene is 400 km wide (courtesy of NASA).

and shock, and to long-term drift, meant that 0.01 mgal or 5 cm were more realistic values (Decker & Kinoshita 1971).

Gravity measurements are as much of interest for what they say about the dynamic changes within the volcano as about topography, and hazardous experiments have been conducted using gravimeters in the search for premonitory indications of sudden magma movement. Repeated chemical analyses of magma and gases have the same end. Spacecraft provide a wide range of opportunities for monitoring volcanoes in various ways. Meteorological satellites such as Meteosat have been found useful for tracing gas plumes from eruptions. In 1994, infrared thermal imaging revealed a thermal anomaly on Teishi volcano off the Izu Peninsula in Japan several days before the ground deformation that preceded the eruption could be detected by GPS.

InSAR is beginning to make its mark on volcano monitoring, as on most aspects of geodynamics. The rates of pre-eruption deformation considered above are easily detected by passes separated by a month, a period over which vegetation or climate is generally slight and coherence is retained. The first application of the method was on Etna, where the most recent major eruption lasted between late 1991 and March 1993, and was captured by ERS-1 five months after it began (Massonnet & Feigl 1998). Thirteen of the images in question were obtained during ascending orbits of ERS-1 and during descending orbits between May 1992 and October 1993. The topographical component was removed by using a DEM with a height uncertainty of 8 m and based on SPOT imagery (Massonnet et al. 1995). About 30 interferograms displayed the coherence required for analysis.

The analysis revealed volcano-wide deflation that could be modelled by a contracting sphere $2 \pm 0.5$ km east of the central cone of the volcano and at a depth of $16 \pm 3$ km. Although the shape or position of the magma reservoir may well be entirely different, the result usefully supplements the levelling work mentioned earlier. During the last seven months of the eruption, subsidence progressed at 21 mm per month; GPS data for the first five months indicated subsidence at 31 mm per month. The good match between the two values tallies with the stable rate of lava production measured in the field. A fresh cycle of inflation and eruption was then traced using 19 interferograms for 1992–6 based on ERS-1 and ERS-2 data, and a DEM with a height uncertainty of 5–10 m (Lanari et al. 1998). The rate of inflation increased in the months before renewed volcanic activity, and modelling the source indicated a depth of 9 km during deflation and one of 11–14 km during the ensuing inflation.

A similar study of Okmok volcano, on Umnak Island in the Aleutians, showed that the centre of the caldera subsided 140 cm as a result of its eruption in 1997. The centre of the caldera had risen 23 cm over the three years before the eruption. The data were collected on ERS-1 and ERS-2 descending-mode orbits in 1992, 1993, 1995 and 1997. An existing DEM was improved using an interferogram created from ERS-1 and ERS-2 images taken one day apart. The deflation could be modelled by a spherical magma chamber 2.7 km deep (Lu et al. 1998). The study demonstrated the potential of the method for monitoring remote volcanoes routinely without benefit of ground checks. It also showed that in Alaska coherence could be maintained for at least two years, provided the images were acquired during summer and autumn (July–November).

# Mountain ranges

In his classic *The Earth*, Jeffreys (1970) comments that the "present relief in mountainous regions is not due directly to the processes involved in their formation". His discussion focuses on the competing contribution of shortening and isostatic adjustment (as he calls it) to the uplift of mountain ranges. Present-day deformation rates are a necessary component of any attempt to disentangle the various contributory processes.

Certain radiometric dating methods (such as K/Ar and Rb/Sr) and the fission-track technique may allow crustal uplift to be derived from denudation rates, as the processes on which they rely are reset when the rock has cooled to a particular temperature. The resulting long-term uplift rates refer either to rock uplift or to surface uplift, according to the minerals and structure at issue, and are generally averaged over $10^5$ or more years (Summerfield 1991). Palaeontological or more direct radiometric dating (say by $^{14}$C or U series) of an orogenic belt rarely provides better resolution unless it refers to a lake or marine deposit that has remained little distorted throughout its rise, such as the marine terraces of the Huon Peninsula in Papua New Guinea (Chappell 1970), and even here the result may harbour an uncertain component of coseismic uplift or of sea-level change.

In thinly populated or difficult regions of no military significance, there may be no instrumental data with which to assess geological estimates, and repeated reference in the literature to the Alpine orogeny as the last major orogenic phase leads many to assume, even in areas that have clearly undergone recent and rapid uplift, that the worst is over and that resurvey is unlikely to yield interesting results. We can be grateful that surveyors have marked and documented their stations with sufficient robustness for reoccupation decades later.

In the Swiss Alps such a resurvey was carried out in 1972, and it demonstrated that symmetrical bulging had occurred over a 50 yr period at a local average uplift rate of $0.6\,\mathrm{mm\,yr^{-1}}$ (Schaer et al. 1975). The result was in good agreement with the fission-track results, which indicated an average for the past 7 million years of $0.5\,\mathrm{mm\,yr^{-1}}$ in a similar pattern of deformation. This is only a start. There is still the possibility that this is a residual effect of isostatic unloading caused by the retreat of the Pleistocene glaciers, rather than the product of active processes. But it shows that a single survey can yield a rate representative of long-term uplift history.

Similarly, a survey line can provide some insight into how regional shortening is accommodated across a mountain chain or at least reveal whether shortening is evenly distributed. In the northwestern Alps and southern Jura (Fig. 7.3), levelling first carried out in 1886–1907 was repeated in 1965–79. Significant postglacial isostatic uplift could be excluded here on the grounds that, although the maximum depression under the Pleistocene ice load was 125 m, it had decayed to a mere 0.3 m (Jouanne et al. 1995), equivalent to uplift at $0.06\,\mathrm{mm\,yr^{-1}}$. An uneven pattern of deformation was found to prevail across the mountains, with maximum uplift rates of over $1\,\mathrm{mm\,yr^{-1}}$, endorsing the idea that movement is distributed over a few major faults.

Where uplift is attributable to interplate processes, as with the Himalaya, the uplift data should be of help in choosing between competing crustal models; however, the

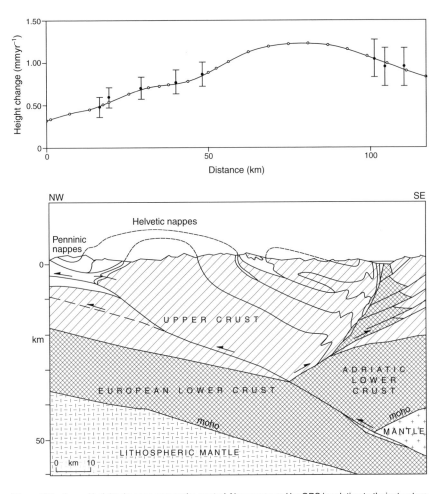

**Figure 7.3** Annual height changes across the central Alps measured by GPS in relation to their structure (after Kahle et al. 1997, with permission).

limitations of space geodesy, compounded by the inaccessibility of many of the critical regions, once again hamper the measurement of vertical movements. In the Himalayas, for example, assessment of any lateral extrusion resulting from India–Eurasia collision is more likely to be detected than any associated crustal thickening. In any case, geodetic lines were not carried from India across the Lesser Himalayas until early in the twentieth century.

A single spirit-levelling line between the Tibetan and Indian borders was measured twice between 1975 and 1991, but many of the observations had to be discarded because monuments appeared unstable. Even so, spirit-levelling data from Nepal for 1977–90 show uplift of the Mahabharat Range and other parts of the Lesser Himalaya (Fig. 7.4) at 2–3 mm yr$^{-1}$ and of the Greater Himalaya at 4–6 mm yr$^{-1}$. Poorer data for 1959–81

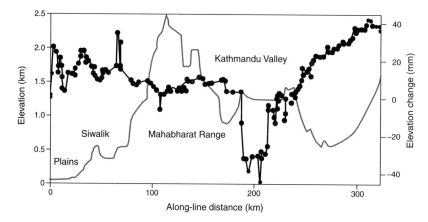

**Figure 7.4**  Elevation change (filled circles, right-hand scale, arbitrary zero) from spirit levelling across part of the Indo-Asian collision zone (after Jackson & Bilham 1994a, © AGU).

indicate uplift of the Himalayan divide at $7.5 \pm 5.6\,\text{mm}\,\text{yr}^{-1}$ relative to central Tibet (Fig. 7.4). Viewing the problem in two dimensions, and with the simplifying assumption that the observed uplift can be explained by two-dimensional elastic processes (Jackson & Bilham 1994a), the pattern of uplift chimes with convergence along a thrust (the Main Siwalik Thrust) dipping north at 3–6° beneath the Greater Himalaya and another (the Higher Himalayan thrust) beneath the Lesser Himalaya and southern Tibet with a similar dip, the two thrusts being linked by a ramp dipping at about 15°.

An important implication is that there is an accumulating slip deficit beneath central Nepal of $5\text{–}21\,\text{mm}\,\text{yr}^{-1}$, equivalent to a return period of 250–1000 yr for earthquakes with 6 m of coseismic slip, such as the 1934 Bihar earthquake. The cumulated results of GPS surveys are thus impatiently awaited not only for improved assessment of the convergence rate but also to remedy the deficient data for uplift rates in southern Tibet. The results secured in 1991–2 across the Nepal Himalayas suggest that, whereas convergence rates may be resolved to 10 per cent accuracy within 5 yr, it will take several decades for secular vertical motions to be resolved using current GPS techniques (Jackson & Bilham 1994b). Additional data up to 1996 show negligible creep in the Lesser Himalaya of Nepal and hence support a recurrence interval for M = 6 events perhaps as low as 300 yr, which is at the lower end of the range originally proposed (Bilham et al. 1998). Parts of the arc have not witnessed a great earthquake for over 300 yr.

These findings also bear on the grander kinematic picture. The geographical pattern of recorded earthquakes suggests that, where continental plates converge or diverge (rather than slide past one another), the resulting deformation may occupy a boundary zone almost as wide as it is long (England & Jackson 1989). Yet 80 per cent of the annual convergence between India and Tibet is taken up by a zone a mere 100 km wide, and 50 per cent of it within 50 km (Bilham et al. 1998). The apparent conflict is not one of incompatibility between surface deformation and deep earthquakes, as the distributed seismicity is mainly shallow and in any case vertical velocities are intimately linked to fault slip. Rather, it is an illustration of the need for complementary data when discussing deformation. Seismicity is generally proportional to fault length but is not necessarily proportional to deformation. The Himalayas may be riddled with earthquakes, but, if the faults are steep, even large displacements may have little effect on the topography. Non-brittle deformation on faults could allow regional strain to be taken up without activating earthquakes or disrupting the topography. Active folding is one possible mechanism, which will be raised, together with the lack of direct correspondence between seismicity and deformation, in a discussion of the Zagros Mountains (p. 125).

For mountain ranges such as the Alps that are growing at ~1 mm yr$^{-1}$ and are ~100 km wide, the annual deformation gradient is too small to be readily detected by radar interferometry (Massonnet & Feigl 1998). If uplift is faster and confined to a narrower zone, as in parts of the Himalaya, the resulting gradient (say $10^{-6}$ rather than $10^{-8}$) is more easily measured, but it will generally refer to rough terrain, the topography of which is difficult to model and where coherence is reduced by snow and active erosion. A possible exception is provided by salt domes (Fig. 7.5) and salt glaciers, which may flow as fast as 0.5 m day$^{-1}$ (Talbot 1998), provided that the surface of the salt does not change too much between images and that it occupies 10 pixels (Massonnet & Feigl 1998).

**Figure 7.5** Salt plugs (dark round blobs) in the southeast Zagros Mountains of Iran. Their alignment suggests basement control rather than a simple association with the pattern of surface folding.

# Submerged ridges and volcanoes

The oceanographic cruises of the nineteenth century, notably that of HMS Challenger, and the laying of the transatlantic telegraph cable, revealed a network of submarine mountains including a series of mid-oceanic ridges. The introduction of sonar to ocean-ography in 1922 gradually exposed their true complexity. By the 1950s the ridges were known to extend over 64000 km and in places to stand several thousand metres above the deep ocean floor. There is now a need to understand (as on land) which parts of the ridge system are active and how.

A rift runs along the crest of the Mid-Atlantic Ridge, and active seismicity betrays its deformation (Karson et al. 1987). Improvements in locating and interpreting earth-quake data show that, in several stretches of ridge, large ridge-axis events are no more than 6 km deep (Fowler 1990), with nearly pure normal-faulting mechanisms on planes parallel to the ridge axis and dipping at 45°.

Deformation can be measured directly by using fibre-optic strainmeters and tiltmeters with a resolution of a few microradians; for horizontal movements over distances of up to 100 km, recent developments include indirect-path acoustic devices positioned by GPS. Multi-beam sonar arrays have been shown to detect bathymetric changes (in the test case consisting of erupted material) on ridge crests provided they are at least 5–15 m thick and occupy an area some 200–300 m in diameter (Fox et al. 1992).

In isolation, bathymetry is inadequate for assessing volumetric change. In the Mari-anas arc a bathymetric survey led to estimates of volcanic production of $9 \, \text{km}^3 \, \text{yr}^{-1}$ over a 500 km section, more than the rate for all the Earth's subduction zones. Later work suggested that the results had been inflated through navigational errors and inadequate coverage (Jackson & Fryer 1991). When in 1996 a swarm of 4000 earthquakes associ-ated with hydrothermal plumes gave rise to a pit crater at Loihi Seamount, off Hawaii, detailed bathymetric surveys were combined with submersible dives and a variety of sampling procedures. Besides the formation of the crater – 600 m across and 300 m below the previous surface – the survey permitted study of shortlived changes in plume temperature and composition, including $^3\text{He}$ enrichment indicative of a magmatic source and temperature anomalies of up to 3.5°C (Loihi Science Team 1997). An ephemeral part of the process was thus recovered. Such datasets highlight the mislead-ing incompleteness of the rest of the record.

The mapping of young lavas will doubtless become as commonplace at sea as on land, but in 1989 it was still thought worth reporting that data obtained by a towed cam-era and by Sea Beam (a multi-beam sonar system) showed a chain of pillow mounds formed by fissure eruption between 1983 and 1987 in the southern Juan de Fuca Ridge, southwest of Vancouver Island. Digital comparison of two Sea Beam surveys demon-strated that an eruption of $0.005 \, \text{km}^3$ had occurred between June 1991 and July 1993 (Fornari & Embley 1995). Such observations evidently become significant when combined with other quantitative data bearing on seismicity or hydrothermal activity. Hydrothermal circulation through the young oceanic lithosphere is an important form of interaction between oceans, the atmosphere and the solid Earth (Baker et al. 1995). It cools hot rock, deposits minerals and modifies ocean chemistry and circulation.

It has long been shown from heat-flow data that the great bulk of the heat and water flux takes place away from the ridges, and thus presumably by low-temperature (<200°C) flow (Stein et al. 1995). Nevertheless, submarine hydrothermal vents have continued to attract great interest since their discovery in 1977, mainly because of their bizarre ecology (Baker et al. 1995), although physical and chemical anomalies indicative of such discharges were recognized 15 years earlier.

The most detailed maps of hydrothermal plumes have been made for the eastern Pacific and especially on the Juan de Fuca Ridge. On the Cleft segment the mapping has been repeated at least once a year since 1986, and it reveals the existence of event plumes that represent bursts of activity: in 1986 one such megaplume, about 20 km in diameter, contained $10^{17}$ J of excess heat, roughly the integrated annual output of a typical ridge-crest hydrothermal system, and released $10^8$ m$^3$ of hydrothermal fluid (Baker et al. 1995). The plume had disappeared when the site was revisited 60 days later, although steady-state venting at greater depth was still evident. A year later a second megaplume erupted 50 km to the north. In the northern Juan de Fuca Ridge a suite of event plumes beginning on 26 June 1993 migrated northwards over a distance of 30 km (Lupton 1995); the event plumes had disappeared by the time a fresh survey of the water column was conducted in August of the same year.

The discovery of volcanic extrusions at the northern megaplume site suggests that the plume had been produced by injection of magma, fracturing of the crust, and emptying of a hydrothermal reservoir during a seafloor spreading event (Lupton 1995). The migrating plumes of the northern Juan de Fuca Ridge likewise appear to result from the injection of dykes. More generally, although seafloor venting occurs on ridges characterized by spreading rates that range from slow to superfast (Baker et al. 1995), production along any multi-segment ridge portion is directly related to the spreading rate.

$^3$He is considered to be primordial helium leaking from the Earth's interior; the $^3$He/heat ratio is thus potentially an indicator of the magmatic and hydrothermal history of the ridge-crest segment (Lupton 1995). On the Juan de Fuca Ridge in 1986 the megaplume had a ratio similar to that of stable hydrothermal systems such as the Galápagos Rift; in the lower steady-state plume it was about 15 times higher, but it declined over the ensuing two years to 30 per cent of the original value. A reasonable interpretation is that magmatic input to a ridge segment provokes major changes in the flux and composition of the hydrothermal fluids, which lead to the sudden release of hot fluids in event plumes and an increase in the steady-state hydrothermal fluxes at the sea floor. The potential impact on oceanic composition is illustrated by Figure 7.6, which shows a plume of $^3$He-rich water on the East Pacific Rise at 15°S an extending >2000 km to the west.

Water-column surveys of plumes, like that used on the Juan de Fuca Ridge in 1993, often employ a tow-yo technique, whereby a hydrographic package is towed in a saw-tooth trajectory through the water column in order to secure an almost continuous record of temperature, suspended particles, chemical constituents and so on. But a mere 10 per cent of the global spreading centres have been examined for evidence of hydrothermal plumes, only a few in sufficient detail for the relationship between hydrothermal and volcanic or tectonic features to be established unequivocally. Nevertheless,

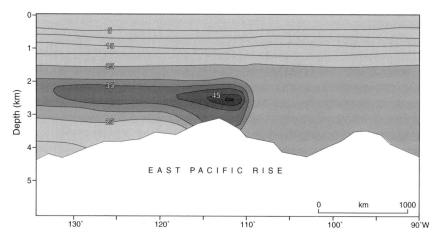

**Figure 7.6** Contours of $\delta^3$He (the percentage deviation of the $^3$He/$^4$He ratio from the atmospheric ratio) above East Pacific Rise at 15°S, showing a plume >2000 km long (after Lupton 1995, © AGU).

the potential for observing magmatic processes (such as lava eruption or dyke emplacement) as they occur – or not many months later – points the way towards global mapping of seafloor extension.

Autonomous underwater vehicles have already proved their worth in mapping a recently erupted lava flow on the Juan de Fuca Ridge (Tivey et al. 1997) and have demonstrated that, thanks to this technology, the study of ocean-floor dynamics stands to benefit from the submergence that has hitherto obscured it: water can provide buoyancy and stability to much larger and more complex remote-sensing platforms than the atmosphere. It has long been accepted that the sea floor is not uniformly cold and inert. The next stage is to map variations in its deformation and to correct the uniformity of motion implicit in long-term average measurements.

CHAPTER 8
# Faults and folds

*E' non è dubbio alcuno che la Terra è molto piú perfetta essendo, come ella è, alterabile, mutabile, etc., che se la fusse . . . un intero diamante, durissimo (ed) impassabile.* ("There can be no doubt that the Earth is much more perfect, by virtue of being changeable, adaptable and so on, than if it were . . . a single, extremely hard and indestructible diamond.")
Galileo, *Dialogo sopra i due massimi sistemi del mondo* (1632)

The techniques of space geodesy and global geophysics have been especially productive in the analysis of such local components of crustal deformation as individual faults and folds. The explanation for this success lies to a great extent in the needs of earthquake research. Fault displacement during earthquakes has been generally recognized since 1893, when Bunjiro Koto published a memorable photograph of a 6 m scarp that had arisen across the Neo valley during the Mino–Owari (Nobi) earthquake of 28 October 1891 (Scholz 1990). Fences and orchard rows in California offset by the 1906 San Francisco earthquake drove home the message. But away from such markers (Fig. 8.1) the size and behaviour of faults have eluded measurement, especially where motion is not seismically advertised and if the task in hand calls for centuries or millennia of narrative. Folded rocks exude a stolidity that seems to imply imperceptible change and, like much else in geology, their development is still generally expressed as an average rate over millions of years. In consequence, we know little about the short-term variations in the rate of deformation that are required to analyze the mechanical properties of the lithosphere.

## Faults

Faults tell us about material properties and about the stress field and its evolution, although the outcome may be strongly influenced by existing fractures. As conduits for fluids, some of which convey valuable minerals or allow noxious substances to escape, and as sources of weakness, they also preoccupy the civil engineer. But their short-term development bears above all on the distribution, severity and timing of earthquakes.

111

**Figure 8.1** Fissure in ritual purity bath (mikvah) in Qumran, Israel, attributed by some to the earthquake of 31 BC and by others to localized subsidence.

The acceptance of faults as the loci of most earthquakes was clinched when H. F. Reid (1910) put forward a persuasive model for strike-slip faulting and showed that geodetic data, collected in California between 1851 and 1906, reflected the storage of elastic energy that was released by the 1906 event. The monitoring of fault displacement soon followed, as there was obvious scope for forecasting events or at any rate identifying structures that were still active.

Strike-slip faults invited attention first because they offered displaced roads, fences, structures and landforms as clues to the extent and possibly the duration of successive movements. Yet the mere juxtaposition of strata across a discontinuity, although readily mapped, is as uninformative as a broken leg. On some faults, for example, creep is increasingly seen or suspected as a component of movement to the point where "silent earthquake" is the appropriate term.

A pioneering account of coseismic deformation is the description by Schmidt (1875) of a crack 2.4 m high, 1.8 m wide and 13 km long, which developed east of Egion on the Peloponnese coast of Greece, during an earthquake (estimated at M = 7) on 26 December 1861 (Fig. 8.2). The feature was long dismissed as nothing more than a landslide effect, understandably so at a time when Charles Lyell (1853) viewed the effects of the Calabrian earthquake in Italy as mainly the products of shaking. A well preserved normal fault south of Egion – well preserved because it was beneath the malodorous town garbage dump – suggested that Schmidt's scarp was indeed on a fault and that an even earlier movement on the fault could account for the mysterious submergence of ancient Helike (now called Eliki) in 373 BC (Mouyaris et al. 1992). Helike is on the downthrown block of the fault and, to judge from the classical literature, it was submerged well

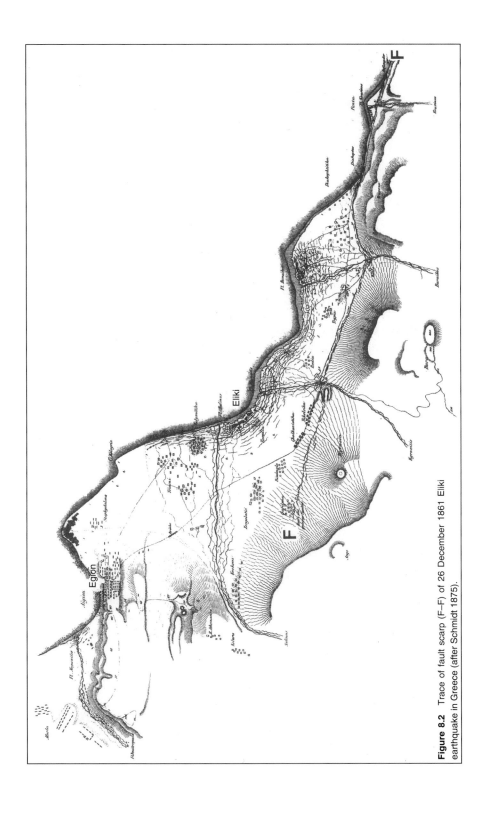

**Figure 8.2** Trace of fault scarp (F–F) of 26 December 1861 Eliki earthquake in Greece (after Schmidt 1875).

enough for boatloads of tourists to gaze down on the town until it was blotted out by silt. The fault is now known as the Helike Fault.

Analysis of surface faulting serves theoretical and applied aspects of seismology, because it provides data on both the extent of movement (and hence on the energy released) and the timing (and hence the spacing between successive events). For all its historical overtones the Helike Fault lacks a well documented account: the 373 BC event is richer in information on the various animals that left Helike before the earthquake than about the earthquake itself. According to Aelian (XI, 19), for example, all its mice, martens, snakes, centipedes, beetles and other creatures left Helike for five days before the earthquake, when an immense wave poured over it, and the city disappeared.

Some archaeological sites are more informative. Consider the earthquake that destroyed the Crusader castle of Vadum Jacob, on the Jordan River, at dawn on 20 May 1202 (Ellenblum et al. 1998). Excavation of the castle supported historical (and geological) evidence for destructive earthquakes on the Jordan Valley part of the Dead Sea transform. It showed an offset of the walls of 2.1 m. Of this, 1.6 m could be attributed to the earthquake of 20 May, which was felt from Iraq to Sicily and for which a magnitude of 7.6 has been estimated from the historical accounts. The remaining 0.5 m of offset, which affected a mosque on the site, occurred during earthquakes in 1759 and 1837. When set against geodetic evidence for no displacement since 1988 and the area's low micro-seismicity, the data imply that the fault segment is currently locked (Ellenblum et al. 1998).

When there is no historical source to hand, reliance is placed on the traditional repertoire of dating methods. Their accuracy is of concern for two main reasons. The causes, or effects, of an event cannot be pinned down if the chronology is sloppy, and the magnitude of an event may be an issue that hinges on whether motion affected a major fault rather than several small ones.

Whatever the question – when did the fault last move, how often has it moved and so forth – the usual obstacles to straightforward dating arise. Cosmogenic dating of surfaces exposed by faulting generally lacks the resolution to supply ages expressed in units shorter than a millennium (Zreda & Noller 1998). Direct dating of the shear zones is hampered by the presence of detrital minerals together with those produced by the faulting event, and by the large error associated with the dating methods, although useful results can sometimes be obtained by applying the $^{14}$C method to charcoal or soil carbon dragged into the gouge by reverse faulting. In the Comechingones Fault of Argentina (Fig. 8.3), soil carbon on the fault plane yielded the first date (~1100 yr BP) so far for a prehistoric earthquake in the Sierras Pampeanas (Costa & Vita-Finzi 1996); in northeast Brazil (Fig. 8.4), AMS $^{14}$C dating of charcoal trapped within a strike-slip fault in basement crystalline rocks shows that the fault was reactivated ~4700 yr ago (Bezerra & Vita-Finzi 2000). Thus, both case studies identified events whose chief value resides in demonstrating the reality and character of coseismic deformation events in prehistoric times.

The issue of earthquake age became of public concern in the northwestern USA, where there was geological evidence for large subduction-earthquake events along the Cascadia coast, but none for the past 150 years. Estimates for the largest events in the

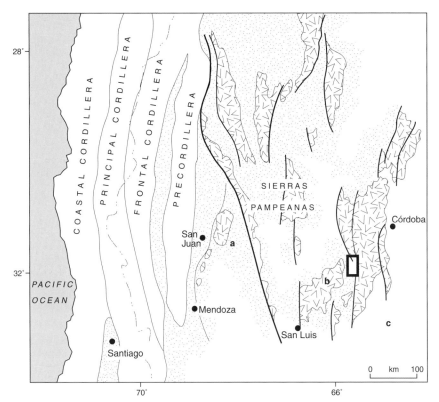

**Figure 8.3** **(a)** Part of Sierras Pampeanas, Argentina. **a**: Caucete earthquake 23 November 1977 ($M_L$ = 7.4), **b**: San Martín earthquake 22 May 1936 ($M_L$ = 6.4), **c**: Sampacho earthquake 11 June 1934 ($M_L$ = 6.0). **(b, c overleaf)**

record ranged from M = 8 to M = 9.5. Careful stratigraphic work, allied with extensive use of high-precision conventional and AMS [14]C dating, has been applied where possible to plants killed by the earthquake or at least to several individual plants that died at about the same time. After calibration to calendar years the results showed rupture by a single $M_W$ = 9 event or a series of smaller events propagating north or south. The time available for rupture of 680 km of the Cascadia zone was less than 20 yr (Nelson et al. 1995), leading to the conclusion that the earthquake magnitude in question was close to 9.

As there were no local historical reports of widespread subsidence, any calibrated [14]C ages more recent than 1850 could be disregarded. That left one plausible candidate: there are written records in Japan for a major tsunami, which struck at 21.00 h local time on 26 January 1700 and which apparently originated in an earthquake of M ≈ 9 (Satake et al. 1996).

Eyewitness and historical accounts of coseismic movement on faults help to identify active structures. They may also reveal the dominant style of deformation. Instrumental data on earthquakes are often ambiguous about the sense of slip on strike-slip faults and, although modelling of the event may reduce the doubt, the best test remains field

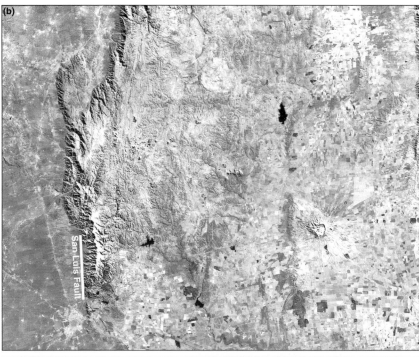

**Figure 8.3** **(b)** The Sierra de Comechingones (including portion in bold box, in **(a)**), like the San Luis Fault shown in Landsat image, is one of several reverse faults in the Sierras Pampeanas dipping east. **(c)** Section of the Comechingones Fault dated by AMS $^{14}$C (black diagonal zone to right of figure). (After Costa & Vita-Finzi 1996.)

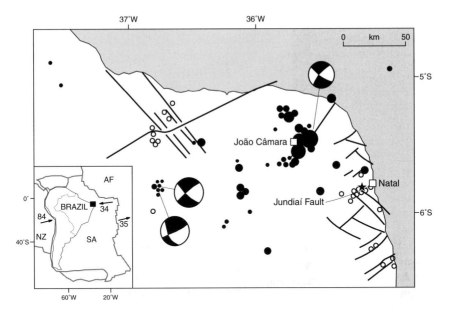

**Figure 8.4** Recent seismicity of northeast Brazil. Large segmented circles are fault-plane solutions indicating strike-slip motion. Filled circles show historical earthquakes, their sizes being proportional to magnitude; open circles denote liquefaction sites; major faults are shown by heavy lines; the star shows the site dated by AMS $^{14}$C. Inset: filled box shows the area of the main map; spreading rates are in mm yr$^{-1}$; SA, South American plate, AF, African plate, NZ, Nazca Plate. (After Bezerra & Vita-Finzi 2000.)

evidence. The amount of displacement is of course a measure of magnitude but a fragile one: great variation may be encountered in slip along a normal fault, the topographical effects of reverse faults may be soon obscured by mass movement, and many faults are too small or too deep to have an obvious topographical effect.

GPS is well suited to tracing the geometry of deformation of a fault by virtue of its speed and its independence of pre-existing baselines. Its potential, in seismology as in volcanology, is greatly enhanced if combined with radar interferometry (Peltzer et al. 1994). As we saw in Chapter 5 (p. 81), the deformation indicated by earthquake records often falls well short of that implied by plate-tectonic patterns, a deficit commonly explained by defective earthquake records, creep or both. The Hayward Fault (California) is one of the few that are continuously instrumented and it has yielded evidence of pronounced aseismic creep. The creep is itself discontinuous, although the discontinuities are generally masked by the search for an average rate.

The first major success of InSAR in fault analysis came with the Landers earthquake, a shallow strike-slip event that ruptured along 85 km of a fault system northeast of Los Angeles. The crucial interference pattern was derived from SAR images acquired by ERS-1 in April 24 and August 7 1992. Geodetic measurements had shown horizontal movements of as much as 3 m, consistent with field and seismic data for slips of up to 6 m and a hypocentral depth of 3–8 km. SPOT images indicated 1 m of coseismic displacement, and field surveys showed up to 6 cm of post-seismic displacement

0     km     20

**Figure 8.5** Synthetic interferogram for the area near the Landers Fault (right). One cycle of gray represents 28 cm of change in the range, i.e. the distance from the spacecraft. (After Massonnet et al. 1993, by permission of *Nature*. See the cover of this book for part of this image in colour.)

(Massonnet et al. 1993). Modelling of the coseismic deformation gave a result that agreed well with both the radar data and the field observations, but not in the immediate vicinity of the fault (Fig. 8.5). Fortunately, repeated satellite passes (every 35 days for ERS-1) allowed very satisfactory mapping of ground deformation close to the fault trace. They revealed sudden variations in fault displacement (Peltzer et al. 1994); three possible cases were considered, namely rigid-body rotations about a vertical axis, tilting, and distributed simple shear. The first was detected at one location, where the pattern of parallel fringes suggested tilting by 1 m of the edge of a block measuring 5 km, equivalent to 0.01° or 190 μrad. A dense pattern of fringes at another site pointed to distributed shear from slip on a blind fault.

InSAR is also used for tracing post-seismic displacements. Interferograms were constructed for three different intervals after the Landers earthquake (Peltzer et al. 1996). The data for the period 41–89 days following the event showed that the 1992 surface rupture included two pull-apart structures. The largest displacement occurred during this time interval and was 20 per cent smaller in the interferogram spanning a 3.4 yr period starting three months after the earthquake.

A later study, which avoided using a DEM by relying on three SAR images (Zebker et al. 1994), obtained values for horizontal displacement that were more precise and indeed on a par with those obtained by GPS, with the bonus of areal (rather than point) coverage. When applied at three intervals in the three years after the earthquake (Peltzer et al. 1996), this approach yielded valuable insights into the processes at work on the fault by revealing that an extensional structure experienced uplift and a compressive subsidence, with a relaxation time of $270 \pm 45$ days and possibly through the transfer of pore fluid.

The Landers earthquake had produced up to 7 m of surface displacement. One of its aftershocks on 4 December created movements measured in tens of centimetres, which were not recorded by other geodetic methods. An interferogram derived from two SAR-1 images of the correct period, after allowing within the model for the effects of the Big Bear earthquake (28 June 1992, $M_W = 6.2$) and the main Landers earthquake, was used to estimate a focal mechanism for the event (Feigl et al. 1995). The solution agreed with seismological estimates in indicating a reverse fault with parameters within the 95 per cent confidence limits of the strike, dip and rake obtained by the alternative procedure, although the inferred-moment magnitude was slightly greater than that measured ($M_W = 5.4$ vs 5.1).

There was an ambiguity about the dip of the rupture plane, but this is a familiar problem in conventional seismology. It was successfully overcome for the Eureka Valley earthquake of 17 May 1993, which nucleated at a depth of 13 km. The aftershocks defined a trend a little west of north, whereas surface breaks recognized after the earthquake were aligned north-northeast and the focal-plane solution indicated a normal fault also striking north-northeast. SAR interferometry indicated subsidence in a basin about 35 km long and 20 km wide, with a maximum depth of 9.5 cm and aligned slightly west of north, its form consistent with slip on a west-dipping fault (Peltzer & Rosen 1995). A likely explanation was that slip on the north-northeast-striking fault plane was on or below a line plunging northwards, so that the long axis of the resulting subsidence would be parallel to the azimuth of the line of maximum slip. Good agreement between the radar observations and the predicted surface deformation was obtained by modelling a fault plane 15 km long, 15 km wide, striking N7°E and dipping 50°W, with 3 cm of slip at the surface in the south and at depth adjusted to match the seismic moment. The method, in short, could "prove quite useful in remote areas without local seismographic networks . . . or, in principle, other planets" (Feigl et al. 1995).

A further illustration of InSAR as a guide to the subsurface came with the 1995 Grevena earthquake in northern Greece ($M_W = 6.6$), which was a normal-faulting event. Five SAR interferograms were produced spanning 2–3 yr, and additional pairs were used to evaluate any problems arising from defective atmospheric propagation (Meyer et al. 1996). (One of the surprises was the recovery of distinguishable fringes even on intensely cultivated terrain, perhaps because the field borders had survived annual ploughing.) The fringe pattern obtained by InSAR could be made to fit the result of dislocation modelling by invoking five fault patches, of which three met the surface along the trace of the faults mapped in the field. The surface break was a mere 2–4 cm over a distance of 8–12 km, which conflicted with a substantial seismic moment estimate based on CMT data of $7.6 \times 10^{18}$ Nm. However, the interferogram yielded a kidney-shape zone with up to 30 cm of subsidence bordering a smaller area affected by up to 5 cm of uplift, which could be modelled by a fault with 1 m of slip at a depth of 4–15 km and dipping north-northwest, with a total seismic moment of $6.4 \times 10^{18}$ Nm. The fringes also indicated two additional faults at the northeast end of the fault and dipping east-northeast. In other words, the deformation pattern endorses the suspicion, derived from the regional setting, that the active fault interacts with the northeast–southwest extension of the dominant regional system.

## Fault systems

The Grevena case study drives home the truism that viewing faults in isolation is of limited value, as they respond collectively, although not necessarily simultaneously, to the regional stress field. Indeed, one of the major benefits of short-term monitoring is that it sometimes reveals the order in which the responses occur. On Mt Etna an EDM survey revealed the location of a set of faults that contribute to deformation of the volcano's uplifting eastern flank (Stewart et al. 1993).

Or consider the island of Sumatra and the Mentawi Islands west of it. The classic picture is that oblique subduction of the Indian plate beneath the Asian plate leads to a combination of shear and shortening. The former is manifested mainly as dextral strike slip along the Sumatra Fault; shortening causes subduction with its attendant trench, back-arc ridge, fore-arc ridge and sediment wedge. As subduction progresses, the wedge contracts along a series of reverse faults (Fig. 8.6a,b), some of which slip far enough to bring the intervening deposits above sea level and create a chain of islands.

Reconnaissance [14]C dating of coastal deposits on Nias and Simeulue (Fig. 8.6c) showed no simple relationship between the age and the height of the various reefs sampled. But the plot of age against height displayed a pattern that was simply explained by episodes of coseismic uplift separated by phases of quiescence about 1000 yr long. A plausible mechanism is for slip on one of the imbricate faults in the sediment wedge to proceed seismically until stress is suitably relieved, to be followed by strain build-up until another fault slips.

As shortening proceeds, the wedge is rotated (clockwise in Fig. 8.6b) so that the faults steepen. Local inhabitants claim that the inshore waters off eastern Simeulue have deepened appreciably since early Dutch colonial days, and recent high-precision dating by U-series shows – granted that only major events produce enough uplift to survive in the record – that coseismic uplift is more pronounced on the southwest than on the northeast coast of Nias (Edwards et al. 1988).

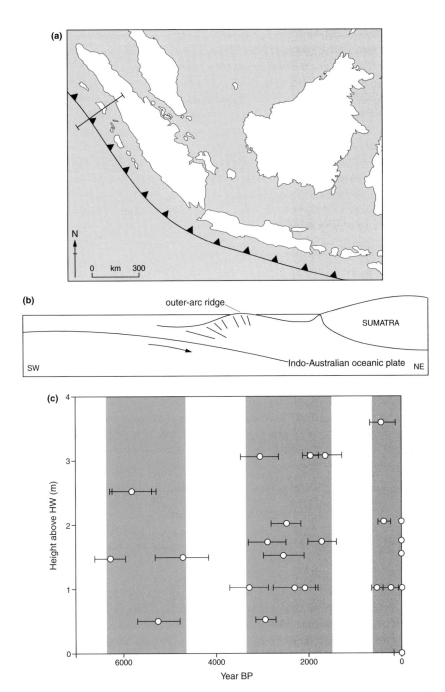

**Figure 8.6** (a) Uplift of outer-arc ridge off Sumatra as a consequence of rotation of faults (clockwise in the figure) (b). Episodes of emergence indicated by [14]C dating of palaeo-shorelines are shaded (c). (After Vita-Finzi 1995.)

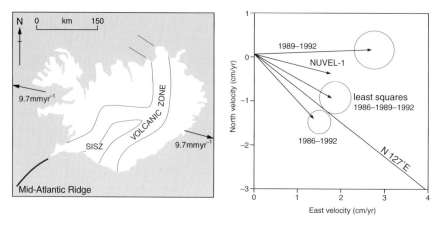

**Figure 8.7** Left: Tectonic elements in Iceland, showing the Mid-Atlantic ridge, the South Iceland seismic zone (SISZ) and NUVEL-1 velocities. Right: The velocity of the Eurasian plate relative to the American plate, showing possible change in azimuth between 1986 and 1989. (After Sigmundsson et al. 1995, © AGU.)

Emergence has also facilitated analysis of the fault systems of part of the Mid-Atlantic Ridge. A study conducted in Iceland between 1986 and 1992 exploited three successive GPS surveys to this end (Sigmundsson et al. 1995).

The area west of the volcanic zone lies on the North America plate, that to the east of the volcanic zone on the Eurasia plate. The relative velocity between them was found by least-squares analysis to be $21 \pm 4\,\mathrm{mm\,yr^{-1}}$ on a bearing of N117°±11°E, close to the NUVEL-1 value of $19.4\,\mathrm{mm\,yr^{-1}}$ at N104°E (Fig. 8.7). The results of the survey showed that these two areas are little deformed and that about $85 \pm 15$ per cent of the relative plate motion is concentrated within a 20–30 km-wide zone broadly corresponding to the South Iceland seismic zone. The shear is accommodated by a series of north–south faults that slip past each other and are rotated anticlockwise (the horizontal analogue of the imbricate faults under Nias and Simeulue) by what is sometimes referred to as book-shelf tectonics. The requisite rotation is $0.5–1\,\mathrm{\mu rad\,yr^{-1}}$ and the slip on the faults, which are 1–5 km apart, is $0.5–5\,\mathrm{mm\,yr^{-1}}$.

It proved possible to consider whether the GPS data have any validity beyond the 16 yr of the survey by comparing the geometric seismic moment release of the north–south fault array during the survey with that indicated by the historical earthquake record. On the assumption that the faults had a moment equivalent to a single transform fault along the seismic zone, the moment for 1986–92 (Hackman et al. 1990) turned out to be very similar to the average annual rate derived from historical events during 1620–1912.

Where deformation is thought to be diffuse, and seismic hazard assessment is a priority, the ideal option is to set up a dense network of permanent, or at any rate frequently occupied, GPS stations. Levelling and tilt measurement are effective especially if they are repeated at short intervals. In the Krafla zone of North Iceland, rifting between 1975 and 1978 was found to display some periodicity separated by inflation, which was presumably caused by magma inflow into a chamber. Levelling had been carried out at 1–2 month intervals in many parts of an extensive network, and was supplemented by data from one water tube tiltmeter, twelve dry tilt stations and, from late 1977, two recording electronic tiltmeters, simple mechanical devices fitted to several fissures, geodimeter measurements, a seismic network and thirty gravity stations (Björnsson et al. 1979). The inflation phases extended over several months with a maximum of 7–10 mm day$^{-1}$ near the centre of the caldera; the rifting pulses lasted a few days and were accompanied by seismicity in the fissure zone and subsidence in the caldera.

The wealth of observation owes a good deal to the economic importance of a geothermal field within the caldera. It reveals pulses too short to be noticed without measuring devices (as confirmed by the limited detail in eyewitness reports of similar events in the eighteenth century) and the connection between caldera subsidence and rift extension. The association comes close to answering the riddle of whether the mid-ocean ridge, of which the Icelandic structures are a visible extension, is jacked open by lava inflow or allows lava inflow passively because it is being extended by other forces. The new evidence suggests that regional plate separation is indeed the primary factor and the flow of magma a secondary phenomenon. It also shows that, like many such questions, the alternatives are posed too starkly: rifting occurred where the mechanical strength of the crust was lowest (i.e. where it contains the magma chamber) and was thus not purely a passive effect of extension.

Discrepancies between different data sources may prove informative. In the Ventura Basin of California the geological estimate for convergence is 20–25 mm yr$^{-1}$, compared with 7–10 mm yr$^{-1}$ measured geodetically (Donnellan et al. 1993). Expanding the area of study does not resolve the conflict, as it yields 17–26 mm yr$^{-1}$ for the geological rate and 11±2 mm yr$^{-1}$ for the geodetic rate. The geodesists had a simple explanation: the geological model is wrong, either because the dates in question are out by a factor of two or because, although the slip rates for the faults bounding the basin are correct, the faults do not flatten out at depth (as had been assumed). Two elastic dislocation models were found to fit the surface data; they have in common reverse faults, which are locked at depths of less than about 2–5 km. In other words, strain is accumulating in the shallow sections; but how much is available for release in the form of earthquakes depends on the proportion of shortening being taken up by folding (Donnellan et al. 1993). In short, the debate has focused attention on a facet of the problem that lends itself to direct (geodetic) observation, but only if the geologists can identify structures capable of the requisite deformation.

Analysis of the 1992 Landers earthquake had benefited from a regional perspective thanks to the permanent GPS geodetic array established in Southern California in 1990. The array comprises five continuously operating receivers; 24 hours of data are collected automatically once a day, and the satellite orbits are placed in a framework based on data from a global network of about 25 permanent stations corrected for polar motion using tabulated predictions. The Landers and Big Bear earthquakes both providentially took place within the three-month test period of the International Global Positioning System and Geodynamics Service (Blewitt et al. 1993).

Ground displacements were monitored immediately before, during and after the 1992 earthquakes with millimetre-level precision up to 200 km from the main rupture

(Simpson et al. 1982, Bock et al. 1993). The analysis showed that the bulk of the observed deformation was coseismic. No significant pre-seismic movement was recorded, but a post-seismic signature of $0.9 \pm 0.3$ mm day$^{-1}$ could be detected for 16 days. Confirmation came from laser strainmeters at the Piñón Flat Observatory, which showed no pre-seismic signal but 1–2 weeks of post-seismic strain.

The Landers earthquake has in fact been proposed as trigger for events on the San Andreas Fault, 25 km away, and also the western Great Basin, over 700 km away. It is claimed that aftershocks occur when Coulomb stresses have risen by 0.5 bar and are inhibited by comparable falls; larger stresses can advance the date of major nearby events (King et al. 1994). Deformation over the same period near the Johnson Valley Fault has been explained by shortening normal to the fault, perhaps reflecting the closure of dilatant cracks and also fluid expulsion, as well as by afterslip at depth. But a post-seismic slip model generated by inverting GPS data obtained at 19 stations in the 6 months after the earthquake yielded synthetic interferograms inconsistent with the SAR images. SAR mapping is uniquely capable of providing a complete map of post-seismic deformation "but, as importantly, it casts new light on poorly understood lithospheric processes" (Massonnet et al. 1996), as will become especially clear in the concluding paragraphs of this chapter.

In 1978–9, dyke emplacement and associated faulting in the Asal Rift of Djibouti, at the junction between the oceanic ridges of the Red Sea and the Gulf of Aden with the northern end of the East African Rift, were mapped geodetically by resurvey of a 1972–3 levelling traverse. The rift had widened by about 2 m and the inner floor had dropped by 70 cm, dimensions consistent with the opening of two dykes. Modelling these data in the light of associated seismicity yielded a map of Coulomb stress changes, which predicted the distribution of seismicity within a radius of 40 km for the ensuing four years (Jacques et al. 1996). Thus, although earthquake prediction using premonitory movements remains beyond the limits of resolution of radar interferometry (Zebker et al. 1994), geodesy allied with stress modelling should soon identify faults liable to slip if they are already close to failure.

# Folds

The folding of brittle rocks is generally thought to be gradual enough to permit deformation of brittle materials elastically or, where it takes place at sufficient depth, by plastic processes. The analysis of individual structures benefits from an historical perspective that assesses both strain rate and mechanism during their development. In many settings one can thus identify an initial stage of elastic buckling followed by one of inelastic buckling until the fold locks (Price 1975). Strain rates will rise to a maximum during this progression and then decline to zero.

Progress in tracing fold development directly, and in treating it in terms of forces and resistances rather than of cumulative net strain, has generally been hampered by the poor time resolution of most deformed rock sequences. Until recently, even when the timespan of the folds was short and deformation could be shown to have taken place in the course of deposition, as in parts of New Zealand and Tunisia (Vita-Finzi 1986), the rate at which it progressed had to be averaged over several millennia. What is more, the average applied only to the part of the fold that had yielded datable material.

The recognition of coseismic folding has shown that in certain circumstances the process is very rapid and can be monitored closely. The El Asnam (Algeria) earthquake ($M_S$ = 7.3) of 10 October 1980 was the subject of one of the earliest descriptions of coseismic folding (Fig. 8.8). Early topographical maps showed that the lake site had been occupied by a marsh, and, on the assumption that this was the remnant of an earlier coseismic lake, there seemed to be excellent prospects of recovering a detailed earthquake chronology by drilling or digging. It was accomplished by trenching (Meghraoui et al. 1988), which revealed at least three events separated by an average of 450 yr.

What this implies for seismic risk is in dispute. As the portion of fault that has been trenched need not be representative of the entire fault system, information on events elsewhere in the region is required. There is also a pressing need for geodetic monitoring in order to identify any strain build-up and also to establish whether the deformation that accompanied the 1980 event has been followed by elastic relaxation, for this could indicate that magnitudes derived from folding are overestimates. A railway line buckled by the 1980 earthquake was repaired with regrettable efficiency within the space of a few days and could not serve as a measure of coseismic shortening.

El Asnam lies at the boundary between Africa and Eurasia, which is here marked by reverse faulting. Where Eurasia collides with Arabia in the Zagros Mountains, surface folding is again associated with motion on reverse faults (Berberian 1995). The mountain belt as a whole is growing by serial-fold development on its southwestern margin. The palaeomagnetic record suggests that convergence between the two plates, after allowing for independent motion of the African plate (Jackson et al. 1995), is at 30 mm yr$^{-1}$ on an azimuth of 015°. $^{14}$C dating of fossil beaches raised above the sea by the growth of coastal folds during the past 6000 yr suggests that their compression represents 20.1 mm yr$^{-1}$ of convergence at 061° (Vita-Finzi 2001). The discrepancy in rate and orientation between the long-term and Holocene averages, although possibly an artefact of inadequate data, could indicate that not all the shortening is concentrated in the frontal folds.

That folding was coseismic is suggested by the large quantities of mollusc shells, including oyster beds, in growth position on the terraces, and the clear offset between the terraces. Analysis of the $^{14}$C ages for three successive terraces suggests that there has been no uplift during the past 1000 yr or so. The pause would go a long way towards explaining the 80–90 per cent deficit between the amount of deformation predicted by plate tectonics and that represented by the earthquakes in the Zagros between 1909 and 1992 (Jackson et al. 1995). It also suggests that, despite a lack of uplift, there may be significant shortening in progress as strain accumulates on subsurface reverse faults (Berberian 1995).

Another coastal area where coseismic folding has been observed is south-central Chile, where the earthquake ($M_W$= 9.5) of 21–22 May 1960, perhaps the greatest recorded instrumentally, produced buckling over an area measuring $1000 \times 200$ km

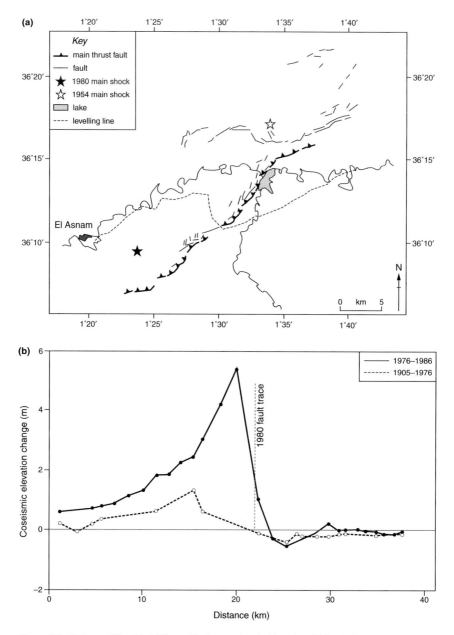

**Figure 8.8** El Asnam (Algeria). **(a)** Normal faults associated with surface folding in the 1980 earthquake. **(b)** Results of levelling for 1905–1976 and 1976–86 along line marked in **(a)** (after Bezzeghoud et al. 1995, by permission of Elsevier Science). **(c, opposite)** Coseismic folding of Chelif bed in Pondeba gorge. **(d, opposite)** Coseismic sandblow in alluvium.

**(c)**

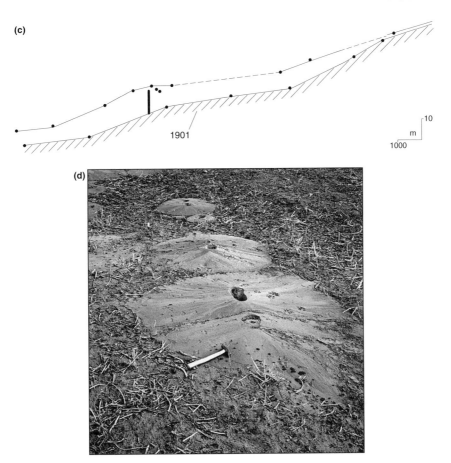

1901

10
m
1000

**(d)**

(Fig. 8.9). Uplift on the coast could be traced with great precision by reference to the upper limit of dead barnacles raised above high water by the earthquake (Plafker 1972), which amounted to as much as 5.7 m. Resurvey in 1966–8 of trigonometrical stations first occupied in 1950–52 provided information transverse to the buckles. Various models that postulated reverse faults dipping southeast or southwest gave satisfactory agreement with the main uplift but did not yield the second minor north–south buckle (Plafker 1972); a simple model based on the buckling of an elastic beam gave good agreement with observation. The elastic model also allows for progressive post-seismic decay of the buckles. Such decay has been observed for the vertical movements that accompanied an earthquake observed by Charles Darwin in 1846.

Elastic buckling will remain a suggestion until geodetic data are gathered to test it. In Taiwan (Fig. 8.10) an extensive network of conventional geodetic and GPS stations (9 monitored continuously and 131 annually) supplemented by field data provide the requisite mix of long and short-term measurements for testing structural models. To mention just one salutary lesson, the predominance of extension in geodetic lines across the southern Central Range probably results from anticlinal folding above buried

127

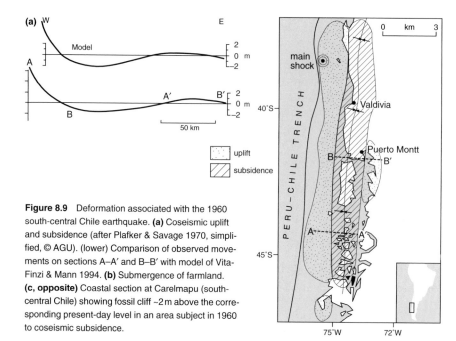

**Figure 8.9** Deformation associated with the 1960 south-central Chile earthquake. **(a)** Coseismic uplift and subsidence (after Plafker & Savage 1970, simplified, © AGU). (lower) Comparison of observed movements on sections A–A′ and B–B′ with model of Vita-Finzi & Mann 1994. **(b)** Submergence of farmland. **(c, opposite)** Coastal section at Carelmapu (south-central Chile) showing fossil cliff ~2 m above the corresponding present-day level in an area subject in 1960 to coseismic subsidence.

reverse faults. In other words it results from shortening. In the Longitudinal Valley and the Fold and Thrust Belt, shortening is unambiguous. The former takes up almost half the interplate convergence of 70–80 mm yr$^{-1}$ between the Eurasian and Philippine plates (Lundberg et al. 1997), but much of it as strike-slip. In contrast the Fold and Thrust Belt contains faults whose geometry is well suited to the storage of seismic strain and its release as major earthquakes, witness the five M > 6.5 earthquakes in the previous century (Vita-Finzi 2000). The Chi-Chi earthquake of 21 September 1999 ($M_W = 7.6$) broke a branch of the Chukou Fault on which GPS data for 1993–7 had indicated rapid strain accumulation. If faults in the Fold and Thrust Belt steepen progressively eastwards, as in the Zagros, away from the collision front between the two plates, and there is a related decline in uplift rate as a fold matures, one would expect a change across strike in the shortening rate. The measured rate for 1993–7 about 10 km west of the Chelungpu Fault was 20 mm yr$^{-1}$, and 20 km east of it 40 mm yr$^{-1}$.

Damaged artificial structures, not being confined to survey lines or the shore, usefully supplemented the geodetic data. In places the thrusting was partitioned into basal slip and hillside steepening, with the latter sometimes taking up over half the slip, so that assessment based solely on offsets at the toe of the thrust would have led to a gross underestimate of fault slip (Bilham & Yu 2000). As in the Central Range, net shortening or extension can conceal a complex pattern of deformation that can be elucidated only by skilled observation on the ground. However, the most effective contribution by manmade structures was in the analysis of fold development. In tropical areas, a dense vegetation cover, paddy fields and standing water are subject to rapid changes that often lead to poor correlation between successive SAR images. An attempt was made to circumvent the problem by focusing on the large urban area of Tainan, at the southwestern margin of the Fold and Thrust Belt, as its buildings would guarantee image coherence.

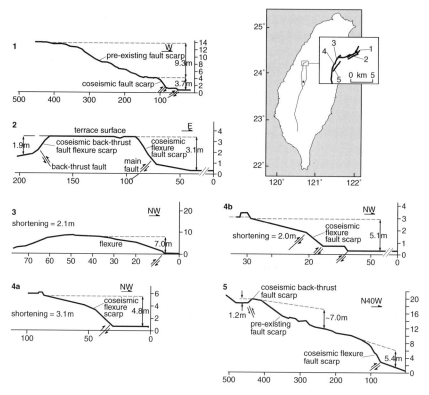

**Figure 8.10** Examples of flexural-slip deformation at the northern end of the Chelungpu Fault during the Chi-Chi (Taiwan) earthquake of 21 September 1999. The variety of topographies produced by the same event is brought out by the two sections (a and b) from location 4. Sections 1 and 5 illustrate attempts to differentiate between pre-existing and coseismic (i.e. 1999) scarps. Vertical and horizontal scales in metres. (After Lin et al. 2001, by permission of Elsevier Science.)

The results for 1996–8 showed anticlinal uplift by 3.2 cm in a tract previously considered to be safely beyond (i.e. west of) the zone of active deformation (Fruneau et al. 2001).

This kind of monitoring can also contribute to the more general question of how the upper crust deforms, particularly in the context of the so-called earthquake cycle. Students of rock mechanics have long acknowledged that descriptive terminologies based on the distinction between brittle and plastic deformation are not always satisfactory, and that, at least when it comes to folding, elastic properties may be obscured by those characteristic of very viscous fluids (Biot 1961, Ramsay 1967). Geodetic studies of areas subject to active extension, such as the Aegean (Clarke et al. 1999), show a pattern of surface deformation consistent with the ductile behaviour conventionally associated with the mantle rather than the crust. The next step is to chronicle the relaxation that follows a major earthquake, both on the fault and throughout the area that serves as catchment for the stored energy.

# CHAPTER 9

# Sediments and surfaces

*The Mississippi is a broad-chested river . . . of mulatto-hued water; more*
*than 400 million tons of mud, carried by that water, insult the Gulf of Mexico*
*each year. All that venerable and ancient waste has created a delta where*
*gigantic swamp cypresses grow from the slough of a continent in perpetual*
*dissolution . . .*
Jorge Luis Borges (tr. Andrew Hurley) *The cruel redeemer Lazarus Morrell*

The acceptance of an Earth history millions rather than thousands of years long owed much to the realization that many rocks represent the products of rock breakdown and its transport by water and wind. Archibald Geikie, for instance, made much of the large sediment load of the Mississippi, the Ganges and the Po in demonstrating the power of subaerial erosion in comparison with that of the sea (Goudie 1995: 2).

Nevertheless, the calibration of these processes into rates was perforce very approximate. Some of the earliest attempts to calculate the time taken to salt the oceans, for example, were crude sums derived from the evaporation of samples of water from the sea and from rivers, on the assumption that the original sea was fresh and constant in volume and that the process had happened only once. Controversies about the severity of soil loss at different times, notably in the context of overgrazing in the American Midwest, were fuelled by estimates of reservoir silting or the depth to which selected structures had been exposed by erosion; such point data were employed to calculate the progress of processes of unknown regularity over large areas and long periods of time. The scarce numerical ages were extrapolated throughout entire depositional units, or the entire globe when it came to major geological boundaries, on the assumption (often reasonable but untested) that the unit had been produced at the same time throughout the area of interest.

Quite apart from errors of measurement, and the great variability that accompanies most natural processes seasonally and sometimes from day to day, extrapolation into the past or future from such measurements is made hazardous by a host of factors, including climate, human activity, and the cumulative effects of the very changes one is seeking to monitor. The classic study by Segerstrom (1950) of gully development on Parícutin volcano in Mexico was privileged in that the volcano had not come into existence until 1943, when it thrust its way out of a maize field. Most other studies of erosion have to allow for thousands or millions of years of environmental change.

Although some of the key recent advances in documenting erosion and deposition depend on conceptual and technical progress in remote sensing, geodesy and dating, others flow mainly from the decision to document what had previously been assumed or interpolated. The most chastening corrections have come from three decades of measurement by simple but effective devices.

## Channels

The Vigil network was established mainly at the initiative of Luna B. Leopold (1962) at the US Geological Survey. Its aim was to set up sites and drainage basins where repeated measurements would be made in order to identify change. The measurements were to include geomorphological, hydrological and biological data, and to be stored in easily accessible form.

By 1965 there were over 60 sites and basins, mainly in the USA, but interest waned at the end of the International Hydrological Decade and was not revived until 1990, when attempts were made to improve access to the data, select additional sites and revisit and update existing ones (Osterkamp & Emmett 1992). By 1991 there were 83 sites or small basins, of which 72 were in the USA, 6 were in Sweden, 3 were in Puerto Rico and one each was in Botswana and Israel (Fig. 9.1). The USA sites were concentrated in Mississippi and Montana; some of them were set up as early as 1931 and later considered suitable for inclusion in the network. There is an understandable emphasis on arid and semi-arid areas, where landscape response to climatic and land-use changes is rapid and often obvious. Many of the stations were designed to trace channel changes by resurvey and by reference to stakes, pins and chains.

The process whose analysis is best served by the network is the incision and aggradation of alluvial channels. One of the most striking features of semi-arid landscapes is the arroyo or gully, and its origin and development have attracted the attention of Earth scientists in the American West at least since the days of Lyell, who described the birth and spread of a gully system following deforestation (Chorley et al. 1964). Gully erosion is a major source of soil loss, dam silting and road damage in the semi-arid world, and the expensive remedial measures often fail because they are based on wrong *a priori* thinking.

Attempts to analyze the climatic contribution to channel change have generally hinged on chronology, on the grounds that synchronous change over a large area is more likely to result from the imposition of an external environmental change than from manmade shifts in the character and intensity of land use. But the chronological test is muddied by the gradual geographical displacement of climatic belts and by changes in agricultural practice following waves of invasion or political reform over extensive tracts of the globe. There is, for example, evidence for widespread valley filling in the Old World, which has been ascribed by some to a shift in the intensity and seasonal distribution of rainfall resulting from the temporary southward displacement of the

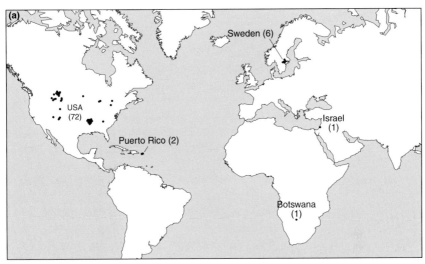

**Figure 9.1** **(a)** Location of Vigil networks (after Osterkamp & Emmett 1992, by permission of IAHS Press). **(b)** Section on Cañada de la Cueva, New Mexico, a typical Vigil site (courtesy of Waite R. Osterkamp, USGS).

depression tracks (Leopold & Vita-Finzi 1998). Others blame misuse of the land and in particular the forest clearing and cultivation of classical antiquity.

The aggradational part of the chronologies (Figs 9.2, 9.3) is generally based on archaeological and radiocarbon limiting ages for the alluvium. The dates for incision are often more precise, as they are derived from eyewitness accounts, photographs and dated maps. But as both aggradation and incision are progressive effects that commonly

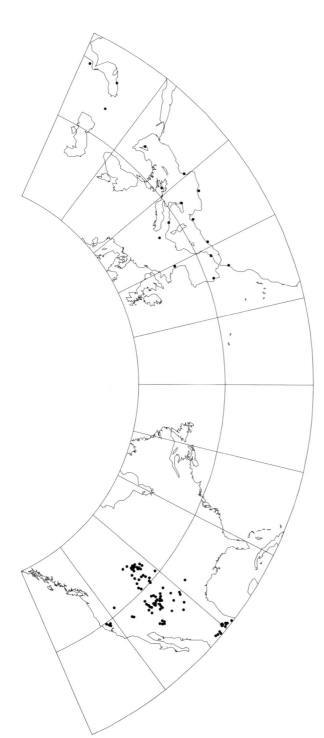

**Figure 9.2** **(a)** Northern Hemisphere river sections that silted up in AD 500–1850. **(b, opposite)** Relationship of $^{14}C$ age of the alluvium with latitude (after Leopold & Vita-Finzi 1998). **(c, opposite)** Postulated path of depressions in the sixteenth century (after Lamb 1962, by permission of the Royal Meteorological Society).

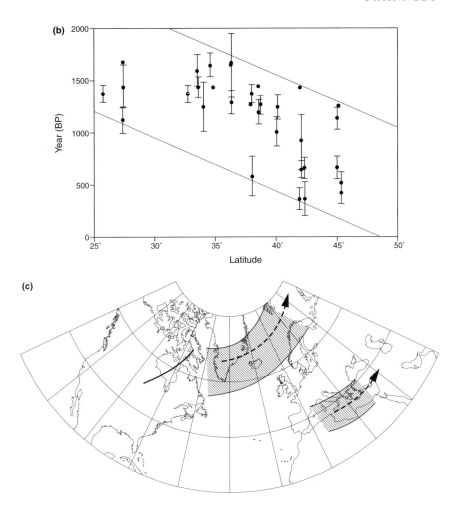

work their way up or down a drainage system, precise point determinations are not necessarily the route to a confident diagnosis. It is here that the Vigil data offer hope of a resolution, although only for the latest part of the record.

In the semi-arid and arid western USA, a period of channel cutting in about 1880 is widely recognized (Emmett 1974), but the explanation is in dispute even though it falls within a reasonably well documented period. The first 10–12 years of the Vigil study were enough to show that arroyo cutting in many parts of the region had given way to aggradation. In one of the channels (Last Day Gully, near Hudson, Wyoming) the survey showed that the main sediment source was hillslope erosion rather than headward incision, and that a third of the material supplied was trapped in the channels. At the measured rate, the channels would fill to the level of the old valley floor in 200–700 yr.

The longest precipitation record in the USA, running since 1849, is for Santa Fe (New Mexico), and it shows no definite cyclicity for precipitation; but nor is the area affected by overgrazing as extensive as in the areas affected by the contentious cut-and-fill sequence. Acting on the suggestion that the critical factor was the intensity rather than the total amount of rainfall (Bailey 1935, Leopold 1951), the average annual intensity was computed. There was a significant decrease in the average intensity of precipitation for 1880–1940; the change to aggradation coincided with a return to the rainfall intensities that had prevailed before 1800. This surprising association – one would expect intense rainfall to produce erosive flash floods – needs to be investigated at other sites, but the preliminary results already demonstrate the advantage of possessing both alluvial and rainfall sequences long enough for trends and their reversal to emerge.

Elsewhere (and for many workers in the southwestern USA too) the extent to which widespread gullying is the product of human activity has remained an unresolved question. In the upper San Pedro River in Arizona, pre-entrenchment alluvium (1450–1900) was laid down by a sluggish low-energy river. Incision, which amounted to 1–10 m and took place between 1890 and 1908, was initiated by a series of large floods and perhaps also by a high-intensity earthquake that fissured the inner valley and disrupted the water table. Channel widening ensued until about 1955 (Hereford 1993), when peak flood discharge decreased, partly as a result of floodplain development and increased channel sinuosity, partly through an increase in the frequency of low-intensity rainfall during the wet season, and partly through improved land-use practices.

Besides the complex interplay of human and climatic factors, there is generally a contribution from the drainage system itself, for it has been shown that channels that steepen beyond a threshold gradient may be prone to cycles of incision and filling in the absence of external triggers (Patton & Schumm 1975). Even so, the contribution made by each major control needs to be understood if the process is to be managed successfully.

**Figure 9.3**  Sands (above pen) deposited by the River Arno during the 1966 Florence floods. Cultivation soon obscured the contact between the old and new deposits.

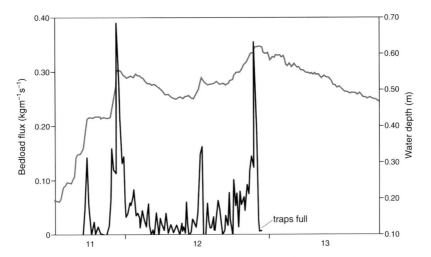

**Figure 9.4** Water depth in the River Tordera (upper curve) and bedload flux averaged over 15 minute intervals during 11–13 November 1996, showing pronounced variability during individual flow events (after Garcia et al. 2000, by permission of Elsevier Science).

Bedload remains the most difficult item to monitor, not least because of the effects on flow produced by the bedload sampler. Portable devices are effective in rivers with sand or fine gravel beds, but by their nature they operate for limited periods at a single location (Fig. 9.4). Various gravel-bed devices have been developed, but continuous monitoring is in progress in only 15 rivers in the world (Garcia et al. 2000). Longer-term averages can be obtained with the help of bomb-derived [137]Cs, and thus only for the period since bomb tests in the early 1950s, or using the [210]Pb inventory, which combines atmospheric fallout with an excess contributed by the transported sediment (Walling & He 1999).

These studies, which generally refer to a limited area and are labour intensive, are increasingly supplemented by repeated imaging from aerial or satellite platforms (Fig. 9.5), which permits close monitoring of river shifts in plan view, while radar interferometry and backscatter data are beginning to be used for the assessment of scour and deposition. Landsat Thematic Mapper (TM) images were available before, during and after the Missouri River floods of 1993, when the river experienced the largest recorded floods in terms of stage, daily discharge and total discharge. Shuttle imaging radar (SIR-C) imagery became available only after the flooding; it was complemented by a SPOT scene. Part of the SIR-C backscatter was found to be controlled by the density of large leafy plants that grew after the flooding, and their abundance was used to estimate the depth of accreted sand.

To determine the extent of erosion caused by the floods, elevations derived by interferometry acquired by the airborne topographical synthetic aperture radar (TOPSAR), with an estimated vertical error of 1–2 m, were subtracted from sections obtained by field survey, using EDM to calculate the total volume of sediment removed by erosion of levees and bottoms (Izenberg et al. 1996). Additional losses could be computed from

**Figure 9.5** Temporary flooding produced by expulsion of water from alluvium during Bhuj earthquake of 26 January 2001 ($M_W$ =6.1), imaged by NASA's multi-angle imaging spectro-radiometer (MISR) (courtesy of NASA).

the destruction of levees by comparing survey maps with TOPSAR data and assuming an average levee cross section and density.

The flood, no surprise, was caused by unusually wet conditions during the autumn and winter of 1992 and the spring and summer of 1993. The detailed mapping revealed the extent to which flood damage was influenced by the addition of artificial levees to the river. Before the channel was modified, the lower Missouri was a complex channel up to 2 km wide, which meandered within a vegetated floodplain 4–10 km in width; during the floods, there was slackwater deposition of fine sediment; high-energy flood-waters then scoured the natural levees and deposited sand and silt. By the 1930s the channel had been dredged and stabilized and the bottomlands exploited for agriculture. The 1993 floods mimicked the earlier pattern, but channel stabilization led to very large discharges, which enhanced erosion and deposition when breaks in the levees occurred.

A more recent application of radar interferometry to fluvial studies is for evaluating the distribution and volume of erosion and deposition during a flood event. The method was tested on a glacier outburst flood in Iceland in 4–7 November 1996 using data from ERS-1 and ERS-2 secured before and after the flood. The two novel procedures were co-registration of backscatter-intensity images to detect changes in morphology and the mapping of interferometric phase correlation in order to identify which surfaces had been modified (Smith et al. 2000).

Net deposition of sediment along the ice margin, compared with net erosion in channels down stream, showed an excess of $13 \times 10^6 \, \mathrm{m}^3$, in agreement with field observations. More to the point, as the original scattering surface is destroyed by fluvial erosion and deposition, correlation is lost and the analysis has to be based on the comparison of DEMs constructed independently. In consequence, the changes that can be detected at present are much coarser than for ice flow or tectonic movements; in this particular example 4 m of elevation change was required for satisfactory results (hence the suggestion that InSAR should be supplemented by laser altimetry); but, in compensation, spatial resolution was 20 m and coverage about $100 \times 100 \, \mathrm{km}$.

The products of satellite imaging feed directly into the concerns of the Vigil operators. In analyzing the effects of flow it is desirable to establish synchronous change, for example the slope of the water surface at a particular moment or the association between incision in the headwaters and deposition down stream. Gauging stations and geological sections cannot provide this information, although they can supply detailed accounts of events at a station. During the 1993 floods of the upper Mississippi, ERS-1 mapping, calibrated with the help of detailed topographical maps, presented an instantaneous flood map for more than 100 km of channel (Brakenridge et al. 1994). It revealed that flood stages were 1.2–2.4 m higher on the western side of the valley than on the east, possibly in response to the entry of the Des Moines River, which is leading to vigorous lateral flow and enhanced deposition on the western side of the valley. The radar data were supplemented by Landsat TM images showing, among other things, plumes of sediment-rich water leaving breaches in levees.

Satellite imaging of exceptional floods holds special interest for planetary scientists because it makes possible the direct recording of the type of cataclysmic floods postulated for some Martian channels. Lake Bonneville released a peak flow of $9 \times 10^5 \, \mathrm{m}^3 \, \mathrm{s}^{-1}$ 14 500 yr ago and Lake Missoula one of $10^7 \, \mathrm{m}^3 \, \mathrm{s}^{-1}$ 17 000–12 000 yr ago; in 1953, the largest known modern flood on the Amazon released $3.85 \times 10^5 \, \mathrm{m}^3 \, \mathrm{s}^{-1}$ (Baker 1994). The peak Missoula flows exceeded by an order of magnitude the average global discharge of all rivers flowing to the sea. The history of exceptionally large palaeofloods is only now being written, and in the southwestern USA it is beginning to reveal intriguing century-scale periodicities.

There is scope for short-term lake studies similar to those carried out during major river floods. A start has been made with playa sedimentation in the Chott el Djerid of Tunisia, using ERS-1 images in order to trace evaporite sedimentation, aeolian processes and channel flow (Wadge et al. 1994). In the absence of image-distorting relief, C-band radar backscatter is sensitive to changes in roughness at the millimetre scale following the growth of crystals of halite and gypsum.

# Mass movement

Remote sensing presents similar advantages for mapping and measuring landslides and mudflows, and it may lead to insights denied to the most perceptive fieldworker. In southern Italy, for example, minor tremors trigger countless slides, the potential instability of which would probably have eluded detection. At the very least the imaging will reveal the timing and extent of mass movement throughout the area.

Analysis of one of the worst engineering disasters of the present century benefits retrospectively from this approach. On 9 October 1963 the Vaiont arch dam, 100 km north of Venice in northern Italy, was overtopped by a flood that went on to sweep away the village of Longarone on the opposite bank of the River Piave (Fig. 9.6). The immediate cause was a landslide, which dropped some $27 \times 10^7 \, m^3$ of material into the dam reservoir. The trigger is uncertain (Semenza & Ghirotti 1998): heavy rain had doubtless waterlogged the slide, and its instability was increased when preliminary sliding was followed by precautionary lowering of the reservoir level.

The established view is that the 1960 slide represented reactivation of an earlier landslide and that it was triggered by heavy rainfall and oscillations in reservoir level. The slide surface is more probably a fault plane. Mylonite, cataclastite and cemented breccia displaying features "considered characteristic of tectonic faulting", as well as striated rock surfaces, have been observed at the slide surface (Hendron & Patton 1985, Semenza & Ghirotti 1998). An uncemented mylonitic zone associated with cataclastites has been traced for 1 km along the Vaiont Valley. The limestone of the slide surface displays many of the large-scale features found on normal faults. Aerial photographs show that alignment of the incised gorge above the dam, which could have resulted from erosion of a narrow fault zone, accords with the regional fault pattern (B. Braghin in Mantovani & Vita-Finzi 2003), as indicated by analysis of aerial photographs, in which north–south and east–west lineaments predominate.

The fault surface would have provided a steep, relatively impermeable plane on which the sodden fault gouge and other debris-slope deposits could readily slide, particularly if pore-water pressure was abnormally high. The proposal raises the possibility that seismicity was a contributory factor. Friuli is undoubtedly one of the most seismically active regions in Italy. The local instrumental record is inconclusive, but there were reports of several events in the vicinity culminating in a series of substantial shocks on 2 September 1963 (Merlin 1997). The tremors have been ascribed by sceptics to the slide itself, but the timing suggests that they preceded it. The dispute between landslide and fault would seem academic, but its outcome bears on a host of issues, including responsibility for the disaster in respect of the dam site and the events of 1963.

Mass-movement sequences are difficult to disaggregate, yet they may reveal a significant periodicity that reinforces this kind of critical connection with climatic or seismic events. With river management in mind, a study was made of late Holocene debris flows in Prospect Canyon, a whitewater reach on the Colorado, using cosmogenic $^3$He and $^{14}$C and repeat photography (Cerling et al. 1999). The debris fans are poor in organic material and archaeological remains, and the investigators combined soil morphology with cosmogenic and radiometric dating to establish a depositional sequence.

**Figure 9.6**  The Vaiont dam; note the incised river channel beneath (courtesy Prof. F. Mantovani).

The photographic record suggests that debris flows in most of the Grand Canyon tributaries have a recurrence of 10–50 yr. The basalt clasts contain olivine phenocrysts, which are efficient traps for cosmogenic $^3$He. The assumed rate of production of $^3$He for this latitude could not be corrected for secular variation or the strength of the Earth's magnetic field, doubtless a refinement that will shortly be possible. Radiocarbon dating

141

was applied to plant remains within debris-flow levees, and the age of the fan surface could be estimated from the vegetation with an uncertainty of ±20 per cent.

Cosmogenic ³He ages of about 3000 yr were determined for boulders exposed on the surface of the highest and oldest deposit, which blocked the Colorado and now has an escarpment 25 m above the river. Eleven later flows were mapped, of which at least one also blocked the Colorado. The oldest event may reflect the production of abundant talus after reactivation of the nearby Toiroweap Fault and followed by unusually large winter floods (Cerling et al. 1999). The remaining ages suggest, not surprisingly, that small flows are relatively frequent, with recurrence intervals of 15–60 yr, and that the rest have recurrence intervals of 200–2000 yr. This result may be compared with the value of 20–200 yr proposed in an earlier study based on six twentieth-century flows and one 500 yr-old event: the contrast is one with which seismologists are familiar, as it shows how large events are often under-represented in the instrumental record and how the inclusion of one such event within recent decades could overemphasize their long-term significance.

Another source of bulk shortlived deposition (Fig. 9.7) that has often to be re-created from circumstantial historical or proxy evidence is explosive volcanism (Briffa et al. 1998, de Silva & Zielinski 1998). Modelling that takes into consideration the height

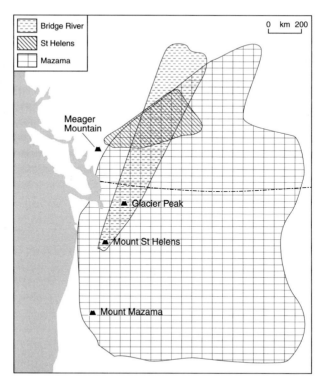

**Figure 9.7** Depositional plumes of three Holocene volcanic ash units in the Canadian Rockies (after King 1995, by permission of Elsevier Science).

attained by the eruption plume and its composition may be obtained by photogrammetric analysis of Landsat imagery. The Geostationery Operational Environmental Satellite (GOES) weather satellite, which operates at 35 800 km and can function day and night, captured an image 13 minutes after the start of the eruption of Mount St Helens on 18 May 1980, and went on taking thermal infrared (IR) and visible images every 30 minutes (Holasek & Self 1995). The elevation of the eruption plume, with a maximum of $31 \pm 2$ km, could be derived from its shadow on GOES imagery. Radar measurements were sometimes lower, perhaps because the technique is relatively insensitive to diffuse portions of the plume.

The resulting account is rich in detail that would have been difficult to obtain in any other way. The initial plumes were probably the product of an instantaneous event, but the rest of the sequence indicated a maintained column, so that plume altitudes could be converted (by reference to equations governing eruption dynamics) to the volume of dense-rock equivalent to the erupted tephra, the result being a total of 0.2 km$^3$. Injection of ash and gas into the middle stratosphere occurred only for 0.5–1 h early in the eruption and briefly late in the eruption. The average downwind velocity was 29 m s$^{-1}$, consistent with a position near the tropopause, where the maximum wind velocities of 28–36 m s$^{-1}$ are encountered. Satellite data for the visible wavelengths showed changes in the nature of the eruption between darker and lighter tones, possibly according to the proportion of fine ash with high reflectance. The former are associated with the violent eruptive style known as Plinian, the finer ashes with entrainment by gas with slow initial velocities. It would seem that the eruption had relatively little impact on the atmosphere (Holasek & Self 1995), partly because the magma that fed it was low in sulphur and partly perhaps because the plume tops remained mainly within the lower stratosphere.

In Sicily, Etna erupted in July 1995 after two years of quiescence, with Strombolian and hydromagmatic activity in the Bocca Nuova and the Northeast Crater, and then varied activity at all of the four summit craters. It produced an eruption column 10 km high. Figure 7.2, from the multi-angle imaging spectro-radiometer on NASA's Terra spacecraft, dates from 22 July 2001. It revealed that there were in fact two plumes, one composed primarily of ash and another of fine droplets of water and dilute sulphuric acid. Etna also expelled water vapour, $SO_2$, $CO_2$ and other gases. Close monitoring of the eruption was thus of benefit not only to local emergency services but also to scientists engaged in assessing the contribution of volcanoes to pollution and climatic change.

Although hazardous and often fortuitous, the direct observation of volcanic eruptions has been practised for over two millennia; submarine mass movement has long eluded it. The Grand Banks earthquake of 18 November 1929, south of Newfoundland, was suspected of triggering a turbidity current because telephone cables continued to rupture as much as 13 hours after the event (Heezen & Ewing 1952). The current flowed for 4–11 h and reached velocities of at least 19 m s$^{-1}$; the volume of sediment transported was more than 150 km$^3$. The slump deposits were first investigated directly by SEAMARC sonar in 1985; in 1999 the site was revisited with the Système Acoustique Remorqué (SAR) high-resolution sidescan and sub-bottom profiler (Piper et al. 1999). Some ground truth was available from submersible dives. The key finding was that the

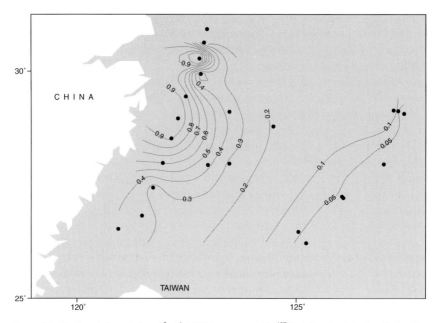

**Figure 9.8** Sedimentation rate (g cm$^{-2}$ yr$^{-1}$) off China measured by $^{137}$Cs dating; the dots show the location of sediment cores (after Huh & Su 1999, by permission of Elsevier Science).

turbidity current was not the product of a single catastrophic slide or liquefaction event: it was triggered by several relatively minor features. Rotational slumps on local steep areas thus gave rise down slope to debris flows that evolved into turbidity currents.

Measurement of light scattering and sediment fluxes makes it possible to observe earthquake-induced sediment transport in progress (Thunell et al. 1999). On 9 July 1997 an earthquake of M = 6.8 occurred on the coast of northern Venezuela. The scattering data indicate that 145 000 tonnes of sediment were transported into the Cariaco basin; the sediment-trap measurements show that the result was a turbidite 2–3 mm thick. $^{210}$Pb dating of the basin deposits suggests that a M = 8.4 earthquake in 1900, west of the 1997 event and thus closer to the basin, left a deposit 3 cm thick near the sampling location, and one in 1929 (M = 6) deposited a turbidite 7 cm thick. To judge from the sediment record of the basin, however, the microturbidites deposited by the 1997 earthquake are more typical of local earthquake deposits (between 1900 and 1997 there were 92 earthquakes of M = 5.0 in the region). The exact contribution of turbidites to the sediment budget is not yet known, but the available evidence reveals the importance of what have been called moderate catastrophes. $^{137}$Cs (and $^{210}$Pb and other isotopes) are being employed to equal effect in tracing sedimentation in the East China Sea (Fig. 9.8) and thus in discovering how effectively deposits brought in by the Yangtze are being dispersed by currents and tides.

# Surfaces

Estimating the age of recent surfaces cut or eroded in solid rock remains much more problematic as, unlike river or lake sediments, the rock is unlikely to contain datable material that is little older than the surface under review. Subjective assessments of freshness, later supplemented by light microscopy and scanning-electron microscopy, have provided comparative measures of exposure history, but their validity is difficult to establish.

The high hopes entertained for dating desert (or rock) varnish appear to have been misplaced. This black and dark-red rock coating consists mainly of iron and manganese oxides, together with clay minerals and small amounts of organic material mostly of airborne origin. Initially, the only age criterion was relative darkness, which permitted some ordering of pictographs of different age if cut in the same rock unit. In the Tibesti Mountains of the Sahara, for example, there is clearly a progression in darkening from prehistoric to recent times (Fig. 9.9). An elaboration of this method was possible if fragments of one of the generations of pictograph were recovered from a dated stratigraphic sequence, as the date could be provisionally extended to all material similar in style.

An alternative approach to rock-varnish dating exploits differences in the rate at which minor elements are leached out of the varnish, and is usually expressed as the $K^+ + Ca^{2+}/Ti^{4+}$ ratio method on the grounds that this increases after the varnished surfaces are stabilized (Dorn et al. 1986). Rocks of known age have been used to calibrate cation-leaching curves for various areas of study, as the results are influenced by climate as well as dust composition and the rate at which the dust is deposited. By 1994 the method had been invalidated by inconsistent results.

AMS $^{14}C$ dating of organic material at the base of the varnish has also proved controversial, not least because the provenance of the carbon was not always established unambiguously (Watchman 2000). Any remaining hopes for varnish (and patina) dating rest with rigorous sampling and in refined techniques exploiting U-series, cosmogenic isotopes and luminescence methods.

Systematic analysis based on radiometrically dated surfaces from the western USA suggests that varnish rarely exceeds a thickness of 200 μm and that the rate of accumulation varies widely, even at the same exposure (Liu & Broecker 2000). Although a patchy varnish takes 3000–5000 yr to form and a heavy coat of varnish takes 10 000 yr, short-term rates range from < 1 to 40 μm per 1000 yr. On the other hand, the presence in desert varnish of lead from vehicle exhausts, zinc from smelters and $^{137}Cs$ from nuclear bomb tests, supported by $^{7}Be$ and $^{210}Pb$ measurements (Broecker & Liu 2001), shows that it is still forming today.

Thermal infrared spectroscopy, an important tool in mapping desert varnish from space, requires initial laboratory measurement for calibrating the emissivity of natural surfaces. The problem of interpreting the signal is compounded by layering. The checkerboard approach is to model a mixed signal from the substrate and the varnish; another is to model transmission through a medium (the varnish). In one set of experiments on varnishes composed mainly of clay materials, the spectral effect of varnish was found to increase linearly with its thickness (Christensen & Harrison 1993). Moreover, the composition of the substrate could be determined from desert varnish that was as much as 4–50 μm thick, and varnish composition could be determined if the nature of the substrate was already known. The survival of varnish may be promoted by salt weathering in the sea-spray zone and by fire, as well as by weathering under sediment (Dragovich 1994). Again, the variable chemistry of superimposed varnishes, say with different proportions of Si, Al, Mn and Fe, or the absence of one of them (Dragovich 1994), may indicate a fluctuating environment.

Yet, strangely enough, weathering was perhaps the earliest geomorphological process whose progress was quantified. Worn inscriptions and monuments provided a convenient maximum age for cumulative decay. Archibald Geikie (1880) reported that marble inscriptions in Edinburgh were faint after 15 yr and completely illegible after 80 yr, and in 1883 a similar state of affairs was reported in Manhattan, in contrast with the good preservation to be found in the unpolluted suburbs (Meierding 1993). The quantification of rock-surface recession rates has become increasingly refined to

**Figure 9.9** Varying thickness of desert varnish in pictographs of different age in sandstones of the Tibesti Mountains, Chad.

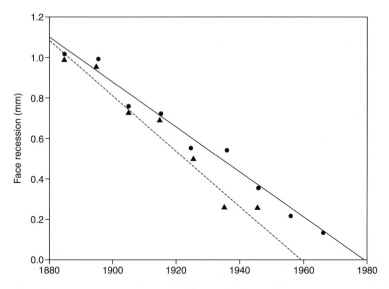

**Figure 9.10** Surface recession rates of horizontal Vermont marble plaques in Virginia and Rhode Island (USA) determined from inscription legibility (after Meierding 1993, by permission of Elsevier Science).

include such matters as reconstruction of the original lettering, analysis of the rock type, and assessment of the degree of degradation (Emery 1941). Close-range photogrammetry, laser profiling, and micro-erosion meters have proved their worth in experimental weathering studies (Inkpen et al. 2000, Williams et al. 2000) and will doubtless permit field monitoring of natural surfaces as well as of worked building stone.

The results are sometimes surprising and they confirm the need for direct measurement. For instance, recession rates for horizontal marble surfaces in Richmond (Virginia) and Providence (Rhode Island) appear to have remained steady since 1880, despite a suspected increase in acid precipitation in recent decades (Fig. 9.10; Meierding 1993). Experimental studies of weathering (Yerrapragada et al. 1994) showed that, in marble protected from rain, the reaction product calcium sulphate exceeded calcium nitrate even when atmospheric $NO_2$ exceeded $SO_2$.

The range and precision of ages obtained by cosmogenic isotopes still rule out the technique for short-term monitoring of rock decay. This is not to deny that it already yields limiting values that can date important events and provide useful mean rates. Meteorite craters are inviting subjects for this kind of analysis because conventional stratigraphic methods generally provide only maximum ages for the impact itself. The first estimate for Meteor Crater in 1932 placed it between two Pleistocene glaciations in the Sierra Nevada. In 1974 the impact was dated to a period of high water table (Nishiizumi et al. 1991), and the oldest talus within the crater was ascribed to the mid-Wisconsin stage, say 55 000–25 000 yr BP. The associated meteorite of El Diablo is an iron meteorite characterized by low $^{14}C$ production; in 1964, gastropod shells from an unspecified depth in lake beds in the crater gave a $^{14}C$ age of $24\,000 \pm 2000$ yr. $^{59}Ni$ dating was first attempted in 1963; in 1985 it gave an age of $< 2.5 \times 10^5$ yr. A $^{36}Cl$ exposure

age for large blocks of dolomite on the rim of the crater obtained in 1991 was
49 200±700 yr. In 1985, thermoluminescence dating of shocked quartz from breccia on
the crater floor gave 49 000±3000 yr for the impact. *In situ* cosmogenic [10]Be and [26]Al
were assayed in 1991 on rocks more than 10 m below the surface before the impact and
were therefore shielded from cosmic-ray production. After correcting for altitude,
latitude and exposure geometry, exposure ages were calculated using production rates
at sea level for [10]Be. The age for the upper surface of large ejecta blocks, which were
exposed after erosion had removed the fallout layer from the crater rim, agrees with the
thermoluminescence age and with several [36]Cl exposure ages (Nishiizumi et al. 1991),
and suggests that 49 000 yr is a good approximation to the age of the crater.

Equally encouraging results have been obtained with [36]Cl dating of faulted bedrock
scarps, which in turn bear on the age of prehistoric earthquakes. The Hegben Lake Fault
in Montana displays a series of surfaces, including those resulting from an earthquake
of $M_S = 7.5$ in 1959. The averaged [36]Cl ages for the successive scarps were statistically
different at the 1 s.d. level; the youngest age, corresponding to the 1959 event, was
400 yr (Zreda & Noller 1998). The needs of seismology and planetary science have
ensured that topographical age, a key issue if not the central issue in geomorphology,
should at long last begin to yield to direct measurement.

CHAPTER 10
# The imprint of life

*[If we] consider that larger portion which is assigned to the aquatic tribes,*
*we discover the great influence of the living creation, in imparting varieties*
*of conformation to the solid exterior which the agency of inanimate causes*
*alone could not produce.*
Charles Lyell, *Principles of geology*

The profound contribution of life to the Earth's atmosphere and, through its $O_2$ and $CO_2$, to weathering and tectonic processes is now generally recognized (Nisbet 1987). The agency of "the living creation" in modifying the solid exterior is likewise given much more prominence than a century ago, on land as well as beneath the sea. Yet its quantification is still hampered not only by inaccessibility in time and location but also by problems of definition, witness the distinction still made, despite the blossoming field of biomineralization, between the inorganic and organic constituents of a mollusc shell.

The destructive impact of living things has been highlighted by human depredation of the land and of the bacterial, animal and plant worlds, but constructive effects may well dominate the biological signature as a whole, to judge from the vast volumes of limestone and the thick organic oozes that fill the ocean deeps. The influence of biological changes in atmospheric composition on the tempo and character of surface processes of erosion and deposition is often starkly noxious; the effect of those changes on the Earth's dynamics, although at present trivial, can no longer be dismissed as purely conjectural.

## Organic stirring

In 1838 Josiah Wedgwood demonstrated to Charles Darwin the effectiveness of earthworms in changing the texture and stratigraphy of soils. In his book on the subject, Darwin (1881) showed that this activity was capable of bringing to the surface as much as $50\,t\,ha^{-1}\,yr^{-1}$, equivalent to a thickness of 5 mm. Most casting species of earthworm are active only in the top 10–20 cm of the soil, as shown among other things by assay of bomb-produced $^{14}C$, but the common earthworm *Lumbricus terrestris* can burrow down to 1.5–2 m. Termites too can bring soil up from depths of several metres (Lee 1985) and thus invert the soil profile rather than merely accentuate it.

A century later, the *Encyclopaedia Britannica* dismissed Darwin's conclusions about the activities of earthworms as "overpublicized". That seems both churlish and wrong. Darwin probably underestimated the outcome. Earthworms can double pore space and increase water penetration tenfold; as the carbon content of worm casts is up to twice that of the soil, and their nitrogen content up to 1.7 times greater, they enrich the surface soil by several grams per cubic metre of organic matter. If soil-profile development is much affected, so is soil erosion: Darwin detected downslope movement of worm casts at Holwood Park in England on slopes as gentle as 1–5°, and reported extensive erosion of worm casts in India during the monsoon. Reworking and the creation of voids may indeed promote soil erosion, but a high density of tube burrows, as well as microbial mucus-binding and enhanced organic content, can stabilize the host sediments. The chemical effects are equally complex (Gage & Tyler 1991). For instance, the accumulation of metals sensitive to reducing/oxidizing (redox) conditions, such as iron and manganese, is strongly influenced by biological activity in burrows.

Photography, observation from submersibles and various kinds of sampling have revealed similar effects on the sea floor at great depths. They include traces of movement, feeding and burrowing. The global distribution of bottom (benthic) biomass is evidently difficult to measure, as the data are uneven and consist of a few small grab samples, but an inverse association between biomass and depth for many animals is well attested. Mixing has been identified from disturbed stratification to depths of 40 cm in carbonate oozes dated by $^{210}$Pb and $^{14}$C (Fig. 10.1). Individual burrows at least 2 m deep have been observed by X-raying box cores (Gage & Tyler 1991).

For the geologist the most significant outcome of bioturbation is the blurring of stratigraphic boundaries. This is an important consideration in the search for high-resolution climatic sequences: the evidence supplied by marine and lake records cannot be wholly replaced by data from polar and glacial ice, which evidently bear mainly on atmospheric conditions at high latitudes and high altitudes.

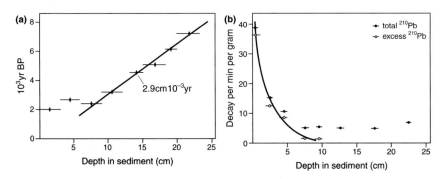

**Figure 10.1** Profiles in marine cores on Mid-Atlantic Ridge: **(a)** $^{14}$C ages and depth showing mixing in top 8 cm and deposition rate of 2.9 cm per thousand years below that; **(b)** excess $^{210}$Pb (after Gage & Tyler 1991, by permission of Cambridge University Press).

# Bioerosion

If human activity is included in the tally, bioerosion is locally dominated by quarrying and accelerated soil erosion. In tracing the sources of erosion, the Earth scientist has often turned to archaeology for insights and information on chronology and land use. Trimble (1999) has demonstrated the power of conventional methods of field archaeology, complemented by direct measurement, in the interpretation of erosional sequences. His area of study, a drainage basin in Wisconsin measuring $360 \, km^2$, was instrumented during the Dust Bowl of the 1930s. With the help of S. C. Happ, who had done some of the original work and co-authored an influential text on man-induced soil erosion (Happ et al. 1940), Trimble located 92 of the 150 original measured sections; he also excavated old roads, railroad tracks and buildings, so that his study is based on 140 yr of data. Contrary to widespread belief, erosion during 1975–93 had declined, at any rate in Wisconsin, to 6 per cent of its 1930s level, possibly through the practice of retaining stubble to reduce runoff and the abandonment of the mouldboard plough. Climate cannot be credited with the change, as the period 1975–93 was wetter than average and included many large storms; flood peaks were reduced by improved land management. On the other hand, net sediment yield changed little in consequence: the upper tributaries became sediment sinks, but the lower main valley was subject to a drastically reduced rate of vertical accretion and, surprisingly, to erosion along river banks that had been reafforested.

The value of chronology for weighing up competing interpretations is also illustrated by an aerial photograph (Fig. 10.2) showing a part of northwest Libya (Tripolitania) that was already seriously gullied by the 1950s. North Africa is often held up as the archetypal victim of widespread soil erosion caused by misguided land use. The photograph, taken in 1953, includes information on both the progress and the probable causes of gullying. It shows a series of north-flowing wadis, which, as the stereoscope soon reveals, are cut into an apron of alluvium sloping from horizontally bedded limestone hills in the south to a series of coastal dunes in the north. The wadis show evidence of cut and fill (e.g. at A); the main channels contain the remains of Roman dams. Gullies cut through field boundaries (G) that date from the period of Italian colonization (1911–40) and also attack land around animal enclosures in the hills (E). Taken in isolation the gullies would justifiably be seen as the product of clean tilling and overgrazing, but the depositional record (Leopold & Vita-Finzi 1998) shows that erosion has been the rule for at least 6000 yr and that recent gullying has simply accentuated an existing trend.

The destruction of coral reefs is another issue to have benefited from advances in chronology. Grazing and boring by marine organisms lead to direct destruction of coral reefs and other limestones; the value of the resulting notches and undercuts as sea-level indicators is enhanced if the ecology of the process is well understood.

In the tropics and subtropics, intertidal limestones are riddled by perforations made by filamentous, mainly blue-green, algae or cyanobacteria. Gastropods graze on the algae and sometimes bring away fragments of rock. Erosion of beachrock in Barbados by the gastropods *Cittarium pica*, *Littorina meleagris*, *L. ziczac*, *Nodolittorina tuberculata*, *Nerita tesselata* and *N. versicolor* has been assessed both directly and by

**Figure 10.2** Stereo pair of northwest Libya showing gully systems of different ages.

analyzing fæcal pellets, which were found to consist of carbonate to over 80 per cent by weight. Granted that the amount of wear produced by grazing will vary a good deal depending on such items as rock hardness, the depth to which the algae have penetrated into the rock, the size of the individual mollusc and so forth, *C. pica* emerged as the most effective species ($2.4\,\mathrm{g\,yr^{-1}}$ per individual) followed by *N. versicolor* ($1.4\,\mathrm{g\,yr^{-1}}$) and *N. tuberculata* ($1.2\,\mathrm{g\,yr^{-1}}$). On a stretch of intertidal beachrock, a population of *N. tesselata* abraded away 154 g of rock within a 1 m$^2$ quadrat in a single year (McLean 1967). On the chalk coast of southeast England (Andrews & Williams 2000), the limpet *Patella vulgata* contributes to the surface lowering on shore platforms by an average of $0.15\,\mathrm{mm\,yr^{-1}}$, with a peak of to $0.5\,\mathrm{mm\,yr^{-1}}$ or 35 per cent of the total.

In the Florida area, chitons (e.g. *Chiton tuberculatus*) may lower the coral rubble on which they graze by $0.18\,\mathrm{mm\,yr^{-1}}$. Clionid sponges (e.g. *Cliona lampa*) in Bermuda can erode $22$–$26\,\mathrm{kg\,m^{-2}}$ of calcarenite per annum (Gage & Tyler 1991) and penetrate 12 cm into coral colonies. Associated amœbocytes etch coral by means of enzymes; the cut material may make up 30–40 per cent of the fine silt on Caribbean and Pacific reefs. Polychaete and sipunculan worms penetrate up to 10 cm into coral skeletons through holes drilled by both mechanical and chemical means. Crustacea, including barnacles, shrimp and hermit crabs, bore and erode reef rock (Glynn 1996).

Bacteria and fungi penetrate coral, shells and barnacles, and thus weaken these materials. The cyanobacteria may etch the surface of limestone crystals and digest the organic matrix of coral to water depths of 75 m. Fungi penetrate into coral skeletons by dissolution. A two-year experimental study at Moorea Island (French Polynesia) included inspection under the scanning electron microscope of internal casts taken of the borings, and computerized image analysis of the borings to estimate the volume of material bored (Chazottes et al. 1995). After two months, during which cyanobacteria and other microborers were the only agents present, macroborers became prominent and their contribution to destruction increased rapidly, but the dominant agents of erosion (89%) were the grazers (Table 10.1).

Experimental studies of bioerosion confirm the high rates inferred in the above studies. Blocks of *Porites lobata* coral and of compact limestone were left in the reefs of the Galápagos Islands at depths of 5–6 m and 11–13 m for 14.8 months (Reaka-Kudla et al. 1996) The contrast was dramatic. General reduction in height was $2\,\mathrm{mm\,yr^{-1}}$ in the limestone compared with $23\,\mathrm{mm\,yr^{-1}}$ in the coral. The former lost 0.7 per cent of its volume in a year to internal bioeroders and 3.9 per cent to external bioeroders, compared with 0.6 per cent and 59.9 per cent respectively for the coral. Indeed, in this particular instance there are fears that the reefs could soon be wiped out by bioerosion.

In the limestones and dolomites of the Musandam Peninsula of Oman (Fig. 5.3), active boring by molluscs, and to a lesser extent grazing by chitons and sponges, contribute to the development of undercuts into the cliffs as much as 5 m deep. The rock is riddled with the burrows of *Lithophaga cumingiana* and *L. obesa* and is therefore easily eroded by wave action. Periodically, the undercut cliff collapses and the process starts afresh (Fig. 10.3). A jetty constructed of local limestone in 1942–3 had been undercut 7.5 cm by 1970, equivalent to $2.5\,\mathrm{mm\,yr^{-1}}$; individual *Lithophaga* burrows in the dolomite appear to have formed at an average rate of $9\,\mathrm{mm\,yr^{-1}}$ (Vita-Finzi & Cornelius

**Figure 10.3** Intertidal notches eroded into dolomite weakened by the burrows of the date-stone mollusc, *Lithophaga cumingiana*, and rimmed by oyster beds (Musandam, Oman).

**Table 10.1**  Rates of bioerosion into limestone (after Glynn 1996).

| Taxonomic group | Max. erosion rate ($g\,m^{-2}\,yr^{-1}$) | Habitat | Locality |
|---|---|---|---|
| *Internal borers* | | | |
| Cyanobacteria | 35 | Lagoon floor | Great Barrier Reef |
| *Porifera* (e.g. clionid sponges) | 23 000 | Subtidal limestone | Bermuda |
| Polychaeta | 1800 | Lagoonal patch reef | Great Barrier Reef |
| Crustaceans | 14 | Fringing reef | Barbados |
| *Sipuncula* | 8 | Fringing reef | Barbados |
| Molluscs (*Lithophaga* spp.) | 9000 | Patch reef | Costa Rica |
| *External grazers* | | | |
| Crustaceans (hermit crabs) | 103 | Patch reef | Panama |
| Molluscs: chitons | 394 | Intertidal coral rubble | Puerto Rico |
| Gastropods | 154 | Intertidal limestone | Bahamas |
| Sea urchins | 22 300 | Reef flat | Galápagos |
| Fish (e.g. parrotfish) | 9000 | Reef flat, slope, lagoon | Marianas |

\* Only the highest erosion rate reported for each taxonomic group is given here.

1973). On the exposed Pacific coast of North America, infestation by the rock-boring clam *Penitella penita* results in an average rate of erosion of $12\,mm\,yr^{-1}$ (Evans 1968).

Borings by subtidal organisms including *Lithophaga* are excellent sea-level indicators in regions with a small tidal range such as the Mediterranean, but they provide only a minimum value for the extent of subsequent emergence if the borers were capable of living at a wide range of depths. Thus, the habitat of *L. laevigata* is at a depth of 6–10 m (Glynn 1996); in the Mediterranean the lower limit of the range occupied by

*L. lithophaga* is not certain, but the upper limit is low tide. Despite some uncertainty over habitat, it is then possible to distinguish between gradual and sudden (possibly coseismic) emergence. In the Corinth area of Greece, the presence of a notch associated with a narrow band of borings suggests that emergence was rapid enough to bring that section out of reach of biological attack (Stewart & Vita-Finzi 1996), so that [14]C dating of dead *Lithophaga* still within their burrows (by AMS, since individual shells total 1–2 g at most) has been used to reconstruct a series of coseismic uplift events.

Even if the reef platform or flat is not diagnostic of a particular depth, it may include an organism with the kind of intolerance that is helpful in shoreline analysis. Many giant clams (notably *Tridacna*) harbour symbiotic algae (zooxanthellae) in their mantle, which, as with hermatypic or reef-building corals, supply organic products to the host and promote $CaCO_3$ synthesis. As these algae are photosynthetic, the clams are largely confined to the zone penetrated by sunlight. The clams themselves dig into the reef or are walled in by fresh coral; their anatomy departs from the molluscan scheme to make it possible for the mantle to face the light. Unlike ages on most corals or molluscs, which may have wide depth tolerance or be easily carried away from their original growth position, those on *Tridacna* thus bear on a clearly specified location within 4 m or so of the former water surface. *Tridacna* have the additional virtue of producing compact shells of cross-lamellar aragonite, which are resistant to contamination.

In West Timor, Indonesia (Fig. 10.4), the evidence of marine microfossils suggests that there was very rapid and substantial uplift in the early Pleistocene, consistent with the suggestion by Price & Audley Charles (1987; Vita-Finzi & Hidayat 1991) that the subducted portion of the Indo–Australia plate then broke away and triggered rapid although shortlived isostatic unflexing of the part of the plate that supports the island. [14]C ages on *Tridacna* show that, whereas oblique convergence between the Indian and Eurasian plates still leads to rapid although discontinuous emergence in the western part of the arc (see Ch. 8), on Timor the process had come to an end by about 12 000 yr ago.

## Construction

The two major constituents of limestone are dolomite $(CaMg(CO_3)_2)$ and calcite $(CaCO_3)$. Dolomite is derived from calcite and its unstable polymorph aragonite, both commonly deposited through the agency of organisms. Algae, including cyanobacteria, play a part in the formation of carbonate sediments, some by secreting $CaCO_3$ in the cell walls, some by reducing the acidity (increasing pH) around them through photosynthesis enough for inorganic carbonate deposition to occur (Thompson & Ferris 1990), and some by trapping sediment. For example, tufa or travertine was long thought to be an inorganic deposit laid down in springs by evaporation promoted by splashing, but the role of algae is now seen to be central to the process. Stromatolites, perhaps the oldest organic construct in the geological record, are subtidal domes produced by bacterial and algal colonies. Dolomites that are finely interbedded with limestones may have been derived from laminae rich in algae with a high Mg/Ca ratio (Holland 1984).

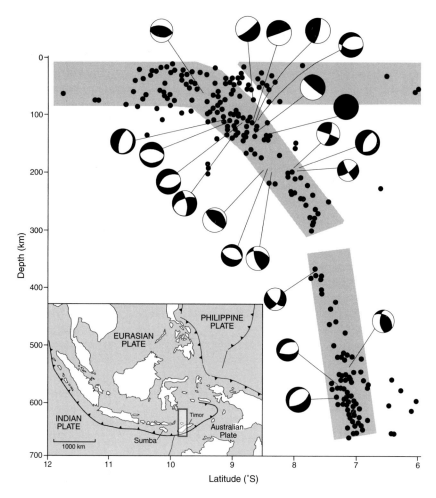

**Figure 10.4** Indo-Australian plate delineated by earthquakes (filled circles) subducted beneath Eurasian plate (rectangle in inset shows area sampled for seismicity). Proposed rupture in slab is obvious. Focal-plane solutions show no clear pattern, but extension seems to dominate in slab, suggesting it is sinking gravitationally both above and below the break.

Chalk is perhaps the most familiar sedimentary rock composed of limestone fragments, in this case predominantly individual foraminifera. The present-day accumulation rate for one of its modern counterparts in the Indian Ocean, *Globigerina* ooze, is 2.5–10 mm per 1000 yr (Ager 1973). Algal blooms measuring thousands of square kilometres sometimes develop at the mouths of major European rivers bringing nitrate fertilizer and sewage into the North Sea (Lovelock 1989). *Emiliana huxleyi*, a common algal constituent of such blooms, is covered by scales or coccoliths of calcite. When one of the blooms dies, the cells clump together and thus sink rapidly; if eaten by crustaceans, they are excreted as fæcal pellets, which also have the capacity to sink rapidly (within about a few weeks) to the sea floor. The coccoliths represent the largest carbonate sinks on Earth (Westbroek 1992).

On exposed coasts, the rock may be armoured by the calcifying activity of coralline algae (Fig. 10.5) and vermetid molluscs (Glynn 1996). At the other extreme in scale are biological edifices, notably coral reefs, which represent some of the most extensive lithological units in the record. Darwin (1842) was surprised at the speed with which coral had grown into a channel excavated a mere decade earlier to allow a schooner to be floated into the lagoon of Keeling Atoll in the Indian Ocean. Experiments reported in 1916 and 1924 suggest that, in favourable circumstances, *Acropora* at reef margins can grow towards the surface at up to $10\,cm\,yr^{-1}$, and *Porites* in lagoons at up to $5\,cm\,yr^{-1}$ (Shephard 1963), although the figures are probably inflated by the contribution of reef constituents other than coral.

Laser measurements of growth in the coral *Acropora grandis* Brooks showed that peak growth was at night, and especially just after sunset, when a rate of $35 \pm 1.75\,\mu m\,h^{-1}$ was measured over a period of 2–3 hours (Hind & Jagendorf 1963, Vago et al. 1997). This disposes of the view that, as in Tridacna, growth in coral is wholly governed by photosynthesis. Of course, marine organisms influence inorganic chemical processes by withdrawing $CaCO_3$ from the oceans or returning it. The acidity of inshore sea water, and hence its aggressiveness towards soluble rocks, may accordingly display a day/night cycle. In Florida Bay the mid-day pH value is reportedly 8.9 compared with 8.0 at night, that is to say almost a tenfold increase in acidity.

**Figure 10.5** Extent of coseismic emergence during the Alaska earthquake of 28 March 1964 (M = 8.4) in southwest Montague island, shown by intertidal algae killed by exposure (white area) when the Hanning Bay Fault (straight line) was reactivated. The fault scarp in the scene measures 3–4.5 m, but both sides of the fault were uplifted relative to sea level. (Courtesy of USGS.)

It is not easy to estimate the rate of accumulation of entire reefs from individual corals, not least because their constituent assemblages are diverse and the outcome is influenced by lithification, erosion and so forth. An alternative route is by $^{14}$C dating of reef sections deemed to be representative of the major accretionary axis. There is remarkable uniformity in the rates for the western Atlantic, with estimates ranging from 1200 to 8500 mm per $10^3$ yr. The figures are in line with the marine transgression of the past 7000–5000 yr (Glynn 1973). Rising sea level is clearly a stimulus to upward growth, witness the rates of 13 mm yr$^{-1}$ reported from the Huon Peninsula in Papua New Guinea at a time of rapid marine transgression 10 000–7000 yr ago (Chappell & Polach 1991). But submergence can promote destruction, especially if associated with an appropriate change in climate and circulation.

The siliceous counterpart to calcareous oozes has long been known to originate in large measure in diatoms, radiolaria and other mainly planktonic organisms. However, the quartz component of marine mudstone deposits is conventionally considered a product of the breakdown of continental crust and should therefore decrease in amount and particle size with increasing distance from the originating coast. Backscattered electron and cathodoluminescence imaging, and oxygen-isotopic analysis of mudstones from the late Devonian of the eastern USA (~370 Myr), suggest that the bulk of the silt was not detrital but had been derived from the dissolution of radiolaria and diatoms and then precipitated in pore spaces early in the diagenesis of the mudstone (Schieber et al. 2000). Here is a challenge to those engaged in monitoring present-day deposition.

# Organic clocks

Even if many other organic processes are only now beginning to yield useful rates, repetitive living processes have traditionally provided tools for tracing variations in global behaviour, and technical advances will merely enhance their precision and reliability.

Tree rings were first investigated in detail for what they could reveal about climatic conditions, especially in semi-arid areas. The classic studies by Douglass (1932) were especially geared to ring thickness as a measure of water availability in the southwestern USA and hence as a device for interpreting erosional and archaeological history. The phases of arroyo incision that punctuate the local alluvial record appeared to coincide with episodes of exceptional aridity, and the resulting falls in the water table, rather than the drought in itself, are sometimes thought to account for the abandonment of terraced fields by the Ananazi people of New Mexico.

Whatever the truth of this suggestion, the potential of dendrochronology for establishing the age of structures and deposits embodying tree remains was soon grasped, and the construction of chronologies from overlapping ring sequences soon became a primary task of tree-ring laboratories. Tree-ring dating has been applied in volcanology as well as in archaeology, as when eruptions were dated by reference to volcanic ashes from Sunset Crater in Arizona in prehistoric pit houses. An unusual application in climatology arose when the provenance of past ocean currents around the coasts of

Arctic Canada and Alaska was established by analyzing driftwood (Dean 1986).

Several important developments have greatly enhanced the role of dendrochronology. Comparison of ages obtained by tree-ring counts with the results of $^{14}$C assay of the ring material itself revealed serious discrepancies. This led to the realization that, as noted in Chapter 4, the $^{14}$C content of the atmospheric reservoirs had fluctuated during the period spanned by the longest tree-ring sequences and presumably before that. There was thus a need – and a means – for calibrating raw $^{14}$C ages. There was also a mechanism to be uncovered.

Bristlecone pine (*Pinus aristata*, now *longaeva*) made it possible to extend the comparison between tree-ring and $^{14}$C ages first to the past 4600 yr and then as far back as 6700 BC. By 1992, intercalibration between several laboratories made possible the correction of $^{14}$C to calendar ages as far back as 7980 BC (Becker 1992). Comparison with U/Th ages on coral should soon add a further 10 000 yr to the calibration. The discrepancies between the two curves bear on solar activity and geomagnetism, as we have seen. Teasing out these interwoven factors is profiting from deuterium ($^{2}$H) measurements on tree rings, and the comparison by visual inspection is of course backed by measurements using X-rays and densitometers, as well as statistical criteria.

At sea a further item that influences the validity of $^{14}$C dating is the apparent age of the sea water in which the dated organisms lived. The radiocarbon content of plants is in equilibrium with that of the atmosphere they inhabit; the fact that atmospheric $CO_2$ is mixed only with the surface few metres of the sea means that ocean water, and the organisms that draw their $CO_2$ or $CaCO_3$ from it, are deficient in modern carbon and thus appear falsely old. The requisite correction depends on location: off Iceland, for example, it is as much as 1000 yr.

Some workers apply an arbitrary value rather than devote an expensive analysis on modern sea water, because they reason that the apparent age at the time in question in any case may well have differed from what it is at the present day. If the hydrography of the area has changed little, if a modern value is available, and if the dated species lived within the well mixed surface layers, the correction is fully justified although always provisional. In the Gulf of Corinth, sea water gave an apparent age of 380 yr; when applied to a series of $^{14}$C ages on fossil *Lithophaga*, the correction increased the Holocene rate of uplift from 1.5 mm yr$^{-1}$ to 2.4 mm yr$^{-1}$ (Soter 1998).

Changes in $^{14}$C level in ocean water are of interest in their own right for the study of oceanic circulation, and the closest marine equivalent to tree rings is provided by banded hermatypic corals and, for recent decades, the calcareous bodies or otoliths found within the inner ear of fish (Kalish 1993). The effect of atmospherically detonated thermonuclear bombs in the 1950s and 1960s is clear in the plot of $^{14}$C against age of otolith calcification (Fig. 10.6).

Finally, the extent to which the $^{14}$C/$^{12}$C ratio (and thus the age) has been distorted by isotopic fractionation of atmospheric $CO_2$ by an organism can be estimated by measuring the stable isotopic $^{13}$C/$^{12}$C ratio (or $\delta^{13}$C) of the sample, preferably from a substantial number of individual members of the species in question to bring out the range of variability (Fig. 10.7). A value of $^{13}$C = –25‰ tends to be used as the standard for all organisms but 0‰ is preferable for marine organisms living distant from possible contamination by terrestrial waters; bulk measurement on a subsample of the material to be used for dating is likewise more representative than one on a fragment of shell taken at random, because an anomalously high or low seasonal growth band could dominate the result.

Growth bands in corals and molluscs nicely illustrate the geophysical potential of real-time geobiology. Calculations of the Earth's decelerating spin rate based on tidal friction alone had yielded estimates of 428 days for the length of the early Cambrian year and 399 for the mid-Devonian. In 1963, Wells showed that, in the outer portion of the hard coral skeleton, ridges appeared to represent daily growth increments and totalled 385–410 days (average: 400) for the Devonian year. He also obtained values of 380 days for Carboniferous corals and ~360 days for a modern specimen (Wells 1963). Scrutton (1965) then identified monthly bands in Middle Devonian corals, and obtained an average of 30.6 days for them, equivalent to 13.04 lunar months for a 399-day year.

As with tree rings, we need to establish when annual bands might be duplicated or skipped, and whether monthly and annual cycles can be identified with confidence. One such study off the island of Oahu (Hawaii) found that the coral *Porites lobata* displayed an incomplete monthly growth record. It concluded that the species was better suited to the analysis of the environment in which it was growing than for the study of lunar and solar periodicities (Buddemeier & Kinzie 1975). Such findings have encouraged the switch to tidal depositional sequences (Williams 1989), which are more widespread and dependable that molluscs or corals.

There is no shortage of potential palaeoenvironmental applications of coral and mollusc periodicities, provided that incremental age is cross checked by independent

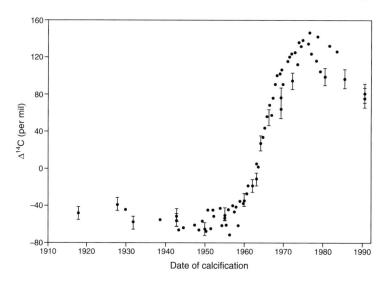

**Figure 10.6** $^{14}C$ of aragonite of fish otolith from New Zealand (dots with vertical error bars) and of coral from the Heron Isles and Fiji (other dots) for 1908–90, showing the potential of otoliths for tracing radio-carbon outside tropical and subtropical waters. (After Kalish 1993, with permission of Elsevier Science.)

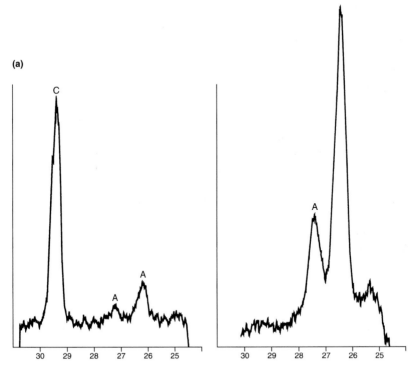

**(a)**

**Figure 10.7** **(a)** X-ray diffractogram of aragonitic shell contaminated by modern calcite (C) (left) and after mechanical cleaning (right). **(b, c, d, overleaf)**

methods. Off northwest Jamaica, the sclerosponge *Ceratoporella nicholsoni* yielded a $^{13}C$ record for shallow waters for the period 1700–1972. Dating was by $^{14}C$ and $^{210}Pb$. The measurements suggested that $CO_2$ from forests and soils contributed 28 per cent to the increase in atmospheric levels of that gas between 1820 and 1972, the rest being the product of fossil-fuel burning (Druffel & Benavides 1986). The point was worth making, especially when the paper was written, as the case for a manmade greenhouse effect was still not generally accepted. Perhaps more important, the study showed that the sclerosponge is a reliable guide to atmospheric $CO_2$ levels because it accretes aragonite in equilibrium with the surrounding sea water. In contrast, the $^{13}C$ record of tree rings, and of marine organisms such as *Tridacna*, which contain symbiotic algae, is distorted by fractionation resulting from photosynthesis.

The increase in $CO_2$ doubtless affects the Earth's rotation, even if imperceptibly, through the atmosphere's density and dynamics. Human activity is capable of influencing the LOD by a further route, through the construction of reservoirs. By the early 1990s the volume of water impounded amounted to $10\,000\,km^3$ ($10^{16}\,kg$), comparable in total to the water in the atmosphere and equivalent to a sea-level fall of 3 cm. The load redistribution produced by 88 major reservoirs with a capacity of $10\,km^3$, which accounted at most for 40 of the total volume impounded by 1995, would have been

161

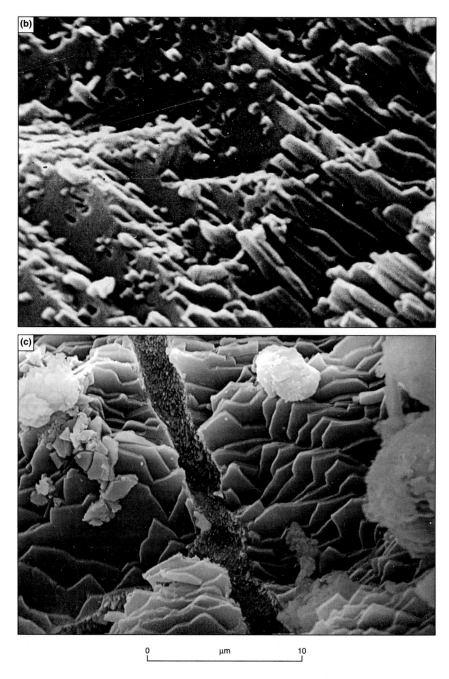

0   μm   10

**Figure 10.7** **(b)** Scanning electron micrograph by B. Walker of the same shell showing calcite over-growths (left) over aragonite laths (right). **(c)** Tubule in mollusc wall showing absence of secondary carbonate.

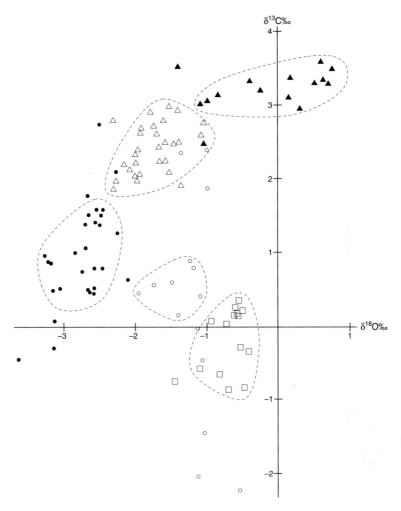

**Figure 10.7 (d)** Stable isotopic composition of Holocene molluscs from fossil beach in Iran showing distinctive signature of different species (indicated by different symbols). Open circles represent modern specimens of *Arca (barbatia) fusca*. The same species from a Holocene beachrock is shown by filled circles.

sufficient to affect both the Earth's moment of inertia and its external gravitational field (Chao 1995b).

The individual contribution by a single reservoir of the stated size will produce LOD changes of 1 µs, a polar motion excitation of 1 mas, and a change in the Earth's dynamic oblateness of $10^{-11}$. But the cumulative effect is substantial. For example, the resulting net movement of water is towards high latitudes, so that both the dynamic oblateness and the axial moment of inertia are reduced; the calculated decrease in dynamic oblateness is about $-1.0 \times 10^{-12}$, only an order of magnitude less than the secular rate of $-26 \times 10^{-12} \, \text{yr}^{-1}$ determined from laser ranging to the LAGEOS satellite and ascribed to

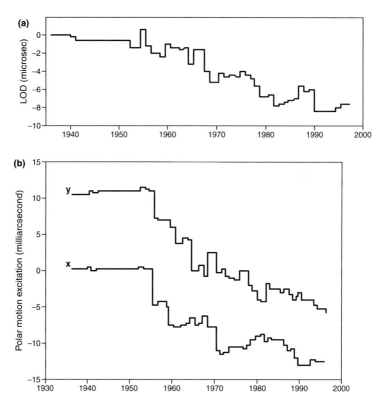

**Figure 10.8** Changes attributable to world's major reservoirs in **(a)** LOD, **(b)** polar motion (y component offset for clarity) (after Chao 1995b, © AGU).

postglacial rebound and polar ice-sheet fluctuations (see p. 52). The corresponding change in LOD amounts to $0.2\,\mu s\,day^{-1}\,yr^{-1}$ in recent decades. The $x$ and $y$ values of polar motion excitation also show a cumulative trend, equivalent to a drift in the rotational pole of $0.5\,mas\,yr^{-1}$ towards 130°W, within the resolution of instrumental observation (Fig. 10.8). Polar drift over the same period, as we saw earlier, is $3.2\,mas\,yr^{-1}$ towards 81°W.

Like the filling of Lake Mead (see p. 98), the reservoir effect amounts to a geodetic experiment, as the key variable is under human control and its impact (on the Earth's oblateness, and ultimately on the LOD) can in principle be measured. But all sectors of physical geology are becoming more experimental because, as the nineteenth-century physiologist Bernard argued, one can observe and reason experimentally even when unable to perform an experiment. Monitoring the Earth then emerges as an essential constituent of creative Earth science.

# Bibliography

Aaboe, A. 1980. Observation and theory in Babylonian astronomy. *Centaurus* **24**, 14–35.

Adushkin, V. V. & I. V. Nemchinov 1994. Consequences of impacts of cosmic bodies on the surface of the Earth. See Gehrels (1994: 721–78).

Ager, D. V. 1973. *The nature of the stratigraphical record*. London: Macmillan.

Alvarez, L. W., W. Alvarez, F. Asaro, M. V. Michel 1980. Extraterrestrial cause for the Cretaceous–Tertiary extinction. *Science* **208**, 1095–1108.

Amato, A. & C. Chiarabba 1995. Recent uplift of the Alban Hills volcano (Italy): evidence for magmatic inflation? *Geophysical Research Letters* **22**, 1985–8.

Ambraseys, N. N. & C. Melville 1982. *A history of Persian earthquakes*. Cambridge: Cambridge University Press.

Anderson, A. J. & A. Cazenave (eds) 1986. *Space geodesy and geodynamics*. London: Academic Press.

Anderson, R. Y. 1992. Possible connection between surface winds, solar activity and the Earth's magnetic field. *Nature* **358**, 51–3.

Andrews, C. & R. B. G. Williams 2000. Limpet erosion of chalk shore platforms in southeast England. *Earth Surface Processes and Landforms* **25**, 1–11.

Argand, E. 1924. La tectonique de l'Asie. *Reports, 13th International Geological Congress*, vol. I, 170–372. Brussels: Vaillant-Carmanne.

Argus, D. F. & M. B. Heflin 1995. Plate motion and crustal deformation estimated with geodetic data from the Global Positioning System. *Geophysical Research Letters* **22**, 1973–6.

Asher, D. J. & S. V. M. Clube 1993. An extraterrestrial influence during the current glacial–interglacial. *Royal Astronomical Society, Quarterly Journal* **34**, 481–511.

Attolini, M. R., S. Cecchini, M. Galli, G. E. Kocharov, T. Nanni 1993. 400-year record of C14 in tree rings – the solar-activity cycle before, during and after Maunder minimum and the longer cycles. *Nuovo Cimento C – Geophysics and Space Physics* **16**, 419–36.

Atwater, B., H. Jiménez-Núñez, C. Vita-Finzi 1992. Net late Holocene emergence despite earthquake-induced submergence, south-central Chile. *Quaternary International* **15/16**, 77–85.

Bailey, M. E., S. V. M. Clube, G. Hahn, W. M. Napier, G. B. Valsecchi 1994. Hazards due to giant comets: climate and short-term catastrophism. See Gehrels (1994: 479–533).

Bailey, R. W. 1935. Epicycles of erosion in the valleys of the Colorado Plateau province. *Journal of Geology* **43**, 337–55.

Baillie, M. G. L. 1999. Putting abrupt environmental change back into human history. In *Environments and historical change*, P. Slack (ed.), 46–75. Oxford: Oxford University Press.

Baker, E. T., C. R. German, H. Elderfield 1995. Hydrothermal plumes over spreading-centre axes: global distributions and geological inferences. In *Seafloor hydrothermal systems*, S. E. Humphris, R. A. Zierenberg, L. S. Mullineaux, R. E. Thomson (eds), 47–71. Geophysical Monograph 91, American Geophysical Union, Washington DC.

Baker, V. R. 1994. Glacial to modern changes in modern river fluxes. In *Material fluxes on the surface of the Earth*, 86–98. Washington DC: National Academy Press.

Bannister, A., S. Raymond, R. Baker 1998. *Surveying* (7th edn). Harlow: Longman.

Bard, E., B. Hamelin, R. G. Fairbanks, A. Zindler 1990. Calibration of the $^{14}$C timescale over the past 30 000 years using mass spectrometric U–Th ages from Barbados corals. *Nature* **345**, 405.

Becker, B. 1992. The history of dendrochronology and radiocarbon calibration. In *Radiocarbon after four decades*, R. E. Taylor, A. Long, R. Kra (eds), 34–49. New York: Springer.

Beer, J. and 12 co-authors 1990. Use of [10]Be in polar ice to trace the 11-year cycle of solar activity. *Nature* **347**, 164–6.

Bell, R. E. 1995. Advances in aerogeophysics and precise positioning: gravity, topography, and high resolution applications. *Reviews of Geophysics*, Supplement, 361–4.

Bendick, R. & R. Bilham 1999. Search for buckling of the southwest Indian coast related to Himalayan collision. In *Himalaya and Tibet: mountain roots to mountain tops*, A. Macfarlane, R. B. Sorkhabi, J. Quade (eds), 313–21. Special Paper 328, Geological Society of America, Boulder, Colorado.

Bendick, R., R. Bilham, J. Freymuller, K. Larson, G. Yin 2000. Geodetic evidence for a low slip rate in the Altyn Tagh Fault system. *Nature* **404**, 69–72.

Benoit, P. H. 1995. Meteorites as surface exposure time markers on the blue ice fields of Antarctica – episodic ice flow in Victoria Land over the last 300 000 years. *Quaternary Science Review* **14**, 531–40.

Berberian, M. 1995. Master "blind" thrust faults hidden under the Zagros folds: active basement tectonics and surface morphotectonics. *Tectonophysics* **241**, 193–224.

Berberian, M. & M. Qorashi 1994. Coseismic fault-related folding during the South Golbaf earthquake of November 20, 1989, in southeast Iran. *Geology* **22**, 531–4.

Bezerra, F. H. & C. Vita-Finzi 2000. How active is a passive margin? Paleoseismicity in northeastern Brazil. *Geology* **28**, 591–4.

Bezzeghoud, M., D. Dimitrov, J. C. Ruegg, K. Lammali 1995. Faulting mechanism of the El Asnam (Algeria) 1954 and 1980 earthquakes from modelling of vertical movements. *Tectonophysics* **249**, 249–66.

Bierman, P. R. 1994. Using *in situ* produced cosmogenic isotopes to estimate rates of landscape evolution: a review from the geomorphic perspective. *Journal of Geophysical Research* **99**, 13885–96.

Bilham, R. 1991. Earthquakes and sea level: space and terrestrial metrology on a changing planet. *Reviews of Geophysics* **29**, 1–29.

Bilham, R. & T-T. Yu 2000. The morphology of thrust faulting in the 21 September 1999, Chi-Chi, Taiwan earthquake. *Journal of Asian Earth Sciences* **18**, 351–67.

Bilham, R., F. Blume, R. Bendick, V. K. Gaur 1998. Geodetic constraints on the translation and deformation of India: implications for future great Himalayan earthquakes. *Current Science* **74**, 213–29.

Bills, B. G. & T. S. James 1996. Late Quaternary variations in relative sea level due to glacial cycle polar wander. *Geophysical Research Letters* **23**, 3023–3026.

Bills, B. G. and 6 co-authors 1994. Hydro-isostatic deflection and tectonic tilting in the central Andes: initial results of a GPS survey of Lake Minchin shorelines. *Geophysical Research Letters* **21**, 293–6.

Bindschadler, R. 1998. Monitoring ice sheet behaviour from space. *Reviews of Geophysics* **36**, 79–104.

Biot, M. A. 1961. Theory of folding of stratified viscoelastic media and its implications in tectonics and orogenesis. *Geological Society of America, Bulletin* **72**, 1595–620.

Bird, P. 1978. Finite element modelling of lithospheric deformation: the Zagros collision orogeny. *Tectonophysics* **50**, 307–336.

Björnsson, A., G. Johnsen, S. Sigurdsson, S. Thorbergsson, E. Tryggvason 1979. Rifting of the plate boundary in North Iceland 1975–1978. *Journal of Geophysical Research* **84**, 3029–3038.

Bland, P. A. and 6 co-authors 1996. The flux of meteorites to the Earth over the last 50 000 years. *Royal Astronomical Society, Monthly Notices* **283**, 551–65.

Blewitt, G. 1993. Advances in Global Positioning System Technology for geodynamics investigations: 1978–1992. In *Contributions of space geodesy to geodynamics: technology*, D. E. Smith & D. L. Turcotte (eds), 195–213. Geodynamics Series 25, American Geophysical Union, Washington DC.

Blewitt, G., M. B. Heflin, K. J. Hurst, D. C. Jefferson, F. H. Webb, J. F. Zumberge 1993. Absolute far-field displacements from the 28 June 1992 Landers earthquake sequence. *Nature* **361**, 340–42.

Bock, Y. and 12 co-authors 1993. Detection of crustal deformation from the Landers earthquake sequence using continuous geodetic measurements. *Nature* **361**, 337–40.

Bonino, G., G. C. Castagnoli, C. Taricco, N. Bhandari 1994. Cosmogenic Ti-44 in meteorites and century-scale solar modulation. *Advances in Space Research* **14**, 783–6.

Bossler, J. D. 1983. The impact of VLBI and GPS on geodesy. *EOS, Transactions of the American*

*Geophysical Union* **64**, 569–70.

Bosworth, W. & M. Taviani 1996. Late Quaternary reorientation of stress field and extension direction in the southern Gulf of Suez, Egypt: evidence from uplifted coral terraces, mesoscopic fault arrays, and borehole breakouts. *Tectonics* **15**, 791–802.

Bott, M. H. P. & D. S. Dean 1973. Stress diffusion from plate boundaries. *Nature* **243**, 339–41.

Brakenridge, G. R., J. C. Knox, E. D. Paylor II, F. J. Magilligan 1994. Radar remote-sensing aids study of the great flood of 1993. *EOS, Transactions of the American Geophysical Union* **75**, 521, 526–7.

Brecher, H. H. 1982. Photogrammetric determination of surface velocities and elevations on Byrd Glacier. *Antarctic Journal of the United States* **17**, 79–81.

Brecher, H. H. & L. G. Thompson 1993. Measurement of the retreat of Qori Kalis glacier in the tropical Andes of Peru by terrestrial photogrammetry. *Photogrammetric Engineering and Remote Sensing* **59**, 1017–1022.

Briffa, K. R., P. D. Jones, F. H. Schweingruber, T. J. Osborn 1998. Influence of volcanic eruptions on Northern Hemisphere summer temperature over the past 600 years. *Nature* **393**, 450–55.

Broecker, W. S. 1992. Discovery of a large offset in the radiocarbon timescale. *EOS, Transactions of the American Geophysical Union* **73**, 11.

Broecker, W. S. & T. Liu 2001. Rock varnish: record of desert wetness? *GSA Today* **11**, 4–10.

Brownlee, D. E. 1985. Cosmic dust: collection and research. *Annual Review of Earth and Planetary Science* **13**, 147–73.

Bruns, P., W. W. Hay, W. C. Dullo 1995. Reconstruction of sedimentation processes using iridium concentration in marine sediments. *Abstracts, International Union of Geodesy and Geophysics XXI*, A239, General Assembly, Boulder, Colorado.

Buddemeier, R. W. & R. A. Kinzie III 1975. The chronometric reliability of contemporary corals. In *Growth rhythms and the history of the Earth's rotation*, G. D. Rosenberg & S. K. Runcorn (eds), 135–46. Chichester, England: John Wiley.

Burroughs, W. J. 1994. *Weather cycles: real or imaginary?* Cambridge: Cambridge University Press.

Calais, E. & S. Amarjargal 2000. New constraints on current deformation in Asia from continuous GPS: measurements at Ulan Baatar, Mongolia. *Geophysical Research Letters* **27**, 1527–30.

Carey, S. W. 1976. *The expanding Earth*. Amsterdam: Elsevier.

Carter, W. E., D. S. Robertson, T. E. Pyle, J. Diamante 1986. The application of geodetic radio interferometric surveying to the monitoring of sea level. *Royal Astronomical Society, Geophysical Journal* **87**, 3–13.

Cavalieri, D. J., P. Gloersen, C. L. Parkinson, J. C. Comiso, H. J. Zwally 1997. Observed hemispheric asymmetry in global sea ice changes. *Science* **278**, 1104–106.

Cazenave, A., K. Dominh, F. Ponchaut, L. Soudarin, J. F. Crétaux, C. Le Prevost 1999. Sea-level changes from TOPEX/Poseidon altimetry and tide gauges, and vertical motions from DORIS. *Geophysical Research Letters* **26**, 2077–2080.

Cebula, R. P., M. T. DeLand, B. M. Schlesinger 1992. Estimates of solar variability using the Solar backscatter ultraviolet (SBUV) 2 Mg II index from the NOAA-9 satellite. *Journal of Geophysical Research* **97**, 11613–20.

Ceplecha, Z. 1992. Influx of interplanetary bodies onto Earth. *Astronomy and Astrophysics* **263**, 361–6.

Cerling, T. & H. Craig 1994. Geomorphology and *in situ* cosmogenic isotopes. *Annual Review of Earth and Planetary Science* **22**, 273–317.

Cerling, T. E., R. H. Webb, R. J. Poreda, A. D. Rigby, T. S. Melis 1999. Cosmogenic $^3$He ages and frequency of late Holocene debris flows from Prospect Canyon, Grand Canyon, USA. *Geomorphology* **27**, 93–111.

Chao, B. F. 1995a. Global change signals in Earth's rotation and gravitational field. *EOS, Fall Meeting, American Geophysical Union, 1995, Abstracts*, F159.

—— 1995b. Anthropogenic impact on global geodynamics due to reservoir water impoundment. *Geophysical Research Letters* **22**, 3529–32.

—— 1996. "Concrete" testimony to Milankovich cycle in Earth's changing obliquity. *EOS, Transactions of the American Geophysical Union* **77**, 433.

Chapman, C. R. & D. Morrison 1994. Impacts on the Earth by asteroids and comets – assessing the hazard. *Nature* **367**, 33–40.

Chappell, J. 1970. Geology of coral terraces, Huon peninsula, New Guinea: a study of Quaternary tectonic movements and sea-level changes. *Bulletin of the Geological Society of America* **85**, 553–70.

Chappell, J. & H. Polach 1991. Post-glacial sea-level rise from a coral record at Huon Peninsula, Papua New Guinea. *Nature* **349**, 147–9.

Chazottes, V., T. Le Campion-Alsumard, M. Peyrot-Clausade 1995. Bioerosion rates on coral reefs: interactions between macroborers, microborers and grazers (Moorea, French Polynesia). *Palaeogeography, Palaeoclimatology, Palaeoecology* **113**, 189–98.

Chorley, R. J., A. J. Dunn, R. P. Beckinsale 1964. *The history of the study of landforms* I. London: Methuen.

Christensen, P. R. & S. T. Harrison 1993. Thermal infrared-emission spectroscopy of natural surfaces – application to desert varnish coatings on rocks. *Journal of Geophysical Research* **98**, 19819–34.

Christodoulidis, D. C., D. E. Smith, R. Kolenkiewicz, S. M. Klosko, M. H. Torrence, P. J. Dunn 1985. Observing tectonic plate motions and deformations from satellite laser ranging. *Journal of Geophysical Research* **90**, 9249–63.

Chyba, C. F. 1993. Explosions of small Spacewatch objects in the Earth's atmosphere. *Nature* **363**, 701–703.

Chyba, C. F. & C. Sagan 1992. Endogenous production, exogenous delivery, and impact-shock synthesis of organic molecules: an inventory for the origins of life. *Nature* **355**, 125–32.

Chyba, C. F., P. J. Thomas, L. Brookshaw, C. Sagan 1990. Cometary delivery of organic molecules to the early Earth. *Science* **249**, 366–73.

Chyba, C. F., P. J. Thomas, K. J. Zahnle 1993. The 1908 Tunguska explosion: atmospheric disruption of a stony asteroid. *Nature* **361**, 40–44.

Chyba, C. F., T. C. Owen, W-H. Ip 1994. Impact delivery of volatiles and organic molecules to Earth. See Gehrels (1994: 9–58).

Clark, J. A., W. E. Farrell, W. R. Peltier 1978. Global changes in postglacial sea level: a numerical calculation. *Quaternary Research* **9**, 265–87.

Clarke, P. J. and 11 co-authors 1999. Some aspects of Aegean continental dynamics inferred from a decade of GPS measurements and a century of triangulations. *Proceedings of the International Union of Geodesy and Geophysics* **XXIIB**, 78.

Clement, B. M. & C. G. Constable 1991. Polarity transitions, excursions and paleosecular variation of the Earth's magnetic field. *Reviews of Geophysics*, Supplement, 433–42.

Cook, D. B., K. Fujita, C. A. McMullen 1986. Present-day interactions in northeast Asia: North American, Eurasian, and Okhotsk plates. *Journal of Geodynamics* **6**, 33–51.

Costa, C. H. & C. Vita-Finzi 1996. Late Holocene faulting in the southeast Sierras Pampeanas of Argentina. *Geology* **24**, 1127–30.

Courtillot, V. & J. L. Le Mouël 1988. Time variations of the Earth's magnetic field. *Annual Review of Earth and Planetary Science* **16**, 389–476.

Crétaux, J-F., L. Soudarin, A. Cazenave, F. Bouillé 1998. Present-day tectonic plate motions and crustal deformations from the DORIS space system. *Journal of Geophysical Research* **103**, 30167–81.

Crittenden Jr, M. D. 1967. *New data on the isostatic deformation of Lake Bonneville*. Professional Paper 454E, US Geological Survey, Denver, Colorado.

Crowley, T. J. & K-Y. Kim 1996. Comparison of proxy records of climate change and solar forcing. *Geophysical Research Letters* **23**, 359–62.

Damon, P. E. and 20 co-authors 1989. Radiocarbon dating of the shroud of Turin. *Nature* **337**, 611–15.

Darwin, C. R. 1842. *Structure and distribution of coral reefs*. Tucson: University of Arizona Press (1984 reprint).

—— 1881. *The formation of vegetable mould through the action of worms*. London: John Murray.

Dean, J. S. 1986. Dendrochronology. In *Dating and age determination of biological materials*, M. R. Zimmerman & J. L. Angel (eds), 126–65. London: Croom-Helm.

Decker, R. W. & W. T. Kinoshita 1971. Geodetic measurements. In *The surveillance and prediction of volcanic activity*, 60–74. Paris: UNESCO.

Delobeau, F. 1971. *The environment of the Earth*. Dordrecht: Reidel.

DeMets, C., R. G. Gordon, D. F. Argus, S. Stein 1990. Current plate motions. *Geophysical Journal International* **101**, 425–78.

——— 1994. Effect of recent revisions to the geomagnetic reversal timescale on estimates of current plate motions. *Geophysical Research Letters* **21**, 2191–4.

de Silva, S. L. & G. A. Zielinski 1998. Global influence of the AD 1600 eruption of Huaynaputina, Peru. *Nature* **393**, 455–8.

Dickey, J. O., T. M. Eubanks, R. Hide 1990. Inter-annual and decade fluctuations in the Earth's rotation. In *Variations in Earth rotation*, D. D. McCarthy & W. E. Carter (eds), 157–61. Geophysical Monograph 9, American Geophysical Union, Washington DC.

Dickman, S. R. 1979. Continental drift and true polar wandering. *Royal Astronomical Society, Geophysical Journal* **57**, 41–50.

Dixon, T. H. 1991. An introduction to the Global Positioning System and some geological applications. *Reviews of Geophysics* **29**, 249–276.

——— 1993. GPS measurements of relative motion of the Cocos and Caribbean plates and strain accumulation across the Middle America trench. *Geophysical Research Letters* **20**, 2167–70.

Dong, D., R. S. Gross, J. O. Dickey 1996. Seasonal variations of the Earth's gravitational field: an analysis of atmospheric pressure, ocean tidal, and surface water excitation. *Geophysical Research Letters* **23**, 725–8.

Donnellan, A., B. W. Hager, R. W. King 1993. Discrepancy between geological and geodetic deformation rates in the Ventura basin. *Nature* **366**, 333–6.

Dorn, R. I. and 11 co-authors 1986. Cation-ratio and accelerator radiocarbon dating of rock varnish on Mojave artifacts and landforms. *Science* **231**, 830–33.

Douglass, A. E. 1932. Tree rings and their relation to solar variations and chronology. *Reports of the Smithsonian Institution*, Washington DC, for 1931, 304–12.

Dowdeswell, J. A., G. S. Hamilton, J. O. Hagen 1991. The duration of the active phase on surge-type glaciers: contrasts between Svalbard and other regions. *Journal of Glaciology* **37**, 388–400.

Dragert, H. & R. D. Hyndman 1995. Continuous GPS monitoring of elastic strain in the northern Cascadia subduction zone. *Geophysical Research Letters* **22**, 755–8.

Dragert, H., K. Wang, T. S. James 2001. A silent slip event on the deeper Cascadia subduction surface. *Science* **292**, 1525–8.

Dragovich, D. 1994. Fire, climate, and the persistence of desert varnish near Dampier, Western Australia. *Palaeogeography, Palaeoclimatology, Palaeoecology* **111**, 279–88.

Drewry, D. J. & E. M. Morris 1992. The response of large ice sheets to climatic change. *Royal Society of London, Philosophical Transactions B* **338**, 235–42.

Druffel, E. R. M. & L. M. Benavides 1986. Input of excess $CO_2$ to the surface ocean based on $^{13}C/^{12}C$ ratios in a banded Jamaican sclerosponge. *Nature* **321**, 58–61.

Dunn, P. J., J. W. Robbins, D. E. Smith 1989. Deformation in the Pacific Basin from LAGEOS. *International Association for Geodesy, Symposium* (Edinburgh) **101**, 96–104.

Dyurgerov, M. B. & M. F. Meyer 1997. Year-to-year fluctuations of global mass balance of small glaciers and their contribution to sea-level changes. *Arctic and Alpine Research* **29**, 292–402.

Eddy, J. A. 1983. The Maunder minimum: a reappraisal. *Solar Physics* **89**, 195–207.

——— 1988. Variability of the present and ancient Sun: a test of solar uniformitarianism. In *Secular solar and geomagnetic variations in the last 10000 years*, S. F. Stephenson & A. W. Wolfendale (eds), 1–24. Dordrecht: Kluwer.

Eddy, J. A., R. L. Gilliland, D. V. Hoyt 1982. Changes in the solar constant and climatic effects. *Nature* **300**, 689–93.

Edwards, R. L., F. W. Taylor, G. J. Wasserburg 1988. Dating earthquakes with high-precision thorium–230 ages of very young corals. *Earth and Planetary Science Letters* **90**, 371–81.

Ellenblum, R., S. Marco, A. Agnon, T. Rockwell, A. Boas 1998. Crusader castle torn apart by earthquake at dawn, 20 May 1202. *Geology* **26**, 303–306.

Emery, K. O. 1941. Rate of surface retreat of sea cliffs based on dated inscriptions. *Science* **93**, 617–18.

Emmett, W. W. 1974. Channel aggradation in western United States as indicated by observations at Vigil Network sites. *Zeitschrift für Geomorphologie, Supplementband* **21**, 52–62.

England, P. & J. Jackson 1989. Active deformation of the continents. *Annual Reviews of Earth and Planetary Science* **17**, 197–226.

England, P. & P. Molnar 1990. Right-lateral shear and rotation as the explanation for strike-slip faulting in eastern Tibet. *Nature* **344**, 140–42.

Evans, J. W. 1968. The role of *Penitella penita* (Conrad 1837) (family Pholadidae) as eroders along the Pacific coast of North America. *Ecology* **49**, 156–69.

Falcon, N. L. 1969. Problems of the relationship between surface structure and deep displacements illustrated by the Zagros Range. In *Time and place in orogeny*, P. Kent, G. Satterthwaite, A. Spencer (eds), 9–22. London: Geological Society of London.

—— 1974. Southern Iran: Zagros Mountains. In *Mesozoic–Cenozoic orogenic belts*, A. M. Spencer (ed.), 199–211. Edinburgh: Scottish Universities Press.

Faure, G. 1986. *Principles of isotope geology* (2nd edn). New York: John Wiley.

Feigl, K. L., A. Sergent, D. Jacq 1995. Estimation of an earthquake focal mechanism from a satellite radar interferogram: application to the 4 December 1992 Landers aftershock. *Geophysical Research Letters* **22**, 1037–1040.

Fitzharris, B. The cryosphere: changes and their impacts. In *Climate change 1995*, R. T. Watson, M. C. Zinyowera, R. H. Moss (eds), 241–65. Cambridge: Cambridge University Press.

Flynn, G. J. 1994. Interplanetary dust particles collected from the stratosphere – physical, chemical, and mineralogical properties and implications for their sources. *Planetary and Space Science* **42**, 1151–7.

Fornari, D. J. & R. W. Embley 1995. Tectonic and volcanic controls on hydrothermal processes at the mid-ocean ridge: an overview based on near-bottom and submersible studies. In *Seafloor hydrothermal systems*, S. E. Humphris, R. A. Zierenberg, L. S. Mullineaux, R. E. Thomson (eds), 1–46. Geophysical Monograph 91, American Geophysical Union, Washington DC.

Foukal, P. & J. Lean 1988. Magnetic modulation of solar luminosity by photospheric activity. *Astrophysical Journal* **328**, 347–57.

Fowler, C. M. R. 1990. *The solid Earth*. Cambridge: Cambridge University Press.

Fox, C. G., W. W. Chadwick Jr, R. W. Embley 1992. Detection of changes in ridge-crest morphology using repeated multi-beam sonar surveys. *Journal of Geophysical Research* **97**, 11149–62.

Freymuller, J. T., S. C. Cohen, H. J. Fletcher 2000. Spatial variations in present-day deformation, Kenai Peninsula, Alaska, and their implications. *Journal of Geophysical Research* **105**, 8079–8101.

Frohlich, R. M. & C. S. M. Doake 1998. Synthetic aperture radar interferometry over Rutford ice stream and Carlson Inlet, Antarctica. *Journal of Glaciology* **44**, 77–92.

Fruneau, B. and 8 co-authors 2001. Uplift of Tainan tableland (SW Taiwan) revealed by SAR interferometry. *Geophysical Research Letters* **28**, 3071–3074.

Fu, L-L. & R. E. Cheney 1995. Application of satellite altimetry to ocean circulation studies: 1987–1994. *Reviews of Geophysics*, Supplement, 213–23.

Gage, J. D. & P. A. Tyler 1991. *Deep-sea biology*. Cambridge: Cambridge University Press.

Garcia, C., J. B. Laronne, M. Sala 2000. Continuous monitoring of bedload flux in a mountain gravel-bed river. *Geomorphology* **34**, 23–31.

Garvin, J. B. 1996. Topographic characterization and monitoring of volcanoes via airborne laser altimetry. In *Volcano instability on the earth and other planets*, W. J. McGuire, A. P. Jones, J. Neuberg (eds), 137–152. Special Publication 110, Geological Society of London, London.

Gehrels, T. (ed.) 1994. *Hazards due to comets and asteroids*. Tucson: University of Arizona Press.

Geikie, A. 1880. Rock weathering, as illustrated in Edinburgh churchyards. *Royal Society of Edinburgh, Proceedings* **10**, 518–32.

Gersonde, R. and 12 co-authors 1997. Geological record and reconstruction of the late Pliocene impact of the Eltanin asteroid in the Southern Ocean. *Nature* **390**, 357–63.

Gilbert, G. K. 1890. *Lake Bonneville*. Monograph 1, US Geological Survey, Washington DC.

Gillespie, A. R. & P. R. Bierman 1995. Precision of terrestrial exposure ages and erosion rates estimated from analysis of cosmogenic isotopes produced *in situ*. *Journal of Geophysical Research* **100**, 24637–49.

Gillespie, A. & P. Molnar 1995. Asynchronous maximum advances of mountain and continental glaciers. *Reviews of Geophysics* **33**, 311–64.

Gillett, N. P., M. R. Allen, S. F. B. Tett 2000. Modelled and observed variability in atmospheric vertical temperature structure. *Climate Dynamics* **16**, 49–61.

Girdler, R. W. & P. Styles 1974. Two stage Red Sea floor spreading. *Nature* **247**, 7–10.

Glynn, P. W. 1973. Aspects of the ecology of coral reefs in the Western Atlantic region. In *Biology and geology of coral reefs* (vol. II), O. A. Jones & R. Endean (eds), 271–324. London: Academic Press.

—— 1996. Bioerosion and coral-reef growth: a dynamic balance. In *Life and death of coral reefs*, C. Birkeland (ed.), 68–95. London: Chapman & Hall.

Goldstein, R. M., H. Engelhardt, B. Kamb, R. M. Frolich 1993. Satellite radar interferometry for monitoring ice-sheet motion – application to an Antarctic ice stream. *Science* **262**, 1525–30.

Goodfriend, G. 1987. Evaluation of amino-acid racemization/epimerization dating using radiocarbon-dated fossil land snails. *Geology* **15**, 698–700.

Gordon, R. G. 1998. The plate-tectonic approximation: plate nonrigidity, diffuse plate boundaries, and global plate reconstructions. *Annual Review of Earth and Planetary Science* **26**, 615–42.

—— 2000. Diffuse oceanic plate boundaries: strain rates, vertically averaged rheology, and comparisons with narrow plate boundaries and stable plate interiors. In *The history and dynamics of global plate motions*, M. A. Richards, R. G. Gordon, R. D. van der Hilst (eds), 143–59. Geophysical Monograph 121, American Geophysical Union, Washington DC.

Gorney, D. J. 1990. Solar-cycle effects on the near-Earth space environment. *Reviews of Geophysics* **28**, 315–36.

Goudie, A. 1995. *The changing Earth*. Oxford: Blackwell.

Grady, M. 1997. Meteorites: their flux with time and impact effects. *Geoscientist* **7**, 8–12.

Grady, M. M., R. Hutchison, G. J. H. McCall, D. A. Rothery (eds) 1998. *Meteorites – flux with time and impact effects*. Special Publication 140, Geological Society of London, London.

Grieve, R. A. F. 1991. Terrestrial impact – the record in the rocks. *Meteoritics* **26**, 175–94.

Grieve, R. A. F. & L. J. Pesonen 1992. The terrestrial impact cratering record. *Tectonophysics* **216**, 1–30.

Grieve, R. A. & E. M. Shoemaker 1994. The record of past impacts on Earth. See Gehrels (1994: 417–62).

Gross, R. S. 2000. The excitation of the Chandler wobble. *Geophysical Research Letters* **27**, 2085–2088.

Gross, R. S. & J. Vondrak 1999. Astrometric and space-geodetic observations of polar wander. *Geophysical Research Letters* **26**, 2085–8.

Grove, A. T. & O. Rackham 2001. *The nature of Mediterranean Europe*. New Haven, Connecticut: Yale University Press.

Gubbins, D. 1999. The distinction between geomagnetic excursions and reversals. *Geophysical Journal International* **137**, F1–3.

Hackman, M. C., G. C. P. King, R. Bilham 1990. The mechanics of the South Iceland seismic zone. *Journal of Geophysical Research* **95**, 17339–51.

Hagstrum, J. T. & E. Champion 1995. Late Quaternary geomagnetic secular variations from historical and $^{14}$C-dated lava flows on Hawaii. *Journal of Geophysical Research* **100**, 24393–403.

Haigh, J. D. 1994. The role of stratospheric ozone in modulating the solar radiative forcing of climate. *Nature* **370**, 544–6.

—— 1996. The impact of solar variability on climate. *Science* **272**, 981–4.

Hanna, E. & P. Valdes 2001. Validation of ECMWF (re)analysis surface climate data, 1979–1998, for Greenland and implications for mass balance modelling of the ice sheet. *International Journal of Climatology* **21**, 171–95.

Hansen, J. E. & E. A. Lacis 1990. Sun and dust versus greenhouse gases: an assessment of their relative roles in global climate change. *Nature* **346**, 713–19.

Happ, S. C., G. Rittenhouse, G. C. Dobson 1940. *Some principles of accelerated stream and valley sedimentation*. Technical Bulletin 695, US Department of Agriculture, Washington DC.

HSCFA (Harvard Smithsonian Centre for Astrophysics) 2000. http://cfa-www.harvard.edu/iau/lists/unusual.html.

Heezen, B. C. & M. Ewing 1972. The role of subaqueous debris flow in generating turbidity currents. *Journal of Sedimentary Petrology* **42**, 775–93.

Heki, K., G. R. Foulger, B. R. Julian, C. H. Jahn 1993. Plate dynamics near divergent boundaries: geophysical implications of post-rifting crustal deformation in NE Iceland. *Journal of Geophysical Research* **98**, 14279–97.

Hempton, M. R. 1987. Constraints on Arabian plate motion and extension history of the Red Sea. *Tectonics* **6**, 687–705.

Hendron, A. J. & F. D. Patton 1985. *The Vaiont slide, a geotechnical analysis based on new geological observations of the failure surface*. Technical Report GL-85-5, US Army Corps of Engineers, Vicksburg, Mississippi.

Hereford, R. 1993. *Entrenchment and widening of the upper San Pedro River, Arizona*. Special Paper 282 (pp. 1–46), Geological Society of America, Boulder, Colorado.

Herman, J. R. & R. A. Goldberg 1985 (1978). *Sun, weather and climate*. New York: Dover.

Herring, T. A. 1995. VLBI data, acquisition, environmental effects. *Reviews of Geophysics* **33**, 345–8.

Herring, T. A. & D. N. Dong 1994. Measurement of diurnal and semidiurnal rotational variations and tidal parameters of earth. *Journal of Geophysical Research* **99**, 18051–71.

Hind, G. & A. T. Jagendorf 1963. Separation of light and dark stages in photo-phosphorylation. *National Academy of Sciences, Proceedings* **713**, 715–22.

Hinks, A. R. 1947. *Maps and survey* (5th edn). Cambridge: Cambridge University Press.

Holasek, R. E. & S. Self 1995. GOES weather satellite observations and measurements of the May 18, 1980, Mount St Helens eruption. *Journal of Geophysical Research* **100**, 8469–87.

Holland, H. D. 1984. *The chemical evolution of the atmosphere and oceans*. Princeton, New Jersey: Princeton University Press.

Hood, L. L. & S. Zhou 1998. Stratospheric effects of 27-day solar ultraviolet variations: an analysis of UARS MLS ozone and temperature data. *Journal of Geophysical Research* **103**, 3629–38.

Huang, S., H. N. Pollack, P-Y. Shen 2000. Temperature trends over the past five centuries reconstructed from borehole temperatures. *Nature* **403**, 756–8.

Huh, C-A. & C-C. Su 1999. Sedimentation dynamics in the East China Sea elucidated from $^{210}$Pb, $^{137}$Cs and $^{239,240}$Pu. *Marine Geology* **160**, 183–96.

Inkpen, R. J., P. Collier, D. Fontana 2000. Close-range photogrammetric analysis of rock surfaces. *Zeitschrift für Geomorphologie, Supplement* **120**, 67–81.

Izenberg, N. R., R. E. Arvidson, R. A. Brackett, S. S. Saatchi, G. R. Osburn, J. Dohrenwend 1996. Erosional and depositional patterns associated with the 1993 Missouri River floods inferred from SIR-C and TOPSAR radar data. *Journal of Geophysical Research* **101**, 23149–67.

Jackson, J. A. 1980. Reactivation of basement faults and crustal shortening in orogenic belts. *Nature* **283**, 343–6.

Jackson, J., J. Haines, W. Holt 1995. The accommodation of Arabia–Eurasia plate convergence in Iran. *Journal of Geophysical Research* **100**, 15205–219.

Jackson, M. C. & P. Fryer 1991. The growth rate of submarine volcanoes on the South Honshu and East Mariana ridges. *Journal of Volcanology and Geothermal Research* **45**, 335–45.

Jackson, M. & R. Bilham 1994a. Constraints on Himalayan deformation inferred from vertical velocity fields in Nepal and Tibet. *Journal of Geophysical Research* **99**, 13897–912.

Jackson, M. E. & R. Bilham 1994b. 1991–1992 GPS measurements across the Nepal Himalayas. *Geophysical Research Letters* **21**, 1169–72.

Jacques, E., G. C. P. King, P. Tapponnier, J. C. Ruegg, I. Manighetti 1996. Seismic activity triggered by stress changes after the 1978 events in the Assal Rift, Djibouti. *Geophysical Research Letters* **23**,

2481–4.

James, T. S. & E. R. Ivins 1998. Predictions of Antarctic crustal motions driven by present-day ice-sheet evolution and by isostatic memory of the last glacial maximum. *Journal of Geophysical Research* **103**, 4993–5017.

Jeffreys, H. 1970. *The Earth* (5th edn). Cambridge: Cambridge University Press.

Jouanne, F., G. Ménard, X. Darmendrail 1995. Present-day vertical displacements in the northwestern Alps and southern Jura Mountains: data from levelling comparisons. *Tectonics* **14**, 606–616.

Joughin, I., D. Winebrenner, M. Fahnestock, R. Kwok, W. Krabill 1996. Measurement of ice-sheet topography using satellite radar interferometry. *Journal of Glaciology* **42**, 10–22.

Jull, A. J., S. Cloudt, D. J. Donahue, J. M. Sisterson, R. C. Reedy, J. Masarik 1998. [14]C depth profiles in Apollo 15 and 17 cores and lunar rock 68815. *Geochimica et Cosmochimica Acta* **62**, 3025–3036.

Kahle, H-G. and 9 co-authors 1997. Recent crustal movements, geoid and density determination: contribution from integrated satellite and terrestrial measurements. In *Deep structure of the Swiss Alps: results of NRP 20*, O. Pfiffner (ed), 251–9. Basel: Birkhäuser.

Kalish, J. M. 1993. Pre- and post-bomb radiocarbon in fish otoliths. *Earth and Planetary Science Letters* **65**, 549–54.

Karson, J. A. and 13 co-authors 1987. Along axis variability in seafloor spreading in the MARK area. *Nature* **328**, 681–5.

Keckhut, P. & M. L. Chanin 1992. Middle atmosphere response to the 27-day solar cycle as observed by Lidar. *Geophysical Research Letters* **19**, 809–812.

Kelly, P. M. & T. M. L. Wigley 1990. The influence of solar forcing trends on global mean temperature since 1861. *Nature* **347**, 460–62.

King, R. H. 1995. Weathering of Holocene airfall tephras in the southern Canadian Rockies. In *Rates of chemical weathering of rocks and minerals*, S. M. Colman & D. P. Dethier (eds), 239–64. New York: Academic Press.

King, G. C. P., R. S. Stein, J. Lin 1994. Static stress changes and the triggering of earthquakes. *Seismological Society of America, Bulletin* **84**, 935–53.

King, G. C. P. & C. Vita-Finzi 1981. Active folding in the Algerian earthquake of 10 October 1980. *Nature* **292**, 22–6.

Kogan, M. G. and 8 co-authors 2000. Geodetic constraints on the rigidity and relative motion of Eurasia and North America. *Geophysical Research Letters* **27**, 2041–2044.

Kolaczek, B., M. Nuzhdina, J. Nastula, W. Kosek 2000. El Niño impact on atmospheric polar motion excitation. *Journal of Geophysical Research* **105**, 3981–7.

Krabill, W., R. Thomas, K. Jezek, K. Kuivinen, S. Manizade 1995. Greenland ice-sheet thickness changes measured by laser altimetry. *Geophysical Research Letters* **22**, 2341–4.

Krabill, W. and 9 co-authors 2000. Greenland ice sheet: high-elevation balance and peripheral thinning. *Science* **289**, 428–30.

Kunzig, R. 1999. *The restless sea*. New York: Norton.

Kusznir, N. J. & R. G. Park 1984. The strength of intraplate lithosphere. *Physics of Earth and Planetary Interiors* **36**, 224–35.

Kyle, H. L., D. V. Hoyt, J. R. Hickey 1993. The 14-year Nimbus 7 solar dataset. *EOS, Transactions of the American Geophysical Union* **74**, 246.

Labitzke, K. & H. van Loon 1990. Associations between the 11-year solar cycle, the quasi-biennial oscillation and the atmosphere: a summary of recent work. *Royal Society of London, Philosophical Transactions A*, **330**, 575–89.

Laj, C, A. Mazaud, J-C. Duplessy 1996. Geomagnetic intensity and [14]C abundance in the atmosphere and ocean during the past 50 kyr. *Geophysical Research Letters* **23**, 2045–2048.

Lal, D. 1991. Cosmic-ray labelling of erosion surfaces: *in situ* nuclide production rates and erosion models. *Earth and Planetary Science Letters* **104**, 424–39.

Lal, D., A. J. T. Jull, D. J. Donahue, D. Burtner, K. Nishiizumi 1990. Polar ice ablation rates measured using *in situ* cosmogenic [14]C. *Nature* **346**, 350–52.

Lal, D., K. Nishiizumi, R. Arnold 1987. *In situ* cosmogenic $^3$H, $^{14}$C, and $^{10}$Be for determining the net accumulation and ablation rates of ice sheets. *Journal of Geophysical Research* **92**, 4947–52.

Lamb, H. H. 1962. The climates of the 11th and 16th centuries AD. *Weather* **17**, 381–9.

Lambeck, K. 1980. *The Earth's variable rotation: geophysical causes and consequences*. Cambridge: Cambridge University Press.

Lanari, R., P. Lundgren, E. Sansosti 1998. Dynamic deformation of Etna volcano observed by satellite radar interferometry. *Geophysical Research Letters* **25**, 1541–4.

Landscheidt, T. 1987. Long-range forecasts of solar cycles and climatic change. In *Climate history, periodicity and predictability*, M. R. Rampino, J. E. Sanders, W. S. Newman, L. K. Königsson (eds), 421–45. New York: Van Nostrand Reinhold.

Larson, K. M. 1995. Crustal deformation. *Reviews of Geophysics*, Supplement, 371–7.

Larson, K. M. & J. Freymuller 1995. Relative motions of the Australian, Pacific and Antarctic plates estimated by the Global Positioning System. *Geophysical Research Letters* **22**, 37–40.

Lassen, K. & E. Friis-Christensen 1995. Variability of the solar cycle length during the past five centuries and the apparent association with terrestrial climate. *Journal of Atmospheric and Terrestrial Physics* **57**, 835–8.

Lean, J. 1991. Variations in the Sun's radiative output. *Reviews of Geophysics* **29**, 505–535.

Lean, J., A. Skumanich, O. R. White 1992. Estimating the Sun's radiative output during the Maunder minimum. *Geophysical Research Letters* **19**, 1591–4.

Lee, K. E. 1985. *Earthworms*. Sydney: Academic Press.

Leopold, L. B. 1951. Rainfall frequency, an aspect of climatic variation. *Transactions of the American Geophysical Union* **32**, 347–57.

—— 1962. The Vigil network. *International Association for Scientific Hydrology, Bulletin* **7**, 5–9.

Leopold, L. B. & C. Vita-Finzi 1998. Valley changes in the Mediterranean and America. *American Philosophical Society, Proceedings* **142**, 1–17.

Levi, B. G. 2000. The decreasing Arctic ice cover. *Physics Today* **53**, 19–20.

Li, Z. 1987. Joint use of the eclipse records in China, Japan and Korea in study of the Earth's rotation. *Beijing Astronomical Observatory* **10**, 1–2.

Libby, W. F. 1952. *Radiocarbon dating*. Chicago: University of Chicago Press.

Lin, A., T. Ouchi, A. Chen, T. Maruyama 2001. Coseismic displacements, folding and shortening structures along the Chelungpu surface rupture zone occurred during the 1999 Chi-Chi (Taiwan) earthquake. *Tectonophysics* **330**, 225–44.

Liu, T. & W. S. Broecker 2000. How fast does rock varnish grow? *Geology* **28**, 183–6.

Loihi Science Team 1997. Researchers rapidly respond to submarine activity at Loihi volcano, Hawaii. *EOS, Transactions of the American Geophysical Union* **78**, 229–33.

Love, S. G. & D. E. Brownlee 1993. A direct measurement of the terrestrial mass accretion rate of cosmic dust. *Science* **262**, 550–53.

Lovelock, J. 1989. *The ages of Gaia*. Oxford: Oxford University Press.

Lu, Z., D. Mann, J. Freymuller 1998. Satellite radar interferometry measures deformation at Okmok volcano. *EOS, Transactions of the American Geophysical Union* **79**, 461–8.

Lupton, J. E. 1995. Hydrothermal plumes: near and far field. In *Seafloor hydrothermal systems*, S. E. Humphris, R. A. Zierenberg, L. S. Mullineaux, R. E. Thomson (eds), 317–46. Geophysical Monograph 91, American Geophysical Union, Washington DC.

Lyell, C. 1853. *Principles of geology* (9th edn). London: Murray.

McCall, J. 1997. Meteorites: flux with time and impact effects. *Geoscientist* **7**, 20.

—— 2001. Keep watching the skies – but not in fear. *Geoscientist* **11**, 12.

McClusky, S. and 27 co-authors 2000. Global Positioning System constraints on plate kinematics and dynamics in the eastern Mediterranean and Caucasus. *Journal of Geophysical Research* **105**, 5695–719.

McElhinny, M. & W. E. Senanayake 1982. Variations of the geomagnetic dipole 1: the past 50000 years. *Journal of Geomagnetism and Geoelectricity* **34**, 163–89.

McGuire, W. J., C. R. J. Kilburn, J. Murray (eds) 1995. *Monitoring active volcanoes*. London: UCL Press.

McKenzie, D. P. 1972. Active tectonics of the Mediterranean region. *Royal Astronomical Society, Geophysical Journal* **30**, 109–185.

McKenzie, D. P., A. B. Watts, B. Parsons, M. Roufosse 1980. Planform of mantle convection beneath the Pacific Ocean. *Nature* **288**, 442–6.

McLean, R. F. 1967. Measurements of beachrock erosion by some tropical marine gastropods. *Bulletin of Marine Science* **17**, 551–61.

McNutt, M. 1996. The 5-million-dollar bumps. *Nature* **379**, 300–301.

McSween Jr, H. Y. 1999. *Meteorites and their parent planets* (2nd edn). Cambridge: Cambridge University Press.

Mann, C. D. & C. Vita-Finzi 1988. Holocene serial folding in the Zagros. In *Gondwana and Tethys*, M. G. Audley-Charles & A. Hallam (eds), 51–9. Special Publication 37, Geological Society of London, London.

Mantovani, F. & C. Vita-Finzi 2003. The Vaiont Fault. *Geomorphology* (in press).

Massonnet, D. & K. L. Feigl 1998. Radar interferometry and its application to changes in the Earth's surface. *Reviews of Geophysics* **36**, 441–500.

Massonnet, D., P. Briole, A. Arnaud 1995. Deflation of Mount Etna monitored by space-borne radar interferometry. *Nature* **375**, 567–70.

Massonnet, D. and 6 co-authors 1993. The displacement field of the Landers earthquake mapped by radar interferometry. *Nature* **364**, 138–42.

Massonnet D., W. Thatcher, H. Vadon 1996. Detection of post-seismic fault-zone collapse following the Landers earthquake. *Nature* **382**, 612–16.

Matthews, P. M. & I. I. Shapiro 1992. Nutations of the Earth. *Annual Review of Earth and Planetary Science* **20**, 469–500.

Matsuzaka, S., M. Tobita, Y. Nakahori, J. Amagai, Y. Sugimoto 1991. Detection of Philippine Sea motion by very long baseline interferometry. *Geophysical Research Letters* **18**, 1417–19.

Mazaud, A., C. Laj, E. Bard, M. Arnold, E. Tric 1991. Geomagnetic field control of [14]C production over the last 80 kyr: implications for the radiocarbon timescale. *Geophysical Research Letters* **18**, 1885–8.

Meade, C. & D. T. Sandwell 1996. Synthetic aperture radar for geodesy. *Science* **273**, 1181–2.

Meadows, J. 1975. A hundred years of controversy over sunspots and weather. *Nature* **256**, 95–7.

Meghraoui, M., R. Jaegy, K. Lammali, F. Albarède 1988. Late Holocene earthquake sequences on the El Asnam (Algeria) thrust fault. *Earth and Planetary Science Letters* **90**, 187–203.

Meierding, T. C. 1993. Inscription legibility method for estimating rock weathering rates. *Geomorphology* **6**, 273–86.

Melosh, H. J. 1989. *Impact cratering*. New York: Oxford University Press.

Merlin, T. 1997. *Sulla pelle viva* (3rd edn). Verona: Cierre.

Merrill, R. T. & M. W. McElhinny 1983. *The Earth's magnetic field*. London: Academic Press.

Meyer, B. and 8 co-authors 1996. The 1995 Grevena (northern Greece) earthquake: fault model constrained with tectonic observations and SAR interferometry. *Geophysical Research Letters* **23**, 2677–80.

Milankovich, M. 1930. Mathematische Klimalehre und astronomische Theorie der Klimaschwankungen. In *Handbuch der Klimatologie* (vol. 1), I. W. Köppen & R. Geiger (eds) 1–176. Berlin: Gebruder Bontraeger.

Milne, J. 1886. *Earthquakes and other earth movements*. London: Kegan Paul, Trench.

Mohr, J. J., N. Reeh, S. N. Madsen 1998. Three-dimensional glacial flow and surface elevation measured with radar interferometry. *Nature* **391**, 273–6.

Molnar, P., B. C. Burchfield, L. Kuangyi, Z. Ziyun 1987. Geomorphic evidence for active faulting in the Altyn Tagh and northern Tibet and qualitative estimates of its contribution to the convergence of India and Eurasia. *Geology* **15**, 249–53.

Molnar, P. & P. Tapponnier 1975. Cenozoic tectonics of Asia: effects of a continental collision. *Science* **189**, 419–26.

Molnia, B. F. 1995. A post-Holocene history of Berin Glacier, Alaska: a prelude to the 1003–1994 surge. *Physical Geography* **16**, 87–117.

Mooney, W. D., M. E. Gettings, H. R. Blank, J. H. Healy 1985. Saudi Arabian seismic-refraction profile:

a travel-time interpretation of crustal and upper mantle structure. *Tectonophysics* **111**, 173–246.

Mörner, N-A. 1976. Eustasy and the geoid. *Journal of Geology* **84**, 123–51.

Morris, C. S. & S. K. Gill 1994. Variation of Great Lakes water levels derived from Geosat altimetry. *Water Resources Research* **30**, 1009–1017.

Morrison, D., C. R. Chapman, P. Slovic 1994. The impact hazard. See Gehrels (1994: 59–91).

Mouyaris, N., D. Papastamatiou, C. Vita-Finzi 1992. The Helice Fault? *Terra Nova* **4**, 124–9.

Muller, R. A. & G. J. MacDonald 1997. Glacial cycles and astronomical forcing. *Science* **277**, 215–18.

Murray, J. B. & J. E. Guest 1982. Vertical ground deformation on Mount Etna, 1975–1980. *Geological Society of America, Bulletin* **93**, 1160–75.

NASA 2001. *Global sea ice extent and concentration.* http://nsdc.org/NASA/SOTC/sea_ice/html.

Nelson A. R. and 11 co-authors 1995. Radiocarbon evidence for extensive plate-boundary rupture about 300 years ago at the Cascadia subduction zone. *Nature* **378**, 371–4.

Nerem, R. S. 1995. Measuring global mean sea-level variations using TOPEX/Poseidon altimeter data. *Journal of Geophysical Research* **100**, 25135–51.

Nerem, R. S., R. J. Eanes, P. F. Thompson, J. L. Chen 2000. Observations of annual variations of the Earth's gravitational field using satellite laser ranging and geophysical models. *Geophysical Research Letters* **27**, 1783–6.

Nerem, R. S. & G. T. Mitchum 2001. Observations of sea-level change from satellite altimetry. In *Sea-level rise*, B. C. Douglas, M. S. Kearney, S. P. Leatherman (eds), 121–63. San Diego: Academic Press.

Newman, A. V., S. Stein, J. Weber, J. Engeln, A. Mao, T. H. Dixon 1999. Slow deformation and low seismic hazard at the New Madrid seismic zone. *Science* **284**, 619–21.

Nisbet, E. G. 1987. *The young Earth*. London: Allen & Unwin.

Nishiizumi, K. and 6 co-authors 1991. *In situ* $^{10}$Be–$^{26}$Al exposure ages at Meteor Crater, Arizona. 1991. *Geochimica et Cosmochimica Acta* **55**, 2699–703.

Norabuena, E., L. Griffin, A. Mao, T. Dixon, S. Stein, I. S. Sacks, L. Ocola, M. Ellis 1998. Space geodetic observations of Nazca–South America plate convergence across the central Andes. *Science* **279**, 358–62.

Nur, A., H. Ron, O. Scotti 1989. Kinematics and mechanics of tectonic block rotations. In *Slow deformation and transmission of stress in the Earth*, S. C. Cohen & P. Vanicek (eds), 31–46. Washington DC: American Geophysical Union.

O'Brien, K. 1979. Secular variations in the production of cosmogenic isotopes in the Earth's atmosphere. *Journal of Geophysical Research* **84**, 423–31.

Ohno, M. & Y. Hamano 1992. Geomagnetic poles over the past 10 000 years. *Geophysical Research Letters* **19**, 1715–18.

Oldfield, F. and 7 co-authors 1978. $2^{10}$Pb, $^{137}$Cs and $^{239}$Pu profiles in ombrotrophic peat. *Oikos* **33**, 40–45.

Oral, M. B. and 6 co-authors 1995. Global Positioning System offers evidence of plate motions in Eastern Mediterranean. *EOS, Transactions of the American Geophysical Union* **76**, 9 and 11.

Osterkamp, W. R. & W. W. Emmett 1992. The Vigil Network – long-term monitoring to assess landscape changes. *International Association for Scientific Hydrology, Publications* **210**, 397–404.

Pacanovsky, K. M., D. M. Davis, R. M. Richardson, D. D. Coblentz 1999. Intraplate stresses and plate-driving forces in the Philippine Sea plate. *Journal of Geophysical Research* **104**, 1095–1100.

Parkinson, J. H., L. V. Morrison, F. R. Stephenson 1980. The constancy of the solar diameter over the past 250 years. *Nature* **288**, 548–51.

Parpola, S. 1970. *Letters from Assyrian scholars to the Kings Esarhaddon and Assurbanipal*. Kevelaer: Butzon & Bercker.

Patton, P. C. & S. A. Schumm 1975. Gully erosion, northwestern Colorado: a threshold phenomenon. *Geology* **3**, 88–90.

Paul, J. and 10 co-authors 1995. Microstrain stability of peninsular India 1864–1994. *Indian Academy of Sciences (Earth and Planetary Sciences), Proceedings* **104**, 131–46.

Pearson, C. F., J. Beavan, D. J. Darby, G. H. Blick, R. I. Walcott 1995. Strain distribution across the Australia/Pacific plate boundary in the central South Island, New Zealand, from 1992 GPS and earlier terrestrial observations. *Journal of Geophysical Research* **100**, 22071–22081.

Peixoto, J. P. & A. H. Oort 1992. *Physics of climate*. New York: American Institute of Physics.

Peltier, W. R. 1996. Global sea-level rise and glacial isostatic adjustment: an analysis of data from the East Coast of North America. *Geophysical Research Letters* **213**, 717–20.

Pelto, M. S., T. J. Hughes, H. H. Brecher 1989. Equilibrium state of Jakobshavns Isbræ, West Greenland. *Annals of Glaciology* **12**, 127–31.

Peltzer, G., K. W. Hudnut, K. L. Feigl 1994. Analysis of coseismic surface displacement gradients using radar interferometry: new insights into the Landers earthquake. *Journal of Geophysical Research* **99**, 21971–81.

Peltzer, G. & P. Rosen 1995. Surface displacement of the 17 May 1993 Eureka Valley, California, earthquake observed by SAR interferometry. *Science* **268**, 1333–6.

Peltzer, G., P. Rosen, F. Rogez, K. Hudnut 1996. Post-seismic rebound in fault step-overs caused by pore fluid flow. *Science* **273**, 1202–204.

Peltzer, G., F. Crampé, S. Hensley, P. Rosen 2001. Transient strain accumulation and fault interaction in the Eastern California shear zone. *Geology* **29**, 975–8.

Piper, D. J. W., P. Cochonat, M. L. Morrison 1999. The sequence of events around the epicentre of the 1929 Grand Banks earthquake: initiation of debris flows and turbidity current inferred from sidescan sonar. *Sedimentology* **46**, 79–97.

Pittock, A. B. 1983. Solar variability, weather and climate: an update. *Royal Meteorological Society, Quarterly Journal* **109**, 23–55.

Plafker, G. 1972. Alaskan earthquake of 1964 and Chilean earthquake of 1960: implications for arc tectonics. *Journal of Geophysical Research* **77**, 901–925.

Plafker, G. & M. Rubin 1967. Vertical tectonic displacements in southeastern Alaska during and prior to the great 1964 earthquake. *Journal of Geosciences* **10**, 53–6.

Plafker, G. & J. C. Savage 1970. Mechanism of the Chilean earthquakes of May 21 and 22, 1960. *Bulletin of the Geological Society of America* **81**, 1001–1030.

Platzman, E. S., J. P. Platt, C. Tapirdamaz, M. Sanver, C. C. Rundle 1994. Why are there no clockwise rotations along the North Anatolian fault zone? *Journal of Geophysical Research* **99**, 21705–715.

Price, N. J. 1975. Rates of deformation. *Journal of the Geological Society of London* **131**, 553–75.

—— 2001. *Major impacts and plate tectonics*. London: Routledge.

Price, N. J. & M. G. Audley-Charles 1987. Tectonic collision processes after plate rupture. *Tectonophysics* **140**, 121–9.

Price, N. J., G. D. Price, S. L. Price 1988. Gravity glide and plate tectonics. *Gondwana and Tethys*, M. G. Audley-Charles & A. Hallam (eds), 5–21. Special Publication 37, Geological Society of London, London.

Puntodewo, S. and 11 co-authors 1994. GPS measurements of crustal deformation within the Pacific/Australia plate boundary zone in Irian-Jaya, Indonesia. *Tectonophysics* **237**, 141–53.


Rabinowitz, D., E. Bowell, E. Shoemaker, K. Muinonen 1994. The population of earth-crossing asteroids. See Gehrels (1994: 285–312).

Ramesh, D. S. & C. H. Estabrook 1998. Rupture histories of two stable continental region earthquakes of India. *Indian Academy of Sciences (Earth and Planetary Science), Proceedings* **107**, L225–33.

Ramsay, J. G. 1967. *Folding and fracturing of rocks*. London: McGraw-Hill.

Reaka-Kudla, M. L., J. S. Feingold, W. Glynn 1996. Experimental studies of rapid bioerosion of coral reefs in the Galapagos islands. *Coral Reefs* **15**, 101–107.

Reid, H. F. 1910. *The mechanics of the earthquake*. Publication 87 (vol. 2), Carnegie Institution, Washington DC.

Riguzzi, F., G. Pietrantonio, M. Crespi, M. Anzidei 2001. True or false GPS-derived deformations? *Annali di Geofisica* **44**, 593–604.

Rignot, E., E. C. Jezek, H. G. Sohn 1995. Ice-flow dynamics of the Greenland ice sheet from SAR interferometry. *Geophysical Research Letters* **22**, 575–8.

Robaudo, S. & C. G. A. Harrison 1993. Measurements of strain at plate boundaries using space-based geodetic techniques. *Geophysical Research Letters* **20**, 1811–14.

Robertson, D. S., W. E. Carter, J. Campbell, H. Schuh 1985. Daily Earth-rotation determinations from IRIS very long baseline interferometry. *Nature* **316**, 424–7.

Robbins, A. R. 1980. Introduction. In *Satellite Doppler tracking and its geodetic applications*, A. R. Robbins, V. Ashkenazi, D. G. King-Hele (eds), 1–5. London: Royal Society.

Rosen, P. A., S. Hesley, H. A. Zebker, F. H. Webb, E. J. Fielding 1996. Surface deformation and coherence measurements at Kilauea Volcano, Hawaii, from SIR-C radar interferometry. *Journal of Geophysical Research* **101**, 23109–125.

Rothrock, D. A., Y. Yu & G. A. Maykut 1999. Thinning of the Arctic sea-ice cover. *Geophysical Research Letters* **26**, 3469–72.

Royer, J-Y. & R. G. Gordon 1997. The motion and boundary between the Capricorn and Australian plates. *Science* **277**, 1268–74.

Rubin, K. H., J. D. Macdougall, M. R. Perfit 1994. $^{210}$Po–$^{210}$Pb dating of recent volcanic eruptions on the sea floor. *Nature* **368**, 841–4.

Rubincam, D. P. 1995. Has climate changed the Earth's tilt? *Palaeoceanography* **10**, 365–72.

Runcorn, S. K. 1974. Some aspects of the physics of the Moon. *Royal Society of London, Proceedings A* **336**, 11–33.

Satake, K., K. Shimazaki, Y. Tsuji, K. Ueda 1996. Time and size of a giant earthquake in Cascadia inferred from Japanese tsunami records of January 1700. *Nature* **379**, 246–9.

Sauber, J., G. Plafker, J. Gipson 1995. Geodetic measurements used to estimate ice transfer during Bering Glacier surge. *EOS, Transactions of the American Geophysical Union* **76**, 289–90.

Sauber, J., G. Plafker, B. F. Molnia, M. A. Bryant 2000. Crustal deformation associated with glacial fluctuations in the eastern Chugach Mountains, Alaska. *Journal of Geophysical Research* **105**, 8055–8077.

Savage, J. C. 1983. A dislocation model of strain accumulation and release at a subduction zone. *Journal of Geophysical Research* **88**, 4984–96.

Savage, J. C. & G. Plafker 1991. Tide gage measurements of uplift along the south coast of Alaska. *Journal of Geophysical Research* **96**, 4325–35.

Scalera, G. 2000. Paleogeographical reconstructions compatible with Earth dilatation. *Annali di Geofisica* **41**, 819–25.

Schaer, J. P., G. M. Reimer, G. A. Wagner 1975. Actual and ancient uplift rate in the Gotthard region, Swiss Alps: a comparison between precise levelling and fission-track apatite age. *Tectonophysics* **29**, 293–300.

Schieber, J., D. Krinsley, L. Riciputi 2000. Diagenetic origin of quartz silt mudstones and implications for silica cycling. *Nature* **406**, 981–5.

Schmidt, J. F. J. 1875. *Studien über Erdbeden*. Leipzig: Scholze.

Scholz, C. A. 1990. *The mechanics of earthquakes and faults*. Cambridge: Cambridge University Press.

Schultz, P. H. & R. E. Lianza 1992. Recent grazing impacts on the Earth recorded in the Rio Cuarto crater field, Argentina. *Nature* **355**, 234–7.

Scrutton, C. T. 1965. Periodicity in Devonian coral growth. *Palaeontology* **7**, 552–8.

Searle, M. P. 1994. Structure of the intraplate eastern Palmyride fold belt, Syria. *Bulletin of the Geological Society of America* **106**, 1332–50.

Seeber, G. 1993. *Satellite geodesy*. Berlin: Walter de Gruyter.

Segall, P. & J. L. Davis 1997. GPS applications for geodynamics and earthquake studies. *Annual Review of Earth and Planetary Science* **25**, 301–336.

Segerstrom, K. 1950. *Erosion studies at Parícutin, State of Michoacán, Mexico*. Bulletin 965A, US Geological Survey, Denver, Colorado.

Semenza, E. & M. Ghirotti 1998. Vaiont-Longarone 34 anni dopo la catastrofe. *Annali dell'Università di Ferrara, Scienze della Terra* **7**, 63–94.

Seno, T. 1977. The instantaneous rotation vector of the Philippine Sea plate relative to the Eurasian plate. *Tectonophysics* **42**, 209–226.

Shackleton, N. J., A. Berger, W. R. Peltier 1990. An alternative astronomical calibration of the Lower Pleistocene timescale based on ODP site 677. *Royal Society of Edinburgh, Earth Science, Transactions* **81**, 251–61.

Sharpton, V. L. and 7 co-authors 1996. A model of the Chicxulub impact basin based on evaluation of geophysical data, well logs, and drill core samples. In *The Cretaceous–Tertiary event and other catastrophes in Earth history*, G. Ryder, D. Fastovsky, S. Gartner (eds), 55–60. Special Paper 307, Geological Society of America, Boulder, Colorado.

Shephard, F. P. 1963. *Submarine geology* (2nd edn). New York: Harper & Row.

Shoemaker, E. M. 1983. Asteroid and comet bombardment of the Earth. *Annual Reviews of Earth and Planetary Science* **11**, 11461–94.

Shoemaker, E. M., P. R. Weissman, C. S. Shoemaker 1994. The flux of periodic comets near Earth. See Gehrels (1994: 313–35).

Shum, C. K., J. C. Ries, B. D. Tapley 1995. The accuracy and applications of satellite altimetry. *Geophysical Journal International* **121**, 321–36.

Sieh, K., Y. Bock, J. Rais 1991. Neotectonic and paleoseismologic studies in west and north Sumatra. *EOS, Transactions of the American Geophysical Union* **72**, 460.

Sieh, K. & D. Natawidjaja 2001. Neotectonics of the Sumatran Fault, Indonesia. *Journal of Geophysical Research* **105**, 28295–326.

Sigmundsson, F., P. Einarsson, R. Bilham, E. Sturkell 1995. Rift-transform kinematics in South Iceland: deformation from Global Positioning System measurements, 1986 to 1982. *Journal of Geophysical Research* **100**, 6235–48.

Silverman, S. M. 1991. Secular variation of the aurora for the past 500 years. *Reviews of Geophysics* **30**, 333–51.

—— 1998. A forgotten proposal for determination of temporal variation of the magnetic declination. *EOS, Transactions of the American Geophysical Union* **78**, 305.

Simpson, R. W., S. A. Schulz, L. D. Dietz, R. O. Burford 1982. The response of creeping parts of the San Andreas Fault to earthquakes on nearby faults: two examples. *Pure and Applied Geophysics* **26**, 665–85.

Sjöberg, L. E. 1986. Determination of the land uplift from old water mark and tide gauge data at Ratan and Lövgrundet/Björn, Sweden. *Neotectonics* **1**, 51–9.

Smith, D. E., R. Kolenkiewicz, P. J. Dunn, M. H. Torrence 1979. The measurement of fault motion by satellite laser ranging. *Tectonophysics* **52**, 59–67.

Smith, D. E. and 8 co-authors 1990. Tectonic motion and deformation from satellite laser ranging to LAGEOS. *Journal of Geophysical Research* **95**, 22013–22041.

Smith, L. C. and 6 co-authors 2000. Estimation of erosion and deposition from SAR interferometry and net topographic change during the 1996 jökulhlaup, Skeidararsandur, Iceland. *Water Resources Research* **36**, 1583–94.

Smith, W. H. F. & D. T. Sandwell 1997. Global sea-floor topography from satellite altimetry and ship depth soundings. *Science* **277**, 1957–62.

Soare, A., G. Cucu, M. M. Alexandrescu 1998. Historical geomagnetic measurements in Romania. *Annali di Geofisica* **41**, 539–54.

Soter, S. 1998. Holocene uplift and subsidence of the Helike delta, Gulf of Corinth, Greece. In *Coastal tectonics*, I. Stewart & C. Vita-Finzi (eds), 41–56. Special Publication 146, Geological Society of London, London.

Sparks, R. S. J. and 19 co-authors 1998. Magma production and growth of the lava dome of the Soufrière Hills volcano, Montserrat, West Indies: November 1995 to December 1997. *Geophysical Research Letters* **25**, 3421–4.

Spence, K. 2000. Ancient Egyptian chronology and the astronomical orientation of pyramids. *Nature* **408**, 320–24.

Spiess, F. N., C. D. Chadwell, J. A. Hildebrand, L. E. Young, G. H. Purcell Jr 1998. Precise GPS/acoustic positioning of seafloor reference points for tectonic studies. *Physics of the Earth and Planetary Interiors* **108**, 101–112.

Steel, D. I. 1995. Collisions in the Solar System, VI: terrestrial impact probabilities for the known asteroid population. *Royal Astronomical Society, Monthly Notices* **273**, 1091–1096.

Steers, J. A. 1945. *The unstable Earth.* London: Murray.

Stein, C. A., S. Stein, A. M. Pelayo 1995. Heat flow and hydrothermal alteration. In *Seafloor hydro-thermal systems*, S. E. Humphris, R. A. Zierenberg, L. S. Mullineaux, R. E. Thomson (eds), 25–445. Geophysical Monograph 91, American Geophysical Union, Washington DC.

Stein, R. S. 1987. Contemporary plate motion and crustal deformation. *Reviews of Geophysics* **25**, 853–63.

Stephenson, F. R. 1978. Pre-telescopic astronomical observations. In *Tidal friction and the Earth's rotation*, P. Brosche & J. Sanderman (eds), 5–21. Berlin: Springer.

—— 1988a. Evidence for solar variability from historical records. In *Solar–terrestrial relationships and the Earth environment in the last millennia*, G. C. Castagnoli (ed.), 133–50. Amsterdam: North-Holland.

—— 1988b. The history of the Earth's rotation as determined from eclipses and occultations. In *Solar–terrestrial relationships and the Earth environment in the last millennia*, G. C. Castagnoli (ed.), 151–65. Amsterdam: North-Holland.

—— 1990. Historical evidence concerning the Sun: interpretation of sunspot records during the tele-scopic and pre-telescopic eras. *Royal Society of London, Philosophical Transactions A* **330**, 499–512.

Stephenson, F. R. & L. V. Morrison 1984. Long-term changes in the rotation of the Earth: 700 BC to AD 1980. *Royal Society of London, Philosophical Transactions A* **313**, 47–70.

Stewart, I. & C. Vita-Finzi 1996. Coastal uplift on active normal faults: the Eliki Fault, Greece. *Geophysical Research Letters* **23**, 1853–6.

Stewart, I., W. McGuire, C. Vita-Finzi, C. Firth, R. Holmes, S. Saunders 1993. Active faulting and neotectonic deformation on the eastern flank of Mount Etna, Sicily. *Zeitschrift für Geomorphologie, Supplementband* **94**, 73–94.

Stothers, R. B. 1992. Impacts and tectonism in Earth and Moon history of the past 3800 million years. *Earth, Moon and Planets* **58**, 145–52.

Stuiver, M. & P. D. Quay 1980. Changes in atmospheric carbon-14 attributed to a variable sun. *Science* **207**, 11–19.

Subrahmanya, K. R. 1996. Active intraplate deformation in south India. *Tectonophysics* **262**, 231–41.

Summerfield, M. A. 1991. *Global geomorphology.* Harlow, England: Longman.

Svetsov, V. V. 1996. Total ablation of the debris from the 1908 Tunguska explosion. *Nature* **383**, 697–9.


Talbot, C. J. 1998. Extrusions of Hormuz salt in Iran. In *Lyell: the past is the key to the present*, D. J. Blundell & A. C. Scott (eds), 315–34. Special Publication 143, Geological Society of London, London.

Tapley, B. D, D. P. Chambers, C. K. Shum, R. J. Eanes, J. C. Ries, R. H. Stewart 1994. Accuracy assess-ment of the large-scale dynamic ocean topography from TOPEX/Poseidon altimetry. *Journal of Geophysical Research* **99**, 24605–617.

Tapponnier, P. 1991. Les satellites et la tectonique en temps réel. In *Tectoscope-positionnement*, 5. Paris: Centre Nationale d'Etudes Spatiales.

Taylor, S., J. H. Lever, R. P. Harvey 1998. Accretion rate of cosmic spherules measured at the South Pole. *Nature* **392**, 899–903.

Tchalenko, J. 1975. Strain and deformation rates at the Arabia/Iran plate boundary. *Geological Society of London, Journal* **131**, 585–6.

ten Brink, U. and 9 co-authors 1999. Anatomy of the Dead Sea transform: does it reflect continuous changes in plate motion? *Geology* **27**, 887–90.

Tett, S. F. B., P. A. Stott, M. R. Allen, W. J. Ingram, J. F. B. Mitchell 1999. Causes of twentieth-century temperature change near the Earth's surface. *Nature* **399**, 569–72.

Thompson, R. & R. Berglund 1976. Late geomagnetic "reversal" as a possible example of the re-inforcement syndrome. *Nature* **263**, 490–91.

Thompson, J. B. & F. G. Ferris 1990. Cyanobacterial precipitation of gypsum, calcite, and magnesite from natural alkaline lake water. *Geology* **18**, 995–8.

Thornton, C. L., J. L. Fanselow, N. A. Renzetti 1986. GPS-based geodetic measurement systems. In

Anderson & Cazenave (1986: 197–218).

Thunell, R. and 6 co-authors 1999. Increased marine sediment suspension and fluxes following an earth-quake. *Nature* **398**, 233–6.

Tinsley, B. A. 1988. The solar cycle and the QBO influences on the latitude of storm tracks in the North Atlantic. *Geophysical Research Letters* **15**, 409–412.

—— 1990. Forcing of climate variations by MeV–GeV particles? In *Climate impact of solar variability*, K. H. Schatten & A. Arking (eds), 249–58. Greenbelt, Maryland: NASA.

Tinsley, B. A. & G. W. Deen 1991. Apparent tropospheric response to MeV–GeV particle flux variations: a connection via electrofreezing of supercooled water in high-level clouds? *Journal of Geophysical Research* **96**, 22283–96.

Tinsley, B. A. & R. A. Heelis 1993. Correlations of atmospheric dynamics with solar activity: evidence for a connection via the solar wind, atmospheric electricity, and cloud microphysics. *Journal of Geophysical Research* **98**, 10375–10384.

Tivey, M. A. and 6 co-authors 1997. Autonomous underwater vehicle maps sea floor. *EOS, Transactions of the American Geophysical Union* **78**, 229–30.

Tralli, D. M. 1991. Spectral comparison of continuous global positioning system and strainmeter measurements of crustal deformation. *Geophysical Research Letters* **18**, 1285–8.

Tric, E. and 7 co-authors 1992. Paleointensity of the geomagnetic field during the last 80000 years. *Journal of Geophysical Research* **97**, 9337–51.

Trimble, S. 1999. Decreased rates of alluvial sediment storage in the Coon Creek basin, Wisconsin, 1975–93. *Science* **285**, 1244–6.

Trupin, A. S., M. F. Meier, J. M. Wahr 1992. Effect of melting glaciers on the Earth's rotation and gravitational field: 1965–1984. *Geophysical Journal International* **108**, 1–15.

Tushingham, A. M. & W. R. Peltier 1991. Ice-3G: a new global model of Late Pleistocene deglaciation based upon geophysical predictions of post-glacial relative sea level change. *Journal of Geophysical Research* **96**, 4497–523.

Vago, R., E. Gill, J. C. Collingwood 1997. Laser measurements of coral growth. *Nature* **386**, 30–31.

van Helden, A. 1995. Galileo and Scheiner on sunspots: a case study in the visual language of astronomy. *American Philosophical Society, Proceedings* **140**, 358–96.

Varekamp, J. C. & E. Thomas 1998. Climate change and the rise and fall of sea level over the millennium. *EOS, Transactions of the American Geophysical Union* **79**, 69, 74–5.

Vermeersen, L. A. & N. J. Vlaar 1993. Changes in the Earth's rotation by tectonic movements. *Geophysical Research Letters* **20**, 81–4.

Vetter, J. R. 1994. The evolution of Earth gravitational models used in astrodynamics. *Johns Hopkins Applied Physics Laboratory Technical Digest* **15**, 319–35.

Vine, F. J. & D. H. Matthews 1963. Magnetic anomalies over ocean ridges. *Nature* **199**, 947–9.

Vita-Finzi, C. 1986. *Recent Earth movements*. London: Academic Press.

—— 1995. Pulses of emergence in the outer-arc ridge of the Sunda Arc. *Journal of Coastal Research, Special Issue* **17**, 279–81.

—— 2000. Deformation and seismicity of Taiwan. *Proceedings of the National Academy of Sciences* **79**, 11176–80.

—— 2001. Neotectonics at the Arabian plate margins. *Journal of Structural Geology* **23**, 521–30.

—— 2002. Buckling of India. *Current Science* **82**, 400–402.

Vita-Finzi, C. & P. F. S. Cornelius 1973. Cliff sapping by molluscs in Oman. *Journal of Sedimentary Petrology* **43**, 31–2.

Vita-Finzi, C. & S. Hidayat 1991. Holocene uplift in West Timor. *Journal of Southeast Asian Earth Sciences* **6**, 387–93.

Vita-Finzi, C. & G. C. P. King 1985. The seismicity, geomorphology and structural evolution of the Corinth area of Greece. *Royal Society of London, Philosophical Transactions A* **314**, 379–407.

Vita-Finzi, C. & C. D. Mann 1994. Seismic folding in coastal south central Chile. *Journal of Geophysical Research* **99**, 12289–99.

Voight, B. and 6 co-authors 1998. Remarkable cyclic ground deformation monitored in real-time on

Montserrat, and its use in eruption forecasting. *Geophysical Research Letters* **25**, 3405–3408.

Wadge, G., D. J. Archer, A. C. Millington 1994. Monitoring playa sedimentation using sequential radar images. *Terra Nova* **6**, 391–6.

Wahr, J. M. 1988. The Earth's rotation. *Annual Review of Earth and Planetary Science* **16**, 231–49.

Wahr, J., D. Han, A. Trupin 1995. Predictions of vertical uplift caused by changing polar ice volumes on a viscoelastic earth. *Geophysical Research Letters* **22**, 977–80.

Walcott, R. I. 1972. Past sea levels, eustasy and deformation of the earth. *Quaternary Research* **2**, 1–14.

Wallace, A. R. 1881. *Island life*. Amherst, New York: Prometheus.

Walling, D. E. & Q. He 1999. Changing rates of overbank sedimentation on the floodplains of British rivers during the past 100 years. In *Fluvial processes and environmental change*, G. A. Brown & T. A. Quine (eds), 207–221. Chichester, England: John Wiley.

Ward, F. A. B. 1970. *Time measurement*. London: Science Museum.

Washburn, A. L. 1973. *Periglacial processes and environments*. London: Edward Arnold.

Watchman, A. 2000. A review of the history of dating rock varnishes. *Earth Science Reviews* **49**, 261–77.

Watts, A. B. & S. F. Daly 1981. Long-wavelength gravity and topography anomalies. *Annual Review of Earth and Planetary Science* **9**, 415–18.

Webb, F. H., M. Bursik, T. Dixon, F. Farina, G. Marshall, R. S. Stein 1995. Inflation of Long Valley caldera from one year of continuous GPS observations. *Geophysical Research Letters* **22**, 195–8.

Weber, J., S. Stein, J. Engeln 1998. Estimation of intraplate strain accumulation in the New Madrid seismic zone from repeat GPSZ surveys. *Tectonics* **17**, 250–66.

Wegener, A. 1929 (1966). *The origin of continents and oceans* (4th edn). New York: Dover.

Wells, J. W. 1963. Coral growth and geochronometry. *Nature* **197**, 948–50.

Westbroek, P. 1992. *Life as a geological force*. New York: Norton.

Wetherill, G. W. & E. M. Shoemaker 1982. Collision of astronomically observable bodies with the Earth. In *Geological implications of impacts of large asteroids and comets on the Earth*, L. T. Silver & P. H. Schultz (eds), 1–13. Special Paper 190, Geological Society of America, Boulder, Colorado.

Wigley, T. M. L. & S. C. B. Raper 1995. An heuristic model for sea level rise due to the melting of small glaciers. *Geophysical Research Letters* **22**, 2749–52.

Williams, G. E. 1989. Late Precambrian tidal rhythmites in South Australia and the history of the Earth's rotation. *Geological Society of London, Journal* **146**, 97–111.

Williams, P. J. & M. W. Smith 1989. *The frozen Earth*. Cambridge: Cambridge University Press.

Williams, R. G. B., J. O. H. Swantesson, D. A. Robinson 2000. Measuring rates of surface downwearing and mapping microtopography: the use of micro-erosion meters and laser scanners in rock weathering studies. *Zeitschrift für Geomorphologie, Supplementband* **120**, 51–66.

Wilson, C. R. 1995. Earth rotation and global change. *Reviews of Geophysics*, Supplement, 225–9.

Wu, P. & W. R. Peltier 1983. Glacial isostatic adjustment and free-air gravity as a constraint on deep mantle viscosity. *Royal Astronomical Society, Geophysical Journal* **74**, 377–450.

Yau, K. K. & K. D. Pang 1995. The Earth's rotation rate in the third millennium BC from analysis of ancient Mesopotamian and Chinese eclipse records. *EOS, American Geophysical Union, 1995 Fall Meeting, Abstracts*, F62.

Yeomans, D. K. & P. W. Chodas 1994. Predicting close approaches of asteroids and comets to Earth. See Gehrels (1994: 241–58).

Yerrapragada, S. S., J. H. Jaynes, S. R. Chirra, K. L. Gauri 1994. Rate of weathering of marble due to dry deposition of ambient sulfur and nitrogen dioxides. *Analytical Chemistry* **66**, 655–9.

Yunck, T. P. 1995. GPS data, acquisition, environmental effects. *Reviews of Geophysics*, Supplement, 349–52.

Zahnle, K. & D. Grinspoon 1990. Comet dust as a source of amino acids at the Cretaceous/Tertiary boundary. *Nature* **348**, 157–60.

Zebker, H. A., P. A. Rosen, R. M. Goldstein, A. Gabriel, C. L. Werner 1994. On the derivation of co-seismic displacement fields using differential radar interferometry: the Landers earthquake. *Journal of Geophysical Research* **99**, 19617–34.

Zreda, M. & J. S. Noller 1998. Ages of prehistoric earthquakes revealed by cosmogenic chlorine-36 in a bedrock fault scarp at Hegben Lake. *Science* **282**, 1097–1098.

Zwartz, D., P. Tregoning, K. Lambeck, P. Johnston 1995. Estimates of present-day glacial rebound in the Lambert glacier region, Antarctica. *Geophysical Research Letters* **26**, 1461–4.

# Index